How to Write a Thesis

SECOND EDITION

How to Write a Thesis

SECOND EDITION

Rowena Murray

Open University Press

Open University Press
McGraw-Hill Education
McGraw-Hill House
Shoppenhangers Road
Maidenhead
Berkshire
England
SL6 2QL

email: enquiries@openup.co.uk
world wide web: www.openup.co.uk

and Two Penn Plaza, New York, NY 10121-2289, USA

First published 2002

A catalogue record of this book is available from the British Library

ISBN-10: 0 335 21968 3
ISBN-13: 978 0 335 21968 1

Library of Congress Cataloging-in-Publication Data
CIP data applied for

Typeset by RefineCatch Limited, Bungay, Suffolk
Printed in Great Britain by CPI Antony Rowe, Chippenham, Wiltshire

This book is dedicated to

Jimmy Walker

And to anyone who's thinking about writing a thesis out of irrepressible enthusiasm for a subject – do it!

Chapter 8 is for Morag.

Contents

Preface to the first edition

In 1995 I wrote a personal statement about my motivation to teach and write about thesis writing. The urge to write this book originated in my own experiences as a student in Scotland, Germany and the USA:

> As a graduate of a Scottish university I made a deliberate choice to enter a PhD programme in what is often disparagingly referred to as 'the American system', as if there were only one system in the USA. As a 'graduate student' in the English Department of the Pennsylvania State University I had the opportunity to take courses, and be examined, on research methods, two foreign languages, a theory course, three years of course work (before starting a thesis, a major piece of original research, on a par with PhD theses in the UK system, a fact which will surprise some academics), with teacher training for higher education, mentoring, observations and evaluations of my own teaching . . .
>
> On my return to the UK in 1984, I felt strongly that there was a need, in the UK system, for postgraduate training of some sort. There was also demand for such training among students; when I offered a thesis writing course at Strathclyde University in 1985 it proved very popular . . . we now have a programme of . . . courses for postgraduates. Some faculties and departments now offer customised induction courses for novice researchers . . . So things are improving.
>
> Yet writing is still neglected; there is often no writing instruction, creating problems for those students who have never done much writing or, if they have, have not done so on the scale of the PhD.
>
> (Lowe and Murray 1995: 78–9)

In addition, having read many other books on 'writing a thesis', it seemed to me that there was still room for a book that covered the whole writing process.

More recent motivation was provided by students in my writers' groups who demanded that I finish this book in time for them use it. Unfortunately, that was not feasible for all of them, for which, having raised their expectations, I apologize. Fortunately, some were able to read drafts of my chapters and their comments improved this book immensely. For that I thank them sincerely. You have made this a better book.

Finally, 'Will supervisors read this book?' I cannot count the number of times I was asked this question by those – students and supervisors – who discussed this book with me and read my draft chapters. The question implies that my exploration of the whole thesis writing process could help supervisors, or, as one student put it, 'Supervisors need to know this stuff too.' While this book is targeted at thesis writers, I recommend that supervisors read it too. Throughout the book I identify topics for student–supervisor discussions, in the hope that this will lead to more – and more explicit – discussions of writing. It is my sincere wish that this will improve the experience of thesis writing for both writers and supervisors.

Preface to the second edition

In evaluations, unsolicited emails and narratives of their experiences, doctoral and masters students tell me that the first edition helped them get started and complete their theses. For example, one supervisor told me that she knew some students who were writing a 'page 98 paper', using prompts in a box on page 98 of the first edition (page 104 in this edition) to draft papers at an early stage in their projects.

However, some students and reviewers requested new material, and I have added this for the second edition: new examples of different sections of a thesis and further definition of features of thesis writing.

Two important topics covered in Chapter 10 – the examination of the thesis and publishing from the thesis – are retained here, and are covered in more detail in my two other books: *How to Survive Your Viva* (2003) and *Writing for Academic Journals* (2005).

Acknowledgements

I would like to thank my editors at Open University Press and the reviewers of the first edition. I must also thank those who advised on the first edition: Liz McFarlan, Gilbert MacKay, Graeme Martin, Professor Portwood, Beth McKay, Pavel Albores, Lorna Gillies, Veronica Martinez, Betsy Pudliner and Alan Runcie.

Chris Carpenter, Carolyn Choudhary, Ellie Hamilton and Enkhjarkhlan Tseyen gave me important insights for the second edition.

Dr Morag Thow provided support, insight and humour.

Overview

Different chapters are constructed in different ways: for example, Chapters 1 and 2 are long and discursive, teasing out ambiguities and subtleties in thesis writing, in order to demystify the thesis writing process, while Chapter 8 is much more compact. It lists steps in a concentrated writing process and has checklists and tasks instead of definitions and explanations. It is also more directive in style.

The Introduction, 'How to write 1000 words an hour', sets out the theory, practice and assumptions that underpin the approaches to writing proposed in this book.

Chapter 1 helps you think your way into the thesis writing role.

Chapter 2 has strategies to start writing right away: writing before you 'have something to say', using freewriting and generative writing.

Chapter 3 is about bringing structure to your writing. A thesis has conventions you can use to shape and progress your thinking and writing.

Chapter 4 marks the first major milestone in writing a thesis: the end of the first phase. Reporting on your work and gauging your progress is the priority at this stage.

Chapter 5 has strategies for regular, incremental writing, for getting into the writing habit. A writers' group is one example.

Chapter 6 marks the halfway point in the writing of your thesis: time to move on to drafting chapters.

'Fear and loathing' were suggested for the title of Chapter 7 by a student who had recently completed his thesis, because they convey the frustration of constant refinements to text. Selected strategies for revising are provided here.

Chapter 8 is either the introduction to the last phase or the condensed version of the whole process, depending on your progress with your thesis. This chapter shows how to pack all the writing into one full-time year or two part-time years.

Chapter 9 covers ways of making your thesis 'good enough' – knowing it can still be improved – and defining what that means in terms of your thesis.

Chapter 10 covers ways of talking about your writing convincingly – during the viva, the examination of your thesis, with suggestions for managing final revisions and publishing from your thesis.

These chapters are arranged to guide you through the thesis writing process, from start to finish, but you can use the techniques described at different phases of thesis writing. Use the contents page initially to get an overview of the whole process and then strategically to locate writing problems or challenges that you face at any given time.

Introduction:
How to write 1000
words an hour

The need for this book • What the students say • A writer's 'toolbox'
• Principles of academic writing • The literature on writing • Disciplinary
differences • Thinking about structure • Prompts • Enabling student
writing • Writing in a second language • Grammar, punctuation, spelling
• Goal setting • Lifelong learning • Audience and purpose • Timetable for
writing • Checklist: defining the writing task

The need for this book

This introduction unpacks the theories and assumptions that underpin this book. It brings together what might seem to be a disparate collection of topics, all of which can impact on your thesis writing. The aim is to help you understand the context for your writing – an important first step in any writing project – and to learn from the literature on academic writing.

Although there is abundant research on writing it has not been fully integrated into the research process:

> . . . what knowledge there is concerning the actual PhD process is scant.
> (Hockey 1994: 177)

The British literature on the academic writing role is similar to that on research: patchy.

(Blaxter et al. 1998b: 290)

The terms 'scant' and 'patchy' suggest that there is work to be done on establishing how best to manage the thesis writing process. In fact, much of the literature emphasizes the importance of 'the research', with the writing process receiving less attention. However, useful lessons can be drawn from existing research, and there are established strategies that you can adapt to the writing of your thesis.

Basic premises of this book are that you have to: (1) find out what is expected of you as a thesis writer; and (2) write from the start and keep writing throughout your research. What this constant 'writing' involves will vary from one person to another, but there are core principles which – if you know what they are – help you to write regularly and effectively.

Writing a thesis is a completely new task for most postgraduate students. It brings new demands. It is a far bigger project than most students will ever have undertaken before. It requires more independent study, more self-motivation. There is much less continuous assessment. It is likely to be the longest piece of continuous writing you have ever done.

However, writing a thesis is not a completely new experience. It does build on your previous studies. Skills you developed in undergraduate years – and elsewhere – will be useful. Time management is a prime example. The subject of your thesis may build upon existing knowledge of, for example, theoretical approaches or the subject itself. The discipline of study, or regular work, is just as important as in other forms of study you have undertaken at other levels.

Early writing tasks

- Noting ideas while reading
- Documenting reading
- Writing summaries
- Critiques of other research
- Draft proposals
- Revising your thesis/research proposal
- Logging experiments/pilot/observations
- Describing experiments/procedures
- Sketching plan of work
- Explaining sequence of work (in sentences)
- Sketching structure of thesis
- Outlining your literature review
- Speculative writing: routes forward in project
- Design for first-year report

Passively accepting that a thesis is one of life's 'great unknowns' is not a sensible course of action; like any other writing task, it can – and must – be defined. One of the first – and best – books to outline the whole process for the PhD is *How to Get a PhD* by Phillips and Pugh (2000). What Phillips and Pugh did for the doctoral process, this book does for the doctoral, and masters, writing processes. The two books can be seen as complementary. This book focuses on that writing process and provides activities, prompts and hints and tips for writing at each stage in thesis writing, right from the start.

Writing a thesis should not be one long catalogue of problems; once you have a repertoire of writing strategies, you can get on with writing, recognizing that at some points in your research you have factual or descriptive writing to do, while at others you have to develop more complex and persuasive modes of writing. You can also use writing to develop your ideas, consolidate new knowledge and refine your thinking. This book gives you strategies for all of these, so that thesis writing becomes a series of challenges that you work through, gradually establishing what type of thesis it is that you are writing. Writing your thesis with these strategies to hand should maintain the intellectual stimulation and excitement that brought you to research in the first place.

Although the terms 'thesis' and 'dissertation' have different meanings in different cultures, the term 'thesis' is used in this book to refer to both undergraduate and postgraduate writing projects. Since these projects can vary in length from 8,000 words, for undergraduate projects, to 20,000 words, for masters projects, to 40,000–50,000 words for professional doctorates, to 80,000–100,000 words for PhDs, readers are prompted throughout this book to develop frameworks and timescales to suit their own projects and within their institutions' guidelines and regulations. Similarly, while the person who works with a thesis writer can have many titles – tutor, advisor, etc. – the term 'supervisor' is used in this book.

What the students say

> *[The researchers] found a discrepancy between graduate students . . . and faculty as to what constituted effective scholarly writing, discovering that students wanted to learn how to write more concisely, follow a prescribed format and use correct terminology. Faculty, on the other hand, felt that students needed to improve their ability to make solid arguments supported by empirical evidence and theory.*
>
> (Caffarella and Barnett 2000: 40)

This is an interesting dichotomy. Then again, why would we expect two very different groups to have formed the same expectations? Presumably research students are still learning what it is they have to learn.

Even when the subject of writing is raised in discussion between student and supervisor or among students – as it should be – there is no consensus about what they need to know. What do those who have started or completed a thesis say, looking back, that students need? The answers to these questions are multifaceted; they may even be contradictory:

Looking back

- It takes a long time to strike a balance between what you want to do and what the supervisor wants. You can waste as much as a year.
- It's difficult to get supervisors to give priority to your project. Supervisors are sometimes not that interested. This is a problem for all students.
- Isolation can be a problem . . . It can come with any of the other items on the list of problems.
- Start with a plan. Six months or a year can drift away very quickly. It's important to write as you go along.

These responses show how writing is related to, and can be influenced by, all sorts of factors:

Problems with writing

- Ownership of the project
- Managing your supervisor
- Isolation
- Planning

Students report that they look for lots of different kinds of advice and help. Many, if not all, of their concerns can be related to their writing. Some will directly affect their writing practices and output. What is provided in the way of support and development for writing seems to vary enormously, from institution to institution and even from supervisor to supervisor.

Some of these problems can be interpreted as the result of students' lack of awareness: of what's expected, of what is involved in writing and of what the educational experience involves. There is, often, the additional problem of lack of research training, although formal training is commonplace in some higher education systems and is becoming more common in others (Park 2005).

We must assume that supervisors want their students to complete their theses on time (as long as the work is up to standard). They are not out to put barriers in your way. However, their role is complex and is sometimes left implicit for too long. Supervisors are not always aware of specific writing problems or established writing development practices. Some admit that they don't know what they don't know about writing. They have all completed a thesis themselves and therefore have knowledge of the writing process. They will have probably published papers and/or books. They may have supervised the writing of many theses. However, the amount of reading they do about academic writing is likely to be variable. Some own up to having forgotten what their own research and writing apprenticeship involved.

This book takes a holistic approach to the total process of writing a thesis. While focusing on writing, some of the related topics raised by students will be addressed. The aim is to help you complete this particular task while, in the process, developing strategies and skills that will be useful in other writing contexts. You can use these strategies at any stage in the process, not just at the start, although they have particular importance at the start, in getting you to start writing.

Students and supervisors who read drafts of these chapters said that what students look for is more direction, not just questions to 'stimulate their thinking'. They want to be directed to good writing style. They want to develop the skills of argument. Students may not be able to say this right from the start; they may not know what they need. They may only understand that this was what they needed when they get to the later stages in their projects, or right at the very end.

This book aims to help you develop your understanding of the writing process – not just the finished product – through reading, writing and discussion with your peers and supervisor(s).

A writer's 'toolbox'

. . .there was a view among the student writers . . . that good writing came spontaneously, in an uprush of feeling that had to be caught at once . . .

I want to suggest that to write to your best abilities, it behoves you to construct your own toolbox and then build up enough muscle so you can carry it with you. Then, instead of looking at a hard job and getting discouraged, you will perhaps seize the correct tool and get immediately to work.

(King 2000: 62 and 125)

These two statements reveal the journey on which this book hopes to take readers. Your point of departure is the popular misconception that good writing happens when it happens, that writers should wait till they are inspired and that, if they do, the writing will 'flow'. Your destination is the development of a 'toolbox' of skills that writers can use for different writing projects and for different stages in any writing project. By the end of this journey you should be able, using these skills, and with the confidence they bring, to 'get immediately to work' on any writing task.

Stephen King's toolbox image chimes with what writers say in writing groups, as they are developing their writing skills over a six- to twelve-month period. They find that they procrastinate less, and they certainly do not wait for any kind of 'uprush' of inspiration, but are content to get something down on paper immediately and then work on that to produce a finished piece. This represents quite a change for many writers: a change in behaviours as much as a change in conceptions of writing.

It may seem inappropriate to use creative writers throughout this book, since they are different from thesis writers in so many ways. They have always wanted to be writers. They write all the time. They have come to know what works for them. How can that help you?

However, what is helpful, particularly when their subject is the writing process, is that they have developed and refined tools and tactics that we can use and adapt. They can teach us that we can fit writing into our lives and still 'have a life'. More importantly, they can show us different ways of learning how to do this.

The material covered in this book has evolved over fifteen years of thesis writing and research supervision courses. It has been tested in writers' groups, where postgraduates and academics have commented on drafts of this book, requesting, for example, that specific topics be dealt with and that lists of cogent questions designed to prompt reflection be replaced with guidance to prompt action.

The book covers the three main stages of thesis writing: Chapters 1–4 deal with strategies for getting started, Chapters 5–7 with working towards closure, and Chapters 8–10 are the endgame, pushing the thesis towards completion. Each chapter in this book takes as its focal point a different strategy for writing.

Of course, a good thesis writing 'toolkit' is more than a source for a certain number of words, just as a thesis is more than a simple total of a number of words. Clearly, length is one – and some would argue the least important – criterion. It gives no indication of the quality of the work or of the writing.

Quality in the writing is far more important than the number of words. However, quality comes through many, many, many revisions. In the early stages of such a long writing project as a thesis, it is not appropriate to aim for that type or level of quality. Early stages, early writings and early drafts will surely lack the qualities expected in the final polished product. Writing that is sketchy, incomplete, tentative and downright wrong is an inevitable part of the research and learning processes. This is why you have supervisors.

Writing is as good a way as any of testing your ideas and assumptions. Learning strategies for and developing a facility for generating text have, in themselves, proved to be important processes, more important, some would argue, than learning the mechanics of writing (Torrance et al. 1993). Being able to write 'on demand' is also a confidence booster for novice writers. It stops them from procrastinating and helps them get started on those early drafts that are, after all, called 'rough' for a reason.

The title of this chapter is so important because it raises one of the key issues: it is possible to become productive, lifelong writers using a variety of strategies. Adopting these strategies will be a more comfortable process for some writers than others; the strategies may initially appear useful at some stages in thesis writing and less so in others. The title of this chapter may also prompt interesting discussion among students and supervisors as to what does constitute 'good' writing practice and a 'quality' written product.

Productive writing, however, may require you to use more than one tool, perhaps several quite different tools at the same time. For example, 1000 words per hour is a feasible rate of writing when you know what the content is to be. If we have a detailed outline, we can 'write to order'. However, for thesis writers who are still learning about the subject, this may not be possible. They will have to sketch structures. They will have to make choices before or during writing in any case. They have to live and write with uncertainty. With thesis writers in mind, this book includes strategies for generating text with and without structure. It also provides prompts for additional thinking about structure, since thesis writers may not be conscious of how to use a generic framework as a starting point; generic frameworks can help you shape your unique thesis structure.

In other words, this book is based on three key principles: (1) learning comes through writing; (2) quality comes through revision; and (3) regular writing develops fluency. With these objectives in mind, it is possible to build up to writing 1000 words an hour, even though the whole thesis is not written in that way. There may be some debate about whether the 'learning' involved is about your topic or about your writing, but both apply. They are, in any case, interconnected.

Over the longer term, perhaps by the end of this book, it will be possible to write 1000 words an hour. This is not just about speed writing. With the strategies and concepts in this book, the writer will be better equipped to decide when, and what, he or she can and cannot write at this rate. Writing 100 or 1000 words in an hour or a day will be an active decision rather than a 'wait-and-see' passive process.

The 'wait-and-see' approach has another potential disadvantage: you may learn less about writing; you may not develop as a writer. There are those who think that writing ability is innate, that it is not learned. However, the fact that writing is not taught – beyond a certain level of school or undergraduate education – does not mean that it cannot be learned. The 1000-words-an-hour method may require a certain level of writing ability; but the argument of this book is that the ability can be developed. This takes time. Like the novice runner who, after a few short runs, asked, 'When does runner's high set in?' – expecting the effect to be immediate – you have to work at it to see the benefits. It might also be a good idea to improve your keyboard skills.

An analogy for word counting is taking your pulse while you are exercising or training: the number of heartbeats per minute tells you more accurately how hard you are working than does your own impression of effort. You may feel that you are really toiling up that hill or round that track, but if your heart rate is already in your training zone – say, 160 beats per minute – then you know that you do not have to increase your workload. You may be working hard enough already to achieve the desired effect. For any number of reasons, you may not be able to interpret 'effort' as actual output. Having a concrete measure can help you adjust your perspective.

With writing, counting the number of words is a way of getting a more accurate measure of output. We may feel that we are, or are not, doing enough writing, yet if we have 1000 or 100 words an hour – whatever the rate we set out to achieve, whatever we judge a realistic rate to be – then we know we are making progress. As with exercise, taking the 'heartbeat' of our writing can save us from trying to do too much and from feeling guilty about not having done 'enough'. More importantly, it can become a way of establishing momentum: we can track the regular flow of our writing. A rate of 1000 words a day produces 5000 words at the end of the week that were not there at the start. This can be a powerful motivator.

Setting a realistic pace, and calibrating it from time to time, is important, as you start to build regular writing into your life. Again, finding some way of measuring output can provide insight into the goals set: are you trying to do too much? If you want to work up to writing 1000 words an hour – having never done so before – should your goal not, initially, be much less than that? How much would be sensible?

A thesis is 'incomplete' for a number of years. It is helpful to have a sense of work that has been completed, even if not to a final stage. Since closure (discussed in Chapter 6) is deferred, again and again, it is helpful to create 'mini-closures' along the way. The writer has to find some way of marking progress.

It does not matter too much which method you choose for defining your writing targets. Do the best you can. Counting words, setting goals and acknowledging increments are ways of recognizing your progress. The beauty of counting is that it is simple and concrete.

Not everyone will be fascinated by numbers of words. There must be some writers who would find this approach too simplistic. Some will be disgusted at the apparent reduction of their highest ideals – original research, tough concepts, first-class writing skills – to a set of sums. But this is just one way of establishing a set of patterns for an extended writing process. It is not the only way. There can be more than one. For me, the fact that I just wrote 442 words of this chapter in 20 minutes, between 9.05am and 9.25am, will not grip every reader, but it does tell me what my actual pace of writing is just now and it does show me that I have achieved something, in writing. In fact, given that 1000 words an hour is a high – in my view – rate of output, I can reassure myself that I am being productive. The question of whether 'productivity' –

with its associations of other contexts – is enough, I ignore for the moment. Quality will come with revisions.

I also recognize that I am – and others may be – able to write this way with some subjects and not others. I have worked on thesis writing for fifteen years, but thesis writers may have worked on their subject for as little as fifteen weeks, fifteen days or fifteen minutes. Theoretically, most students and supervisors will probably say 'Thesis writers need more thinking time; they can't just churn out text at the rate of 1000 words an hour.' They – students and supervisors – might add, 'And it's just as well – it would all be rubbish.' It might, in one sense, be 'rubbish': students might, in the early stages, rush out writing that is tentative, full of uncertainties, rambling and wrong. But is this 'rubbish?' Another way of reading such writing is to say that the student is still learning to write and using writing to learn.

Rambling writing may indeed signal rambling thinking, but it may also be a first step, for students, in understanding their subject. I can hear supervisors and students saying things like 'But what is the point of doing bad writing?', and my response would be, 'Isn't producing writing that you're not happy with, that you know you have to redraft many times before you submit it for public scrutiny, an acceptable part of the writing process?' Does this make our writing 'bad writing'? Or is it more accurate – and helpful to the novice – to call it writing-on-the-way-to-being-good-writing, i.e. a draft? But if not this, then what?

The 'arithmetic of writing'

- How will you measure your written output?
- How will you identify the pace of writing that suits you?
- How will you establish momentum in your writing?

There are many ways of doing this, but if counting words, or pages, seems so unusual – if not wrong – to a thesis writer or supervisor, what does this say? What does it suggest about how they conceptualize writing? How will they define increments and stages? How will they break that down into actual, daily writing practices? These questions are not simply meant to be rhetorical – although they are frequently treated as such – but are meant to prompt discussion so that thesis writers develop their own answers.

Whether this point represents a real shift in thinking – even reconceptualization – about writing or whether it's just a way of renaming things, there is a point to be argued here about making explicit what are often left as assumptions about writing practices and products. Opening up the multiple draft writing process for discussion, for example, can boost students' confidence. They realize that producing 'bad writing' is sometimes part of the process and may, at times, be such a necessary part of the process that we would do well to find another name for it.

Supervisors shape thesis writers' conceptions of writing, but students can develop a number of different tools for writing without going against what their supervisors recommend. It is not the purpose of this book to create conflict between students and supervisors. However, given the potential for debate about writing, perhaps it is understandable if writers do not agree all the time about what works best. Given the range of strategies available – though supervisors and students may not have heard of them all – it is inevitable that there will, and should, be discussion of 'what works best', what that means and how we know.

It is to be anticipated that out of any set of new strategies one, or more, will seem immediately sensible and practical to the individual writer, while another will seem pointless and inappropriate for a thesis. For example, writing on demand is a theme of this book. Helping students to find ways to force their writing, throughout the three or six years, is one of its goals. If we accept that having a range of strategies – or at least more than one – is, in principle, a good idea, then there is every chance that some of the strategies in this book will not only be new, but may also seem counter-intuitive.

We have been writing in our own particular ways for so long; presumably, something has to change if we are to write a much larger and much more complex document. However, initially that 'change' in writing approaches, that simple broadening of our options, can seem uncomfortable and just too challenging. A thesis requires the writer – or provides opportunities for writers – to experiment with new techniques. If a thesis is different from any other kind of writing, you need to consider other strategies.

When asked to try specific activities for forcing writing by writing without stopping for five minutes, writers often ask, 'What can I write in five minutes?' In fact, this question is frequently rhetorical: 'What can I *possibly* write in five minutes?' Many people report that it takes them thirty minutes to 'get into' the writing. Before we go any further, that is worth noting as a future talking point in itself: what are people doing in those thirty minutes of 'warm-up' time? Do they have routines for getting themselves started? Does that really have to take all of thirty minutes? Can that really be the only way? Aren't other options available?

The purpose of this activity is to prompt writing, even at an early stage, when the thesis writer may not have a clear idea of where his or her project is going. The temptation at this stage – for obvious reasons – is to aim for a coherent proposal statement and thereafter other formal writing. However, examining – and adapting – your writing practices and assumptions is an important part of the writing process. For this activity you can also take time to react to the propositions so far covered in this chapter and to consider how they might help you write your thesis.

Writing activity

What can I write in five minutes?

1 Write continuously, non-stop, in sentences on this question:
   What do you think of the idea of writing 1000 words in an hour?
2 Count the number of words you wrote.

You may not be able to write 1000 words an hour yet. The point is that you can write – to order – X number of words when given a prompt and a time limit. This effect can be extended. Using all the tools in this book, it is feasible to write 1000 words in an hour, even for a thesis.

Forcing writing, writing quickly without stopping, writing immediately without planning has potential benefits:

> There's plenty of opportunity for self-doubt. If I write rapidly . . . I find that I can keep up with my original enthusiasm and at the same time outrun the self-doubt that's always waiting to set in.
>
> (King 2000: 249)

The point is not just to keep up enthusiasm for writing – though that, too, is important – but to keep a focus on what you are thinking, forcing yourself to find a way to ignore – or defer – any 'self-doubt' that may occur. There is, of course, nothing inherently wrong with self-doubt, unless it constantly stops you writing. In fact, self-questioning is probably a key skill for researchers.

Principles of academic writing

There are principles of writing in each academic discipline. It is up to you to locate and learn them. Find out what they are. You can do this by reading examples – publications and theses – and discussing your developing understanding of core principles in your discipline with your supervisor and peers. As you read examples of academic writing in your discipline, it might help to ask the following questions:

- What are the conventions of writing in this discipline?
- What language – nouns, verbs, links, etc. – do writers use?
- How are debates represented?
- How is the researcher represented, if at all?

- How is structure revealed?
- What are the options in style and structure?

Just as there are dominant issues in the debate in your discipline, so there are terms that are in and out of current use. Whether you see this as a matter of intellectual 'fashion' or not, it is up to you to recognize the language in which the conversation you are entering is being conducted and to use, interrogate or challenge it as you see fit.

The literature on writing

I presume that most thesis writers do not need a detailed survey of the literature, but might query approaches that are not underpinned by research and scholarship. The relevant literature is wide-ranging in approach and outcome, and the following overview is intended to demonstrate different schools of thought.

- Boice (1990) found that a daily regimen of writing makes academics productive writers.
- Brown and Atkins (1988: 123) defined the problems thesis writers face:
  - Poor planning and management of the project
  - Methodological difficulties in the research
  - Writing up
  - Isolation
  - Personal problems outside the research
  - Inadequate or negligent supervision.
- Elbow (1973) challenged the traditional view that we must first decide what we want to write and then write about it, arguing that we can use writing to develop our thinking.
- Emig (1977) argued that writing is a mode of learning.
- Flower and Hayes (1981) argued that cognitive processes – how you think – affect composition.
- Herrington (1988) defined the functions of writing tasks in educational settings, indicating, perhaps, what we might expect to have learned from them as undergraduates:
  - Introducing academic conventions
  - Introducing professional conventions
  - Showing knowledge of relevant conventions
  - Exercising independent thinking, actively engaging with the materials of knowledge (pp. 133–66).
- Hockey (1994) explored the psycho-social processes of thesis writing and the doctoral experience.

- Lee and Street (1998) argued for an 'academic literacies' approach, suggesting we should set about systematically learning the discourse of our disciplines.
- Murray (1995, 2000) argued that many different approaches and practices, working together, are needed for the development of a productive writing process, i.e. cognitive, psycho-social, rhetorical.
- Swales (1990) made a case for learning the 'genres' of academic writing and Swales and Feak (1994) demonstrated a genre-based approach in a textbook for non-native speakers of English that has relevance for native speakers.
- Torrance et al. (1993) found that neither learning about the technical aspects of writing nor developing cognitive strategies for writing were as effective as strategies for 'generating text'.

A theme in the literature is that there are writing tasks throughout the thesis process, aimed at developing the thesis as an integral part of the research process. If this integration is successful, the student can become a 'serial writer', i.e. develops the writing habit, learns to find ways to fit writing into a busy schedule and makes writing one of the parallel tasks of professional life.

Developing fluency and confidence requires regular writing. When we write regularly, writing is still hard work, but not as intimidating. Other writing tasks become easier to do; it becomes more difficult to procrastinate. The key is learning how to focus. The end result is that you can be confident about your writing, knowing that you can meet deadlines.

Herrington's (1985, 1992) naturalistic (i.e. looking at what student writers actually do) studies show how students construct themselves in the discipline, but also show that each course represents a distinct discourse community. It could be argued that each thesis is potentially situated in the same way: the thesis sits not just within the distinct discourse community of the discipline but, in fact, within a smaller, though no less complex, sub-set of that disciplinary discourse.

Should supervisors explicitly, not just implicitly, seek to develop these different knowledges and functions in their students' writing? Herrington (1992) has provided evidence that academics do take on this role in undergraduate education, through guiding, posing questions, making suggestions for revision processes that are familiar in the traditional student–supervisor relationship.

Disciplinary differences

[On] questions of theory and method, in particular, I would remind readers that these concepts mean very different things in different disciplines ... In most subject areas, however, the synergy between hypothesis, theory and method is absolutely central to the thesis's success.

(Pearce 2005: 74)

Even the words 'theory' and 'method', so central to research, can have very different meanings in different academic disciplines. Within your discipline there may appear to be a particular meaning attached to each, and you may find writing about them straightforward. Alternatively, you may find that these words denote areas of complexity that you do not yet understand. Writing about these core terms may, therefore, depend on which discipline you are working in, the type of work you are doing and the method – if that is the word you are using – that you use in your research. Some of these issues you will work out in your discussions with your supervisor. For your thesis, the important question is not whether there are disciplinary differences – there are – but what the characteristics of writing in your discipline are:

How to analyse a thesis

- Scan the contents page.
  What type of structure is used?
  Experimental/narrative/other form of logical progression?
  What are the approximate relative lengths of chapters?
  Is this structure reflected in the abstract?
- Read the introductory paragraphs of each chapter.
  How is progression from chapter to chapter established?
- What are the main differences between chapters?
  Look at structure and style: long/short sentences and paragraphs.
  Look at the language used: what are the key words?
  Types of verbs used: definitive, past tense or propositional?

If you are coming to research and thesis writing after a gap from study, then you may benefit from a kind of 'academic writing induction'. Your supervisor may be prepared to provide you with an overview of writing in your discipline and may help you with analyses of completed theses. If so, the trick is to focus not on the content, which is tempting when the thesis is in your and your supervisor's area of study and research, but on the way in which the content is articulated. You may find that this type of discussion produces more questions than answers. Do not be afraid to ask what you might think are fairly simplistic or superficial questions:

Ask your supervisor

- Why does the author use this term in this sentence?
- Why is that phrase repeated so often?
- Why is that section so long?
- Why is this other section so short?
- Why is that chapter divided up into so many sections?
- Will using the word 'limitations' not weaken the thesis?
- Why does the author not just say what he/she means?

Once you start to analyse thesis writing in your discipline, you will notice that there are certain ways of writing about certain subjects. You may also notice that there are differences between different sections: there may be a factual, descriptive style of writing for reports of experimental studies or individual analyses of texts or transcripts, and a more discursive style for interpretations and syntheses of results. The more factual writing can be done as you do your experiments or analyses, so that details and differences are recorded as you do the work, and, potentially, more accurately than if you let time elapse between experiments and writing.

Noticing such differences can help you see where different elements of your thesis will go and how you will write them. Of course, your thesis may be unique, unlike any other thesis, even in your discipline, yet it may share certain features that will help your reader find his or her way around it. At the end of the day, you can use existing thesis writing conventions as a framework or formula for your thesis, or you can transform existing conventions. The key is to write, in your introduction, what you do in your thesis, how it is set out and, perhaps, why you chose to do it that way. In some disciplines, such freedom is not an option, but in others you can, literally, invent your own structure.

However, there may be a set of core elements that examiners look for: some kind of forecasting statement at the start, for example, or certain kinds of linking and signposting devices between sections or, more importantly, a clear indication of your thesis's contribution and how you have laid out evidence for that claim throughout the thesis.

In the humanities and social sciences one of the challenges that thesis writers face is locating writing: where is writing? In the sciences and engineering, the structure of writing more closely mirrors the research process and writing practices may be more integrated in research. It can be easier to see that for every research task there is a writing task. However, in the humanities and social sciences students have to invent not only their own research question and thesis structure but also find the writing practice appropriate to their work. They have to find a place for writing in their research.

In certain disciplines there are assumptions about student writing. For example, in the humanities it may be assumed that students who are about to start writing a thesis have certain writing abilities already:

Assumptions about thesis writers in the humanities

- They can already write well.
- Attempts to improve writing are remedial.
- The first writing students submit to supervisors is a draft chapter.
- Progress is indicated and assessed in terms of completed chapters.
- They are natural 'loners' and independent thinkers.
- With good students, supervisors make few comments on writing.
- Students know how to correct problems in writing when they are pointed out.
- Drafting is key (but rarely discussed).

Some of these assumptions may operate, of course, in other disciplines. Some of them may be closer to the truth than the word 'assumption' implies. With any unspoken assumption, it is difficult to know how generally accepted it is. However, because they are not all helpful to the thesis writer, it is worth discussing these assumptions with supervisors. Exploring your and your supervisors' reactions to these assumptions might be a useful way to initiate more detailed and relevant – to your thesis – discussions. You might find that you learn a lot about thesis writing, specific to your discipline, in this way.

In the visual – and other – arts, there are other forms of thesis, other definitions of what constitutes 'research' and other modes of examination. Thesis writing may involve a form of 'active documentation' (Sullivan 2005: 92). You may not have to provide as much justification of your work as is the norm in other disciplines. However, as with any discipline, it is your responsibility to check the institutional requirements and, probably, you will still have to demonstrate some knowledge of the culture of research. Beyond that, you may not simply have to give an account of the context for your work but also to define its creative component.

Defining what is required in the written form is, as for any discipline, a key initial task. The thesis writer has to find answers to

questions about how practice-based research might be conceptualized as a dissertation argument, and where this theorizing might be located: within the realm of the artwork produced, within a contextual form such as a related 'exegesis,' or in some combination of the two.

(ibid.: 92)

'Exegesis' refers to an explanatory text which some see as unnecessary, because the art work should speak for itself and stand on its own, but which others see as requiring the intellectual apparatus of any other advanced study or research:

> *Exegesis* is the term usually used to describe the support material prepared in conjunction with an exhibition, or some other research activity that comprises a visual research project . . . exegesis is not merely a form of documentation that serves preliminary purposes, records in-progress activity, or displays outcomes: *It is all of these.*
>
> (ibid.: 211–12)

In one sense, this is quite like the research and writing produced in any discipline; in other senses, and perhaps in practice, it can be very different. Like other disciplines, the visual arts use many different forms of inquiry and frameworks for conceptualization.

Students often feel that they have to start from scratch in designing their theses, with each student inventing a new structure. However, some would argue that, in terms of structure, the differences between one thesis and another are minor, even superficial. In fact, one reader has asked, 'How are these different?'

Nevertheless, the headings on the right-hand side will look alien to some students in the humanities, social sciences and business. Yet there are similarities with the left-hand column. Some will see the two columns as completely different; others will see them as much the same.

Generic thesis structure

Humanities and Social Sciences	Science and Engineering
The subject of my research is . . . It merits study because . . .	*Introduction*
My work relates to others' in that . . . The research question is . . .	*Literature review*
I approached it from a perspective of . . .	*Methods*
When I did that I found . . .	*Results*
What I think that means is . . .	*Discussion*
There are implications for . . .	*Conclusions*

The point is that we can adapt the generic thesis structure – on the right in this box – to many different contexts. It can be used as a framework for many different types of study. Its apparent 'home' in science and engineering should not prevent us from making use of it as a starting point, at least. Nor is this structure just for experimental research. Every study has a method. Every study produces 'results' – outcomes of analyses, of whatever kind.

Some writers, in some disciplines, may feel that 'translating' the scientific template is not a valid option; the headings do not translate into chapters, and this is unhelpful. That may well be true. You might not have such chapter headings and divisions. However, it is a starting point. It can be seen as representing the 'deep structure' of many different types of thesis. It may, therefore, help writers develop initial statements on what are key issues for any thesis.

The generic structure is a tool for writing and thinking. As a template, it can help us answer the key questions for a thesis. Whether or not this shapes chapters is another question. We may not all be drawn to it – some will be alienated by it – but even if you use it as an antagonist, it will prompt you to sketch alternative structures. If this structure and strategy seem wrong to you, that may be because you already have the germ of an idea for your thesis structure. Capture that on paper now. You then have some ideas you can discuss, and possibly develop, with your supervisor.

Thinking about structure

In order to develop further your thinking about structure, at an early stage, you could discuss the following questions with other writers and, of course, with your supervisor:

- Does your discipline have an implicit/explicit generic structure?
- Are there any books/support materials on thesis writing in your discipline?

If the idea of 'generic structure' strikes you as strange – since each thesis is different – then it might be a good idea to discuss this concept further.

- Have you discussed the overall structure of your thesis with your supervisor and/or peers?
- If you think it is too early, in your research, for this discussion, think about and discuss how the work you do in the early stages relates to the production of a thesis.

If you do want to use a 'non-generic' structure, then you should research – and discuss – that too.

- Will you be inventing a completely new structure?
- What are the precedents for this in your discipline?

Prompts

At the very start of the thesis process, most writers feel they have nothing to write about. The instruction to 'just write' seems absurd. Many will feel they have not really 'started' anything, while they are still reading and thinking about their project. The problem with this state of mind – or concept of thesis writing – is that it can continue for just a little too long. It is possible to think that you 'have nothing to write about' for many months. In fact, the more you read, the more certain you may become that you have nothing to contribute to the debate, and therefore nothing to write.

In order to combat this reluctance to write – since it cannot continue indefinitely – the chapters of this book have 'What can I write about now?' sections. These are to be used as prompts – by students and/or supervisors – for writing throughout the thesis, from start to finish. Any prompt can be used at any time. They can be adapted, or rewritten, to suit the individual. The main point is that writing occurs, text is generated.

This approach antagonizes some supervisors and students: the word 'quality' is the focus of their concern. Will the writing activities proposed here produce 'good writing'? Possibly not. But, as was proposed earlier – and it is worth repeating because the 'quality question' is paramount – we have to question the practice of applying the 'quality' criterion so early in the thesis writing process. Is quality – in structure, style and content – feasible at this stage? The quality of your writing – on all of these criteria – will be a focus for later discussions and revisions. This means that you should determine and discuss what the 'quality criteria' are at any given stage in your thesis writing process.

However, it cannot be assumed that this issue, or the proposed discussion, is straightforward. The concept of differentiating 'quality' criteria may not be central to your supervisor's practice, in providing you with feedback on your writing or, more importantly, in establishing criteria for you before you write. This means that you may come up against surprise, incredulity or open hostility to the concept. Alternatively, your supervisor may respond very positively to the news that you have been reading and thinking carefully about thesis writing. It is likely, however, that some of the concepts and practices proposed in this book will be new to some supervisors and you may find that, as with other aspects of your research, you have to participate in a debate about writing matters. Discussing the pros and cons of thesis writing strategies is no bad thing; you may in the process gain additional insights from your supervisor's experience and practice as a writer.

Naturally, your supervisor may at any time alert you to any features of your writing that need to be improved. These early writing tasks often act as a kind of diagnostic test. Your knowledge of and ability in writing will be tested at every stage. You may feel that hard criteria are unfairly applied to very early writing; alternatively, you could be thankful that you have a supervisor who is willing and able to give you feedback on the quality of your writing.

Some writers say that they can only write when they have a clear definition of the purpose of the writing task, but you may benefit from writing about quite general questions at this stage:

What can I write about now?

1 **What I am most interested in is . . .**
The books/papers I have enjoyed reading most are . . .
The ideas I want to write about are . . .

2 **What I want to do with this is . . .**
What I want to look at is . . .
The idea I keep coming back to is . . .
Here are my ideas . . . views . . . feelings . . . on the topic . . .

3 **The main question that interests me is . . .**
What I really want to do is . . .
What I really want to say is . . .
I want to find out whether . . .

This writing activity helps thesis writers (1) find topics and (2) focus on them. Establishing a direct link to your own interests, using plain English and the first person – 'I' – and actually writing about them are the key features of this exercise.

Simply thinking about these questions, running over them again and again in your mind, will, arguably, not have the same effect. Writing will help you to develop your idea one step further. Not writing – over the longer term – may erode your confidence in your fledgling idea.

Enabling student writing

Here is a set of expectations that you might have of your supervisor, specific to your thesis writing process. It might be a good idea to articulate your expectations or, if that does not suit you, to use these statements as a trigger for your discussions:

• Supervisors should give you feedback on your writing.

Feedback will be variable. It might be helpful to discuss feedback on writing at an early stage, even if you have not written much. The discussion will give you insights into what your supervisor is looking for and, perhaps equally importantly, it will give them insights into how you see writing.

- Supervisors should help their students set writing goals from the start of the thesis and all the way through to the end.

This will help you to see the writing process as a whole, perhaps even to see the stages ahead of you and to see how you can plan time for them. Long-term goals can help you to plan your writing, while short-term goals make it manageable. Whatever the goals, the key point is that they are discussed and agreed by you and your supervisor. Otherwise, everything remains undefined, many aspects of writing are unspoken and you may form the impression that you just don't write well.

- Supervisors should motivate students to start writing and to keep writing throughout the project.

However, your supervisor may not want to put you under too much pressure. Your supervisor may feel that you have enough to do setting up the research or reading piles of books and papers and may agree to defer writing to a later stage. This may be a mistake. If writing is part of learning, you will miss out on an opportunity to develop your understanding. If writing is a test of learning, you may have no measure of how you are building your knowledge.

This section can be summarized as a series of prompts for you to take the initiative with your supervisor so that he or she is able to 'enable your writing'.

Writing in a second language

Non-native speakers of English may require extra help with thesis writing; alternatively, you may have more knowledge of English grammar and usage than native speakers. The code of practice on *The Management of Higher Degrees Undertaken by Overseas Students* (CVCP/CDP 1992) states that overseas students may require more supervision than others, perhaps for more than just the language differences, since there are other layers of cultural difference that create specific challenges. However, is each supervisor (1) aware of this code and (2) able to give extra time to overseas students? Is it fair to expect this? How will you find out what you can expect from your supervisor?

The highest standard of clarity and correctness is required in a thesis, and this does require some knowledge of grammar and punctuation rules. While all students are admitted to a university on the basis of satisfactory perform-ance on one of a number of standard tests, the complexity of the thesis –

process and product – puts new demands on writers. You may find that you require further writing development or support.

You are unlikely to know what you need, if indeed you need any further development or support, unless you have some form of diagnostic test. This need not be a formal test, just a writing task which lets your supervisor assess the standard of your writing. If your supervisor does not provide this, or does not ask you to write in the first few weeks or months of your project, you should offer to do some writing, so that you can get such feedback early. Then, if you do need to attend a course on English for Academic Purposes, for example, you will still have time to do so. If you need some other form of additional support, you will have time to find out where you can get it. If you need individual instruction, again, you will have time to find someone to provide it.

Your spoken English may be equally important for the development of your research and in your relationship with your supervisor and peers. If you are an overseas student who is not yet entirely fluent in English, it is vital that you find out who is going to help you, particularly if you are not speaking English at home. Again, if your supervisor or department is prepared to take limited responsibility for helping you, you must check out what other sources of support your university offers. Many universities have a language support service dedicated to helping overseas students. Be persistent till you find what you need. Continuing without additional support is not a wise option.

- Does your supervisor see this as his or her role? How will you know? How can you find out?
- Will your supervisor be prepared to give you writing support in the earlier stages? He or she may do so, but may want to see that you can learn some of these things by yourself.
- Will your supervisor be prepared to give you detailed editing in later stages? Again, perhaps – but you must check. However, your supervisor will probably not be happy to continue to correct the same errors over and over again in your drafts. You have to take some action to improve your writing.

Grammatical correctness in English often seems less important to students, but it has an important effect on your argument, particularly in the later stages. Poor sentence structure, for example, will obscure your line of thought and may even make your writing appear incoherent.

Grammar, punctuation, spelling

If you do not know the difference between the passive voice and the active voice – or if you thought it was the active 'tense' – then you may need to learn some of the key terms used in defining, and useful for discussing, the qualities of academic writing. You may need to study this area. Otherwise your discussions with your supervisor may be confusing, as they use terms that you do not really understand, although you know you should, and they may expect you to. You can always ask them to explain them to you, but Strunk and White ([1959] 1979) combine definitions with illustrations to such good effect, in such a short book, that there is no need to go into such discussions completely unprepared. There are many other texts that cover this area. Your supervisor may recommend another text and may use other definitions of grammar that you will have to connect to your reading about it.

More importantly, you might not understand what your supervisor is saying in any comments on your writing. How will you respond to this feedback if you do not fully understand it? Will you just press on with your writing and revising and hope for the best? Will you make some kind of revision without really knowing if you have responded to the feedback or not? This will breed uncertainty that you can undoubtedly live without.

There are a number of terms you should be able to define and recognize in practice – in reading and writing.

Here are ten questions that you can use to test your knowledge:

Quick quiz

1 What are the definite and indefinite articles?
2 When and how do you use a semi-colon?
3 What is a personal pronoun?
4 What is 'the antecedent'?
5 What is subject–verb agreement?
6 What are the essential elements of a sentence?
7 Give examples of sentences using the passive and active voices.
8 What is the difference in meaning between the two?
9 Define 'sentence boundaries' and say why they are important.
10 What is a topic sentence?

If you know the answers to all of these, you are probably a student of literature or foreign languages. Perhaps your first language is not English, as it often seems that 'non-native speakers' have more knowledge of grammar. However, if you can answer only five – or none at all – this suggests that you have some work to do in this area. How much work, and how you will learn about these subjects, may be worth discussing with your supervisor.

Remember that your goal is to produce excellence in your writing; it is not simply an exercise in pedantry to require that your subjects and verbs agree. Likewise, if your sentences are not well bounded your argument will appear confused. You will appear confused. If you do not know exactly what you are doing when you are revising your own writing, this could undermine your confidence as you write the thesis. That is exactly the opposite of what the process is meant to achieve.

If you do not know the answers to the ten questions, you need to read one of the many texts or sites on grammar and punctuation or find some other mechanism for learning about these topics:

- Strunk and White (http://www.diku.dk/students/myth/EOS)
- *Fowler's Modern English Usage* (Fowler [1965] 1984)
- Websites on writing
- Online writing courses (e.g. at American universities)
- Ask for help
- Attend a course.

Goal setting

This topic takes us right back to the question of why you are writing a thesis. You choose this track. You wander into the department. Before you know it, you have a stack of books and papers to read, meetings to attend and classes to teach. Alternatively, you may have large chunks of unplanned time, which can be just as intimidating. The point is that however clear your goal was, you may have lost sight of it, not for the last time. It helps to have some way of reminding yourself of where you are going and why you chose to go there.

Goal setting is about managing the long and short term. We can use a goal-setting process to help us to focus on both the immediate goal – the writing that we are doing now – and the long-term goal – the thesis that we have to produce. Somehow, we have to develop a commitment to both goals and deal with the tension between the two:

> Having the long view is being both energized and relaxed; enthusiastic and patient. It's knowing in the marrow of your bones this one paradoxical fact: Writing's been around a long time and will probably continue at least as long, and yet it always happens in the here and now.
>
> (Palumbo 2000: 93)

What does this mean? Holding two contrary views in our minds, throughout the project, from now until it ends? What is, for each writer, the 'long view'? You have to form your own long view. Take a few minutes now to write (five minutes, in sentences) about yours.

Our goal may not be to 'become a writer', but the thesis writing process goes on for long enough that writing has to become a major part of our lives:

Seeing things whole, having the long view, is the only way to live the writer's life. It's committing yourself to a concept of writing as an integral, ongoing part of your life, instead of just a series of external events.

(Palumbo 2000: 93)

We have to see our writing process both as a long-term process and as a 'series of external events'. We have to keep one eye on 'what's in it for us' and the other on 'what they want me to do'.

In addition, there is value not only in seeing the project as a whole, but also in imagining the text of the thesis as a whole. We also need to construct an image of our life as a whole with writing in it. We then have to find a way of putting that into practice. In other words, there is more to goal setting than simply listing a sequence of actions; there is more to monitoring than ticking a box as we complete each task.

The principle at work here is bringing definition to the thesis writing process. We create stages in the writing process; these stages are a construction. We can play the numbers game, setting very specific writing goals. The student has responsibility to create a series of writing milestones.

Most people have heard of 'SMART', a snappy way of defining a good goal. In fact, there are two versions of this: one identifies external features of goals, representing goal setting as an objective process, and the second links goals to internal motivation (based on James and Woodsmall 1988).

SMART Version 1

Effective goals are

- **S**pecific: detailed enough to be measurable and convincing
- **M**easurable
- **A**chievable
- **R**ealistic: with no limiting factors
- **T**imescaled

Version 2, because it focuses less on the outputs and more on values and emotions may be more effective for creating writing goals that work:

SMART Version 2

- **S**imple: immediately understandable by you
- **M**eaningful: to you, aligned with your core values
- **A**s if now: you can make it real to you, in all areas of your life
- **R**esponsible: for everyone involved
- **T**owards what you want: not someone else's goal

Both supervisors and students may have reasons for shying away from goals: the supervisor may think this is too personal an approach, and may not want to put pressure on the student so early on; the student may be more comfortable talking about research goals than writing goals. However, there is evidence that goal setting improves performance in many different areas. Goal setting and self-efficacy beliefs can work in symbiosis (Seijts et al. 1998). It may be up to you, once you have a general goal from your supervisor, to make it more specific, more workable:

Writing goals

- Define the purpose of the writing task.
- Choose a writing verb: review/evaluate/summarize.
- Define your audience.
- Define the scale and scope of your writing.
- Decide on the number of words you will write.
- Decide how long you will take to write it.

These approaches usefully remind us to adopt behavioural approaches, since changing and monitoring our behaviours – not just our thoughts – are what make up this new writing challenge. Hence the value of 'the arithmetic of writing': it sets concrete targets and gives real measures of output. Vague writing goals can cause problems: not only is it difficult to ascertain whether or not we have achieved them, but a vague writing goal is difficult to start. If the writing task is not sufficiently defined, the writing process is itself ill-defined:

Poor writing goals

- **Do five minutes' writing practice daily.**
  Too big a change. Purpose not clear.
- **Clarify topic.**
  Scale and scope of the writing task unknown.
- **Get feedback on writing.**
  Type of feedback not defined. Recipe for misunderstanding.

Writers who have used the 'SMART' process are only too well aware, once they step back to appraise their own goals, that they have left them ill-defined. They quickly realize that there has to be much more definition:

Good writing goals

- Do five minutes' writing practice today at 9.45 am.
- Define the topic in 500 words (two pages). Give it 30 minutes.
- Ask supervisor: is the topic becoming more focused?

Not everyone works best by setting specific goals; some find approximate goals more effective. Whatever you choose to do, it is important not just to have the long-term goal in view, but the short-term too. Not just the long-term goal of 'finishing' but the short- and medium-term goals of starting, keeping going, losing the way, failing, changing direction, productive periods of writing, etc., i.e. all the unpredictable phases of a large writing project.

How does your supervisor want you to set, and monitor, your goals? He or she may think the 'SMART' stuff is too gimmicky for higher education, or find the second version too personal, but if you find it useful, there is no reason not to use it to work out what your goals are. It is your goals that you have to agree with your supervisor, not your personal processes for working them out.

Your goals provide a number of topics for discussions with your supervisor. If you are not confident enough to talk about your writing goals, you can at least discuss – and agree – your research goals, although you should define writing outputs for your plan of work.

It is important to put your goals down on paper and get focused feedback on them. Goal setting requires feedback and monitoring, otherwise you will have no real sense of whether or not you are progressing. You will have to see how your supervisor wants you to set and monitor goals, but you may also have to take the initiative, indicating that you are ready for this discussion and, above all, ready to include writing in this discussion.

A research methods group, or writers' group that includes new students and those who are further along, can help students see how goals are set, what constitutes an effective goal and what the whole thesis writing process involves.

Lifelong learning

Academics . . . should know better. Researchers have been nervous to let go to notions of 'scholarship', 'academic' or 'pure research', 'specialisms', 'expertise' and the 'scientific method'. We perpetuate the myth that education is a practice, and in so labelling it we separate it from what is everyday and for everyday.

(Elliott 1999: 29–30)

Elliott reminds us that individual learners have the responsibility to make sense of learning in their own environment.

You did not stop learning about writing when you completed your first degree. You are expected to have a high level of written and spoken English at the start of your second degree, but it is likely that you will develop these skills further in the course of the months and years to come.

Writing a thesis can be seen as a development process:

Five minutes' freewriting

How do you want to develop as a writer over the long term?

Five minutes' writing
In sentences
Private writing

It would be interesting to look back at your answer to this question at the end of your thesis.

You will continue to learn throughout the thesis writing process. Some students get frustrated that they still have not quite 'made it' in their writing, but that is a feature of the protracted learning process and the growing recognition that since we are always writing for new audiences, we are always learning about writing. Our relationship to our audience also changes, as we become more knowledgeable – and more known – in our field.

You may notice an emphasis on process in the course of your study, prompting you to think about, and perhaps document, the learning that you do in the course of writing your thesis:

An emerging theme in doctoral discourse in the UK is the switch from content to competence, driven by a shift in emphasis towards the PhD experience for the student, and away from simply the outcome (award of the degree) or the product (thesis).

(Park 2005: 199).

Whether you are doing a doctorate or a masters or undergraduate thesis, you may have to think about what 'transferable skills' you can learn in the process.

Audience and purpose

Audience and purpose are always the key in any communication act. What we write is shaped by the identity of whoever we are writing for and by our purpose in writing for them. For example, we present our research differently to departmental groups, to work-in-progress presentations and at conferences, where we create the impression of closure.

The audiences – since there are more than one – for a thesis are analysed in Chapter 2. However, it is important to consider how problematic audience can be for new thesis writers: thesis writers have to write with authority, when they may feel that they have none.

While we know that we are not expected to produce high-quality writing – and thinking – in our first, or 'rough' drafts, we have internalized the expectation of high-quality writing. This can present writers with a conflict. It can stop them writing anything. This is, therefore, an important talking point: what are the criteria for early writings, i.e. in the first few weeks and months? Is there adequate definition of the writing task: length, scale, scope, etc.?

While much of the writing that you do in this phase – and most of the activities proposed in the early chapters – is not intended to generate text to be shown to your supervisor, it is important that you address the requirements of that audience too.

Remember that when you write for your thesis you are joining a debate. Anything you write can be challenged, not because your argument is weak or your writing is poor, but because that is the nature of the context. Entering the debate tentatively is probably a sound strategy. See yourself participating in, rather than 'winning' or 'losing', the debate. See yourself making your point clearly, rather than demolishing – or impressing – the opposition. Expect some to agree and others to disagree with your points; this is inevitable in debate.

This introduction has explored the theoretical underpinnings of this book. It has demonstrated how we can become regular writers: by writing regularly. More importantly, it has begun to shift the responsibility for defining the writing process to the thesis writer. How others, including the external examiner, define writing will be covered in the next chapter. It defines the whole thesis writing process.

Timetable for writing

Phillips and Pugh (2000) provide a graphic illustration of the timescale of the PhD (p. 88), showing 'writing' as a continuous and 'iterative' element. 'Iterations' have to be designed by the individual writer. If writing is iterative then some tasks will appear more than once in your timetable:

- Revise proposal.
- Start constructing list of references.
- Summarize readings.
- Sketch background theory.
- Write research aims/questions.
- Write about two or three possible methods of inquiry.

Take time to develop your timetable:

- Writing task
- Deadline
- Writing time.

Discuss your plan of work, including writing, with your supervisor. How will you monitor your progress towards your goals?

As you gradually grasp what is required for a thesis – and how your supervisor interprets that requirement – revise your short- and long-term goals. Any – perhaps every – timetable is there to be changed.

Checklist

Defining the writing task

One student said she liked having checklists for chapters: 'You need to have checklists.' They provide a route map on a long and complex journey.

Some students say that they are so exhausted all the time that they need checklists to make it all manageable; checklists clarify what needs to be done.

- Start writing now.
- Discuss writing, explicitly, with your supervisor.
- Read one book on writing in your discipline.
- Make up a rough timetable for writing.
- Set long- and short-term writing goals (not just research goals).
- Find out about punctuation rules. And grammar.
- Define audience and purpose for your writing.
- Discuss all of these subjects with your supervisor.
- Consider taking typing lessons. If you don't already have one, consider buying/using a laptop.

1

Thinking about writing a thesis

Doctorate or masters? • What is a doctorate? • New routes to the PhD
• Why are you doing a doctorate? • Internal and external drivers • PhD or
professional doctorate? • Full-time or part-time? • What will you use writing
for? • Regulations • How will it look on the page? • Demystification: codes
and guides • How will my thesis be assessed? • What are the criteria?
• Defining 'originality' • What is the reader looking for? • IT processes and
needs • Reasons for not writing • Peer discussion and support • Your first
meeting with your supervisor • Questions for reflection • Prompts for
discussion • Writing timetable • Checklist: pre-planning

Doctorate or masters?

While several sections of this chapter focus on the doctorate, the issues and questions that are addressed are relevant to other levels of study. For example, finding out about institutional and departmental context and regulations is a crucial step in defining your task as a thesis writer. If you are intending to do a masters before your PhD, then this chapter will help you to think through your options and possible directions. The type of doctorate you intend to do in the future may influence the type of masters you do now. For example, if you want to use a particular research method, you might want to do a masters that provides the training you need, and then do a more independent form of doctorate, without research training, if you feel you are ready.

This chapter proposes a structured approach to writing a thesis, promoting the idea of integrating writing into the research process. There is an overview of what this involves, including reflections on many strands of the writing process: psychological, social and rhetorical.

Arguments for writing throughout the thesis are proposed and strategies for writing at the early stages defined and illustrated, using examples of real student writing. Commentary and annotations on these writings point out valuable strategies. Questions students usually ask about such arguments and strategies are addressed. The aim is to take readers, and writers, through a progression of skills, since it is assumed that the research process includes writing development.

First, however, there are several sections of definition: what do the terms that frequently feature in research discussion really mean? What are the contextual factors affecting thesis writers? What structures, practices and processes are typical of the doctoral thesis? To what extent are these relevant to masters and undergraduate thesis writers?

These initial sections of this chapter are intended to help prospective doctoral students choose the programme that suits them best and to help new students find their way in the programme they have chosen. This should help both groups to find a place for writing in their research.

What is a doctorate?

The 'old' or the 'new'? Traditionally, the doctorate in the UK has consisted of three years of independent research; more recently, there is some interest in what is perceived as 'the American doctorate' (although American higher education offers many variations of the doctorate), meaning four years, including one or two years of course work and research training.

The pros and cons of each form of doctorate (and masters programme) will no doubt continue to be hotly debated; the question is, which one suits you? Do you feel ready for independent research?

> The UK system assumes undergraduate education provides students with all they need to know to begin researching. It is debatable whether that is still true, particularly as universities try to keep up with the latest advances.
>
> (Plomin 2001: 1)

Can you do – or do you want to do – a one-year masters to prepare you for your doctorate? There is also the one-plus-three mode: one year of training, plus three years of research. For example, the Wellcome Trust has a four-year course that allows students to gain experience in more than one lab, as they make up their mind which project to do for their doctorate. There is a precedent for this mode in psychiatry:

> We got a lot of training in modelling and statistics, but the main thing was being able to take part in various experiments. With other PhDs, you would have to say, 'This is the title of my project' and been stuck with it three years later. Here you can work out what you want to do.
>
> (Mike Galsworthy, third-year PhD student,
> commenting in Plomin 2001)

However, this mode may not suit everyone; those who know exactly what they want to do, and who want to get their doctorate started and finished as quickly as possible, may prefer the three-year mode.

The UK government has called for more formal training in the doctorate, partly in order to improve the research training component, but partly also to increase employability in sectors beyond higher education, i.e. the argument is that the doctorate should prepare people to conduct research in different areas, not just their area of specialization. Even in the humanities, the set of disciplines most wedded to the three-year model, the Arts and Humanities Research Board (AHRB), supports programmes that include some form of 'research preparation', either in a taught masters or a tailored MA by research.

Consequently, this may, or may not, be an explicit goal of an institution or an individual student or supervisor. It may be a factor in funding, programme selection and student recruitment. This may influence the writing project considerably. For example, there may be a requirement to demonstrate knowledge of wider applicability of methods and analyses (Park 2005).

On the other side of the debate are those who argue that 'We demand too much from the traditional PhD.' Gillon (1998) puts the representative case that 'A PhD should prepare a person for one career, not all possible careers':

> At the present time those involved in the PhD process are over-stretched. Students are no longer simply expected to carry out research leading to a substantial and original contribution to knowledge. On top of that, they are required to undertake teaching that is often tied to the award of a bursary, publish academic papers . . . acquire and develop transferable skills such as those of communication and project management, and, of course, write an in-depth and coherent thesis in the space of three years. To fit in so many tasks is difficult and often leads to deficiencies [in one] or more of these areas. While PhD graduates have to endure the criticism arising from such deficits, surely the blame lies more squarely upon the unfocused, haphazard process itself.
>
> (Gillon 1998: 13)

There is another way of looking at this allegedly overloaded agenda: it would be surprising if a doctoral student were not encouraged, for example, in addition to writing a thesis, to submit papers for publication during the doctorate.

Whether or not there is evidence of such 'deficiencies' is a question to which we do not have an answer in Gillon's short piece. It may be logical to assume that where there is course work, research training and teacher training for higher education, there will be less time for the thesis, as some would argue; however, that logical assumption, if it is not normally, formally part of your doctoral programme, will have to be well planned, perhaps by you.

Many supervisors will have been involved, though some not enough, in these transformations of the doctorate – proposed or real – at the local level. It is supervisors who still, in theory and in practice, develop the 'curriculum', if that is the right word, for each doctorate. The value of this system is that the doctorate can be customized for the individual student, or supervisor, but the downside is that there may, as Gillon argues, be too much of a good thing, too many contradictory demands on the student.

American universities have, for some considerable time, been combining the various elements, listed by Gillon as excessive, into coherent programmes. That type of programme, managed well, makes for an outstanding and comprehensive learning experience for the novice researcher. It is not, therefore, that the broader doctoral curriculum cannot be done well, just that it probably has to be managed at a 'Graduate School' level in order to become a coherent programme. Can an individual supervisor be responsible for 'mapping the [doctorate] onto the demands of students and the requirements of employers'? Or is that the work of another, possibly strategic, grouping in a university? This too is the subject of much debate.

A key question for prospective postgraduates would be, for example, to ask if you will be given a teaching load – a good opportunity to develop both skills and knowledge – and if you will also be able, or required, to attend a course on teaching. If there is such a course, for postgraduate tutors, then this is a sign that that element of the broader curriculum has been thought through, is being supported and is more likely to be well managed. Then you can ask, is the course or programme that you will be taking accredited, or not?

A specific question that you can use to unpack the rationale of particular doctoral programmes would be, 'What are the learning outcomes of the doctorate?' In any case, this is an important question for individuals to engage with themselves before signing up to the doctorate: what learning outcomes are you aiming to achieve?

The fact that Gillon referred to the PhD as the 'traditional' form raises the question of whether there ought to be, or already are, different forms of, or 'new routes' (plural) to, the PhD.

New routes to the PhD

The traditional PhD model is now being challenged by a growing diversity of types of doctoral degree, including PhD by publication, Professional Doctorates, and New Route PhD. Traditional expectations of the PhD are being challenged by the new context within which research degrees are now situated and evaluated.

(Park 2005: 190)

While Park's paper on 'New Variant PhD' focuses on the UK, there are issues here worth raising before you commit to one mode of study, and some of the research-teaching and professional-academic tensions might also feature in masters programmes. You might, as Park suggests, think beyond your research and your thesis to where it is that you want to get to professionally, after you have completed your research.

In most countries there are many 'routes' to the doctorate. Even universities in the same country or state will offer variations on the theme. Each has its own appeal. The trick – for the individual applicant – is to find the programme that suits your needs and aspirations.

One new route developed by the Higher Education Funding Council for England (HEFCE) is designed as an improvement on the 'traditional' UK PhD. Its explicit economic aim is to compete with the 'American PhD', but it has educational appeal too. It combines a research project with 'a coherent programme of formal coursework' in a 'seamless programme' of all components. The rationale provided by HEFCE, who are sponsoring it, combines market-oriented and employability arguments:

Why a New Route PhD?

The knowledge-based economy of today puts far greater demands upon Doctoral graduates. There will always be a need for the subject specialist, but the competition for jobs in all sectors . . . is increasing and many find that having specialist knowledge . . . is not sufficient. Increasingly, the traditional PhD is seen as too 'narrow' and students wishing to study for a PhD must carefully consider how employable they will be on graduation.

(www.newroutephd.ac.uk/Pages/why.html)

While this rationale – taken from the 'New Routes' website – sounds a bit ominous, it does appear to offer more choice, although there is some evidence that student views have not been included in the design of this 'new route' (Johnston and Murray 2004: 42). Ten universities were initially invited to offer this new type of PhD. Their websites, accessible through this one, give details of what is involved. These university websites illustrate the content of, for example, the 'PhD with Integrated Study' at the University of Birmingham: http.//www.prospective.bham.ac.uk/newroutephd.htm.

This route will take four years. Thirty to 40 per cent will be taught discipline-specific and interdisciplinary modules. The taught element includes skills training, e.g. communication skills, management training, etc.

Perhaps more important, for prospective students – and universities – is HEFCE's statement about the future of this route: they propose that all PhDs will use this model.

While this new route aims to compete with the American PhD, it is not offering the same components as are available at many US universities, although it must be remembered that American higher education is an extremely diverse system, and therefore any generalizations about it have to be carefully considered. However, it may offer the nearest thing to it in the UK. It may attract more international students, thus creating a more cosmopolitan peer group.

Independent evaluation provides more information on the effectiveness and experiences of this new form of the PhD. On the basis of that information, you can judge the success – and suitability – of this route.

For individual doctoral students, the question of whether or not to follow this route may be decided by the simple fact of whether or not it is offered in their subject area or in the university they want to attend.

This chapter provides summaries of and commentaries on such developments in the form of the doctorate. It might be worth checking the websites and publications of the different groups involved in order to keep up to date on what is available.

Why are you doing a doctorate?

Do you have an answer to this question? Have you discussed this with those close to you, with those who are most likely to be affected, directly or indirectly, by your studies? Do you have their support?

What is your personal motivation? Is this a career-enhancing thing? Or are you seeking a post in higher education, for which this is usually a required qualification? Are you aware of the very small percentage of doctoral graduates who actually find employment in higher education?

How much time and energy you see yourself spending on your doctorate is related to why you are doing it in the first place. What are you prepared to give up in order to make time for this?

Are you interested in learning more about a subject? Or do you want to extend your knowledge of the whole field? A key factor – some would argue 'the' key factor – in sustaining meaning and motivation through the long doctoral process is the subject you choose. It has to be something in which you have a genuine interest.

These questions are relevant to the writing of your thesis, since your sense of why your research topic is important should appear in some form in your introduction.

More importantly, your answer to the question of 'why' may strongly influence your choice of 'where' and 'with whom'. Leonard provides a useful reminder to intending students that they can pick and choose:

> If you are a good student, man or woman, home or international, and even if you are older than 'normal', you can be selective. It is therefore worth taking time and shopping around. Women in particular may lack self-confidence and feel flattered by, and accept too readily, early offers. However, it is a really important decision.
>
> (Leonard 2001: 85)

Leonard's chapter on 'Where to Study: Finding the right supervisor and the right university' talks readers through the key issues.

Internal and external drivers

Do you feel excited about your research? Are you genuinely interested in finding out the answers to your questions? How will completing a doctorate change you, during and after the process? Are others ready for this change?

- What's in it for you?
- Do you stand to gain anything by doing a doctorate?
- Are you really doing it for yourself?
- Is there anyone else who wants you to do a doctorate?
- Who cares whether you succeed or fail?
- Do you have to do it?
- Do you have to do it for yourself?
- Or do you feel compelled or forced?
- How much will it cost?

It is important to have both internal and external drivers, to have both intrinsic and extrinsic motivation. Goal setting, in the previous chapter, has hopefully revealed, for you, links between the two.

PhD or professional doctorate?

These two degrees have different purposes and offer very different experiences: do you see yourself as, or do you want to be, a 'scholarly professional' or a 'professional scholar' (Doncaster and Thorne 2000: 392)? The PhD is a three- (or four-) year piece of independent research; the professional doctorate usually includes course work and research training, along with a shorter research project, usually shorter and smaller in scale, or a portfolio. The PhD is primarily an induction into an academic career; the professional doctorate emphasizes personal and professional development, within the context of any profession. The PhD aims to make a contribution to knowledge; the professional doctorate is usually focused on improving practice within the profession that is the subject of the research.

The professional doctorate is usually a structured programme, including both course work (at Level 5, i.e. the level above the highest level of under-graduate study) and a thesis. For the PhD you work on a larger, independent project, with little or no course work. Some people confuse the UK professional doctorate with 'the American PhD', but the two are very different.

The professional doctorate may involve a substantial 'reflective' process or piece of work, with you reflecting on your career or professional self. You could be asked to engage in searching dialogue about your professional development, values and aspirations: 'dialogue encourages critical reflection' (Doncaster and Thorne 2000: 396).

What is the relationship, for you, between 'dialogue' and 'critical reflection'? This sounds like there would be ample opportunities to test your growing knowledge in peer group discussion. There may be more peer support here, built into the programme.

Is the assessment any different for the professional doctorate? Ruggeri-Stevens et al. analysed 16 DBA (Doctor of Business Administration) pro-grammes in the UK to see if the assessments matched the intended learning outcomes and what they found was 'tension':

> The main conclusion is that there is a tension in the assessment methods employed by DBAs through their relationship with the traditional PhD. The tension is captured in the question: should programme developers follow the assessment methods of the 'gold standard' PhD or should they use assessment methods that assess the learning outcomes of the DBA that distinguish it from the traditional PhD?
>
> (Ruggeri-Stevens et al. 2001: 61)

Over time, this 'tension' may resolve, but who knows how? The PhD, which in some contexts holds higher status, may cease to be the one and only 'gold standard'; in fact, there may be several such standards already. Much more important, if you are contemplating either of these routes, may be the relevance of the particular degree – PhD or professional doctorate – to what you want to learn and research. If you are keen to make a contribution to the body of knowledge of practice – rather than to fill a gap in the literature – then the professional doctorate will be the more appealing option.

If the difference in the length of the professional doctorate thesis proves captivating – 40,000 words, as opposed to 80,000 words, approximately – it may be worth adding up the total words required in assignments and thesis for the professional doctorate. Often, and quite intentionally, they come to around 80,000 words, i.e. about the same as the traditional PhD.

There may be possibilities for publishing papers from your professional doctorate assignments. In fact, some professional doctorates explicitly include a module on writing a scholarly article, that is then submitted to a journal. Once you have one or more papers submitted or published, you may be tempted by the option of PhD by publication, and you may find that it is relatively straightforward to transfer from the professional doctorate to PhD by publication. In other words, consider – before you start, or during your programme – the relative flexibility of different routes to the qualification and written outputs that you seek.

At the end of the day, the similarities between the PhD and the professional doctorate may be as important as the differences:

> Whilst the DBA like the PhD may have a programme of complementary studies, it is not held to be a taught programme as its primary mode of assessment is through the production of a thesis.
>
> (Ruggeri-Stevens et al. 2001: 67)

The authors are here quoting the Association of Business School guidelines on the professional doctorate (1997). The key words are 'like the PhD'. Their conclusions show that assessment in the professional doctorate proved to be less like the intended learning outcomes and more 'like the PhD':

> Our summative assessment is that the espoused assessment requirements of DBAs compare well with those of the traditional PhD, less well with Guidelines [of the Association of Business Schools] and least well with the espoused learning outcomes of the DBA programmes themselves.
>
> (Ruggeri-Stevens et al. 2001: 70)

For an excellent attempt to clarify matters, see Sarros et al. (2005):

> The distinction between the DBA and a PhD, while understood implicitly, needs to be articulated unambiguously to potential examiners to avoid pre-conceived opinions of the DBA report as being similar to but lesser than a PhD compromising the ability of examiners to perform their role dispassionately and appropriately.
>
> (Sarros et al. 2005: 161)

This suggests that, while you might think it premature, it might be a good idea to look at assessment criteria – i.e. those that are sent to and used by external examiners – when choosing between one programme or another. In addition, you may find that the growing number of doctoral and masters degrees in your discipline has been subjected to critical scrutiny or analysis. For example, in nursing, different forms of doctorate, their underpinning concepts and 'current understandings' have been studied by an international group of scholars and educators (Ketefian and McKenna 2005: 163).

Which mode?

- Which mode are you best suited to?
- Do both modes provide preparation for study?
- What new competencies will you be expected to develop?

For consideration of the criteria for the professional doctorate, see Winter et al. (2000). For consideration of the differences in writing for each mode, see some examples of completed projects: ask yourself the question, 'Is there a difference between 40,000 and 80,000 words of sustained writing, in the proposed discipline and department, other than the obvious one that the professional doctorate is usually shorter?'

There are, therefore, many issues to consider, as you make the choice between professional doctorate and PhD: time, curriculum, supervision, flexibility, status, structure and organization, among others. However, the final choice may also be influenced by the state of your finances or your judgement about how much you want to invest in your education:

> It seems evident that the capacity to pay rather than the underlying purpose and structure of the degree will become the prime differentiating feature between professional doctorates and the PhD.
>
> (Neuman 2005: 186)

'Capacity to pay' may be affected by government policy, in the sense that national or local authorities can decide to fund one type of study but not another, so it is probably a good idea to keep an eye on funding trends, and, of course, to assess the extent to which any funding sources would focus, or restrict, your study choices.

Full-time or part-time?

While there are obvious advantages to studying full-time, and part-timers often say they envy those who do, there are drawbacks. For example, going full-time means giving up pension years. You will have to buy back three or more years and there is no guarantee that you will get a job – and the pension that goes with it – immediately after you graduate.

On the plus side, you will have all of your time to devote to your research, unless, of course, you take on teaching, marking, networking, staff development and finding a job, etc., as many research students do. The idea that you will have nothing to do but research and write may be less true now than it used to be, but many still consider the full-time route easier than combining it with a full-time job.

The part time route presents a different challenge. Part-timers often have different priorities from full-timers. It is tempting, but not helpful, for part-timers to compare themselves with full-timers. You have to learn not to overreach, to move at your own pace.

> Part-time study for a higher degree has become the fastest growing sector of Higher Education. Funding is becoming ever more elusive, and the financial strain of taking years 'out' of employment often renders part-time study the only route back into higher education.
>
> (Greenfield 2000: i)

Part-time study will not make you a second-class citizen. There will be many others doing the degree this way. The trick will be to make contact with them.

- 'It's a nightmare part-time.'
- 'In my situation it wasn't even part-time; it was my own time.'
- 'I only got two hours' remission from teaching.'
- 'There was no protected time at all.'

You may have less control over your time. Other priorities may nudge your research and writing aside, with more feelings of disruption, more gaps in the process. Design them in, plan for them. Take time to get back on track after a break, top-and-tailing for continuity, using restarting strategies after a period of inactivity. You will have to take control of time: 'University attendance, research and writing have to be carefully planned and scheduled with nothing left to chance' (Greenfield 2000: i).

The part-time/full-time decision has many factors; many people will not have the luxury of choice in any case. The main thing is to be aware of how the two differ and not to get distracted by the 'path not taken'. There is sometimes an element of 'the grass is often greener on the other side', in the views each has of the other.

What exactly does 'part-time' mean?

What 'part' of your life can you give to your doctorate?

- A day a week?
- All day Saturday?
- Sundays?

You will have to develop routines and regimens for writing regularly, strategies that are covered in Chapter 5. There is even more need for writing routines when you are juggling a higher degree and a full-time job.

What will you use writing for?

Doing a higher degree requires a fair amount of writing. What will you be using writing for? What do you see as its purpose – what purpose will writing serve for you, not just for the degree?

- You are writing to learn.
- You are writing to explore your research topic.
- You are writing to document.
- You are writing to report.
- You are writing to persuade.

Is writing – for you – primarily a means of learning? Learning what? Learning what you know? What you do not know? To discover the limits of your knowledge? Or the limits of your apparent ignorance? Do you believe that we learn about what we think when we put our ideas down in writing? Do you agree that our thinking develops as we write our ideas down in formal ways? Are you setting out to learn from the feedback you get on your writing? Is writing something you see as a tool for recording what you think and do in your research? Is writing therefore a documentary process?

All of these are relevant to the learning process that is part of the writing process. Each involves a different form of writing. Each assumes a particular response from the reader, assuming that either the reader knows your purpose and/or that you have specified it in your writing.

It is also important to recognize that all of these ways of thinking about writing are in stark contrast to the more 'instrumental' ways in which it is frequently regarded: i.e. as simply a means of communicating the 'results' of research; that is only part of the thesis writing process.

It is always a good idea to make the audience and the purpose specific, by writing it on the first page, and this is as valid for thesis writing as for other forms of writing: 'This piece/draft/paper has been written for . . . The purpose is to [verb].' That way, as your paper drifts away from its presently obvious context, as time passes, as your supervisor takes it home, as more time passes, as your supervisor sits down to read it in the airport/train/office, your writing will be read within the context you intended it. Probably. The supervisor is still likely to read it within his or her context, in relation to his or her ideas and experiences.

All of the forms of writing covered in this section will shape how you write: for how long, how often and in what form(s)?

These forms do not occur in a linear sequence, first one, then the other. However, they are probably all relevant for all theses. As the writing progresses they are probably all occurring at the same time, in parallel. All the more reason to say explicitly, in writing, on the writing, which one you are doing at any one time. Of course, you may mix the different forms in any one piece of writing. Again, this is another reason for making specific what your purposes are in any piece of writing.

Regulations

The most important document for a thesis writer is the university's 'higher degree regulations', or whatever they are called in your context. This will define what you are required to do. It will also explain the procedures for doctoral study and examination.

Equally important, if your university has one, is the Code of Practice for Postgraduates, or for Research Students, or, again, whatever it is called in your institution. Some universities provide ample information and support material on the web. Some of it is extremely helpful, although it should probably come with a 'health warning' for you to check that it is relevant to your own institution's practice.

You may find both regulations and guidelines – there is a difference – or both on such key topics as 'Responsibilities of the student' and 'Responsibilities of the supervisor', 'Length of study', 'Examination', 'Appeals'. Departments may also have their own codes. Sometimes these are a reprint or photocopy of the university code; sometimes they have few or many major or minor changes that will affect you. You have to check: compare them carefully. Work out what they mean.

Between the university's regulations and code, you should have the answer to most of your questions:

Your university's regulations and codes

- Do I have to register initially for an MPhil, and then convert to PhD? Or not? What are the criteria for 'upgrade' to PhD?
- What are the responsibilities of the supervisor?
- What are my responsibilities?
- What is the university's policy on supervision? Is there a policy of joint supervision? Are new supervisors mentored by experienced supervisors?
- What are the procedures for monitoring my progress?
- Whom do I go to if I have problems (other than supervisors)?
- What are the procedures for assessment?
- What are the grounds for appeal?

As you study your institution's, or supervisor's, answers to these questions, compare notes with other students: what have they found out? What has been their actual experience? What does the UK National Postgraduate Committee – or other national student bodies – say about it all? A thesis writing group can use some or all of these questions as talking points at one of their meetings .

Thesis writing group discussion

- What answers have your peers found to these questions?
- How have responsibilities, assessment, etc. been defined?
- How are the answers reflected in your plans of work?
- Have any questions not been answered?
- Do you have other questions?

The question about 'upgrade' from MPhil to PhD is one of the most important, and is often seen by students as one of the more obscure, procedures in doctoral studies. Having students register for an MPhil first gives the university – and the student – an early warning system. If, after one or two years, a student's work is not up to standard he or she can be halted at this point. The advantage for students is that they do not walk away empty-handed from a year or two's work. If the work is up to standard, then the student's registration is 'transferred' to PhD or to some other doctorate.

The regulations and Code of Practice should be given to you when you register, unless there is some other form of communicating such information to you, on a website or some other form of publication. It may be up to you to check. You may also want to make sure that you get hold of a copy for each year of your registration, as regulations can change over time.

Clearly, there will be many potential talking points for you in the Code, or whatever document your university uses, for you, your peers and your supervisor. Note that while Codes begin to define many aspects of the doctorate, each element is subject to further definition. For example, if the code states that the student is responsible for 'maintaining regular contact with the supervisor', this only begins to define the role, raising further questions about the definition of 'regular' and 'contact' that will be expected and used by any individual student or supervisor. It is not unusual for both student and supervisor to have different definitions in mind, at least initially. Presumably these definitions can change over time, as the student becomes more expert and experienced, and as the study moves towards completion. At later stages, a key question will be what is meant by 'monitoring of progress' – how will your progress be monitored? It would be as well to have established and agreed milestones and goals at an early stage.

There may also be department processes: you may have to provide an annual report, or it could be at nine or eighteen months.

Writing your annual report

- What are the absolute requirements: length, contents, structure?
- How much writing is required?
- Can you see examples of written reports?
- How will it be assessed? What are the criteria?
- What kind of feedback can you expect? From whom? When?
- Will there be any follow-up?
- An oral examination?
- How will performance outcomes be recorded?
- Will your deficiencies be constructively identified and addressed?

The idea of having more than one oral examination may sound tough, but the early report plus 'mini-viva' process can be more useful than anything else at teaching you what you know and what you need to do next. Students who have been through such a process report that it made them really make sure that they understood what they were writing. They also found the mini-viva useful practice for the real thing (Murray 1998).

There will also be guidelines on layout for the thesis. Start using them in all your writing, right from the start:

What is the required layout?

- What is the required size of left and right margins?
- Where must page numbers appear on the page?
- How much space is required at the top and foot of the page?
- Are there regulations about 'widows', etc.?

While the final copy of your thesis will be single-sided and double-spaced, you can probably get away with single-spaced for your drafts, but it is worth checking with your supervisor. How does your supervisor want to see your writing? In addition to your university's guidelines, you will be required to follow a particular style sheet. This has detailed rules that you have to follow in presenting your text, references, etc. It is crucial that you find this out before you do much – or any – writing, since changing it all later, when you do have a fair amount of text, will simply be a waste of your precious time.

How will it look on the page?

You may think it is a bit early to be thinking about final layout, but there are certain requirements. Certain features of your thesis are fixed. If you do not use the required format from the start you will waste a lot of time later – just when you feel you have least time – changing format, layout, etc. More importantly, this is another facet of defining your writing task.

For the final layout, see your university's guidelines or 'higher degree regulations' or library requirements (for the final bound copy). They will probably specify required – not optional – margins, page numbering system, title page layout, etc. Follow this to the letter. Even minor differences from the required format can cause your thesis to be rejected by the library. For example, if you are required to write the university name on the title page in a particular way, such as 'The University of Strathclyde, Glasgow', then that is exactly what you do. None of the following is acceptable:

- The University of Strathclyde at Glasgow
- The University of Strathclyde Glasgow
- The University of Strathclyde in Glasgow

That comma must be there. That is how detailed your attention to the requirements must be. It is as rigorous a process as submitting your manuscript to a publisher, which, in a sense, is exactly what you are doing. Although the university is not actually a publishing house, nevertheless the university's name is attached to, and forever associated with, your thesis. The university has to uphold the highest standards, right down to the presentation of the finished thesis that will sit on the library shelves and be accessed by other researchers.

Demystification: codes and guides

The criteria for success and failure in the PhD cannot be reduced to a set of written rules, however explicit.

(Delamont et al. 2000: 40)

Knowledge of regulations, codes and guides does not guarantee success, but it does begin to demystify the thesis writing process. Students are often unaware of how codes of practice can affect their writing process. Supervisors are sometimes unaware of the content, or even existence, of such codes. Students and supervisors alike have been known to assume that these are 'not relevant in our discipline'. It is worth checking that.

For the purposes of this book, I assume that students will not be interested in the competing policies and politics of all the organizations that shape the current state of postgraduate study in the UK and beyond. However, selected codes and guides are useful in that they define the research process and requirements for the thesis. They define modes of monitoring and/or criteria for assessment. Taken together, they are part of the demystification process.

In any system of higher education, in addition to regulations for the degree, there are bound to be codes of practice and guidelines. These are issued by a number of different bodies with different interests in research and educational outputs: government offices, the universities' associations, employers, professional groups, students' associations (national and local) and quality assurance groups who may represent, and may or may not be staffed by, any of these other groups, playing a particular role.

These provide the ground rules. They also direct you to writing that you can do in the early stages. You can translate questions they raise and criteria they recommend into prompts for writing.

Any code or guide produced by your university must be central to your research and your writing:

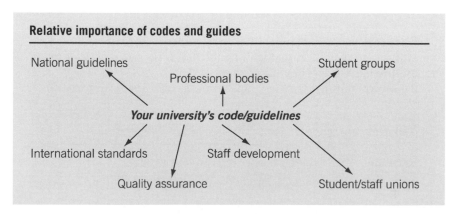

Relative importance of codes and guides

National guidelines   Student groups
             Professional bodies
   Your university's code/guidelines
International standards   Staff development
      Quality assurance   Student/staff unions

What follows in this section is an overview of some of these groups in the UK context. There will be other such groups in other national contexts. Each of these codes and guides is examined for their potential influence on thesis writing.

A number of different agencies and groups issue codes and guides that may or may not be relevant or useful for your study or writing. Some are more official than others. Some prioritize students' interests; others are concerned with quality assurance, also of importance to students, but whose importance is not always obvious to students. A key question, for all students, would be which one(s) are operating in your institution, if any. A likely priority would be to get hold of your institution's Code of Practice.

The **Quality Assurance Agency (QAA)** produces a *Code of Practice for the Assurance of Academic Quality and Standards in Higher Education* (QAA 1999):

> With effect from the year 2000, QAA will expect that individual institutions will be in a position to demonstrate how they are meeting the expectations contained in the precepts of this Code (p. 4).

The 'precepts' are a set of statements, given a little further definition in a few 'guidelines'. Twelve topics are covered:

1 General principles
2 The research environment
3 Promotional information
4 The selection and admission of students
5 Enrolment and registration of research students
6 Student information and induction
7 The approval of research projects
8 Skills training
9 Supervision
10 Assessment
11 Feedback
12 Evaluation complaints and appeals.

Some of these may seem of more interest to students than others, but it can be interesting to see what it is that your institution is supposed to be doing in all the administrative stages of your degree.

The most interesting topics are skills training, supervision and assessment:

8 Skills training

. . . institutions will wish to consider the development of: . . .

• language support and academic writing skills . . .

9 Supervision

Supervisors should possess recognised subject expertise ... Institutions should consider:

- the provision of training for supervisors and continuing staff development ...

Research students should receive support and direction sufficient to enable them to succeed in their studies.

Institutions will wish to consider how to ensure that: ...

- there is a framework for regular supervisor/research student interaction, with a minimum frequency of (and responsibility for initiating) scheduled review meetings between the student, supervisor(s) and, if appropriate, other individuals;
- students are introduced to other researchers (and appropriate academic bodies and societies) in their field;
- participation in institutional and external discussion forums is encouraged, with the presentation of research outcomes where relevant; . . . (pp. 10–11).

The words 'should consider' clearly indicate that this is not about enforcement, but it is becoming more and more common for universities to require some form of training of new supervisors. Continuing staff development for supervisors would, I expect, be more rare. The second section indicates that monitoring, a critical process, should follow some kind of 'framework'.

10 Assessment

Postgraduate research assessment processes should be communicated clearly and fully to research students and supervisors.

Institutions will wish to consider: . . .

- the mechanisms used for communicating procedures relating to the nomination of examiners, the examination process (including any oral examination), the process and time taken to reach a decision and the potential outcomes of the assessment.

Postgraduate research assessment processes should be clear and operated rigorously, fairly, reliably and consistently.

Institutions will wish to consider:

- the mechanisms used for the identification and maintenance of standards of research student achievement (p. 12).

These may seem too general to be helpful. In some ways that has been seen as an advantage, allowing institutions and departments – and students? – to be flexible and autonomous. However, if these terms are taken to refer to your doctorate, you can immediately see the need for further definition of each of the precepts in practice.

Ask your department what they will provide

- What skills training, supervision and assessment will be provided by your department?
- How will you be able to feed your experience of them back into the system?

The **National Postgraduate Committee** (**NPC**) aims to represent and improve the conditions of postgraduates in the UK. You can read their constitution at http://www.npc.org.uk/committee.constitution.html. They provide an update on 'Recent policy developments and issues' and have several useful publications:

- *Guidelines for the Conduct of Research Degree Appeals* (NPC 1995)
- *Guidelines on Codes of Practice for Postgraduate Research* (NPC 1992).

The latter provides more specific guidance than the QAA code, again revealing for students how the institution/department works:

The Department will keep a portfolio containing a comprehensive record of the student's progress. This would include notes on discussions between supervisor and student on instructions, level of performance, etc. . . .

A programme of work is essential. The research topic should be agreed as soon as possible and a programme drawn up and approved by the supervisor during the first semester. The supervisor should ensure that the student is aware of the basis of the supervisor's assessment of progress and understands the amount of work involved. The programme must include:

a provisional outline of the thesis . . .
a statement of the research and sources to be examined
a provisional timetable . . . (p. 9).

The NPC is usefully attempting to bring further definition to the doctoral process. An even more interesting publication, *Questions for Prospective Postgraduates* (Gillon and Hoad 2000), is designed for those who are thinking about doing a doctorate and have still to decide where, although some of the questions could usefully be asked by enrolled students. The NPC have drawn up a list of questions to help people choose the place that is best for them and to avoid 'common problems'. The questions about the (prospective) supervisor are particularly thought-provoking:

The supervisor is the most important person in the academic life of a research student

You should find out:

• What are his/her research interests?
• What has he/she published recently?
• What is his/her experience of supervising research students? If this is their first time acting as supervisor, what are the back-up provisions?
• How much time will your supervisor have for you? . . .
• Will you be able to get on with this supervisor? . . .
• What kind of role does the supervisor expect to take and does that fit with your pattern of working?

While these are not explicitly about 'writing', they have obvious implications for your writing, given that the supervisor is, or will be, the immediate audience for your writing. There are other questions you can ask, before or after you start your programme of study, about the programme, about the institution and the department, about resources, and so on.

The NPC *Guidelines on Accommodation and Facilities for Postgraduate Research* (1995) provide an interesting set of issues that will also have potential to affect writing (see http://www.npc.ord.uk/page/1003802081). You can use these to make comparisons between different institutions in terms of facilities provided to support your research and your writing.

Looking to the bigger picture, the NPC site also includes essays on 'Developments in higher education'. For example, Martin Gough's paper on 'The future wellbeing of postgraduate communities' has some interesting thoughts on three models of higher education (drawing on Southwell and Howe):

1 ivory tower, which is knowledge-based, aiming for intellectual development;
2 market driven, which is vocational, skills-based, aiming for employability;
3 mature HEI [higher education institution], which is about flexibility, pleasure, is learner-centred and aims for 'true understanding'.

These are interesting theoretical standpoints; they may have shaped the rationale of the doctoral and masters programmes at a particular institution. However, it would not be surprising to find a university that claimed to be aiming for all three. Again, there is the question of how this will affect the thesis writer: is the university looking for all three dimensions in your forthcoming education – and in your thesis? – or will one of these dimensions do?

The UK Council for Graduate Education also sets out to promote graduate education in all disciplines, but while the NPC comes from the student's perspective, this body is a collection of academics, supervisors and various working groups (http://www.ukcge/). Like the NPC, they produce interesting and useful publications, for example, *Graduate Schools* (UKCGE 1995) and *The Award of the Degree of PhD on the Basis of Published Work in the UK* (UKCGE 1996).

The thesis-by-publication mode interests many postgraduates – particularly if it means not writing a thesis – although you should note that a survey revealed that in countries where this route to the doctorate is well established, published papers are frequently not the sole requirement; there is often a requirement for a critical report on the work (5000–10,000 words). Here it refers to gathering papers that have already been published. Some of the administrative procedures are outlined. They also found that this option is mainly taken up by academic staff, registered at the institution where they work. There can be problems with this mode: the publications may not be detailed enough for an assessment to be made; there may be little or no raw data. The future of this mode, the authors conclude, lies in some kind of fusion, involving some published work and a kind of mini-thesis to pull the publications together so that they form, to some extent, a body of work.

The British Standards Institution has produced a standard format for the thesis, which some universities endorse: *Recommendations for the Presentation of Theses*, British Standard 4821 (BSI 1990). Although it is registered on the website as 'withdrawn', it is still circulating in some universities. Some students still ask for it, but as a guide to written presentation perhaps it should now be regarded as out of date.

For international students there is also a Code of Recommended Practice on *The Management of Higher Degrees Undertaken by Overseas Students* (CVCP/CVP 1992). Though not brand new, and perhaps not in wide circulation currently, it is worth noting – by students and supervisors – for at least one of its recommendations about cultural differences in perception of supervision: 'It should be borne in mind that some overseas students may need more supervision time than others, at least in the early stages of their course' (p. 4). Whether or not this is an accurate statement about 'some' of this group – and whether or not such 'time' is provided – will be the subject of some debate. I can imagine that many supervisors would reply that this statement could apply to any student, wherever they come from: some will need more supervision than others. However, the fact remains that many, if not all, international students will need time to adjust. This is not just a matter of tuning their written and spoken English. American students, for example, can find the UK system very foreign, just as UK graduate students can find the US system alien, at least initially.

Other groups, such as professional bodies or associations, Royal Societies, Research Councils and others, produce their own codes and guides. Some are more specific than others, but if you are studying psychology, for example, you would be well advised to read the British Psychological Society's *Guidelines for Assessment of the PhD in Psychology and Related Disciplines* (BPS 2000). Even if you are in a 'related discipline' you will find these guidelines helpful, as they do define many aspects of the doctoral experience. They cover the PhD by publications.

Key questions

1 What is the status of these codes and guides in my institution?
2 How can they support my research?
3 How will they support my writing?
4 Where can I get a copy of my institution's code?
5 Will revised versions be sent to me automatically?
6 The university code of practice: contract or agenda?

The code may represent a tacit or real contract between you and the institution, but to what extent can it be legally binding on you or your supervisor? A code of practice is a starting point for discussions at the start of the doctorate. In that sense, it offers students and supervisors an agenda for their discussions.

How will my thesis be assessed?

While supervisors provide feedback all the way through the research and thesis writing process, the final assessment takes the form of an oral examination, known as the 'viva', 'viva voce' or 'oral defence'. There will – usually – be an external examiner, an internal examiner, and supervisors can attend, but usually – check the institution's procedures – they have no formal role and in some institutions have no speaking role. The conduct of this examination and the place of thesis writing in it are covered in Chapter 10.

What are the criteria?

There is a lot of mystique, and not much research, about the thesis examination. While many students are unaware of the criteria that will be used in the oral examination, the *Handbook for External Examiners in Higher Education* (Partington et al. 1993) may give more than a clue. The handbook helpfully outlines general features of the examiner's role and, for students, can help them to see their work from the examiner's perspective. While each doctorate is different, the approach taken here is that the process of examination is 'generalizable' to all doctorates:

> Many, if not most, colleagues in higher education see themselves primarily as subject specialists. They will often maintain that their subject is unique and that what applied to other courses does not therefore apply to them. This is true to a limited extent only. This handbook is written in the belief that assessment techniques are to a large extent generalisable: the issues raised here are those which external examiners could raise as appropriate in any department or course.
>
> (Partington et al. 1993: 1–2)

In other words, while you may see your thesis as 'unique' – and in some ways it is – there is a set of core criteria – and behaviours – that can be said to cross disciplinary boundaries. This means that you do not have to adopt the 'wait-and-see' position with your examination, but can anticipate, and prepare to answer, specific types of questions.

This handbook guides examiners through their initial and detailed readings of a thesis, all the way to the examination itself. Examiners are advised to read the completed thesis and form an initial, holistic impression of the strengths and weaknesses of the work. Next, they are prompted to move on to 'systematic reading with questions in mind'. These questions are designed to focus the examiner's detailed reading and, possibly, to identify questions for the viva. There are lists of questions for each chapter of a thesis (pp. 76–7):

The external examiner will scrutinize . . .

- Review of the literature
- Design of the study
- Presentation of the results
- Discussion and conclusions

There is an additional set of questions in section 4.7 of Partington et al. (1993: 76–7). The chapter headings listed there may at first sight appear to be more appropriate for a science or engineering doctorate; however, it could be argued that they are relevant to other disciplines, particularly when you see the specific questions listed for each 'chapter'. Some of these are bound to be relevant to theses in other areas:

Review of the literature

- To what extent is the review relevant to the research study?
- Has the candidate slipped into 'here is all I know about *x*'?
- Is there evidence of critical appraisal of other work, or is the review just descriptive? . . .
- Does the candidate make explicit the links between the review and his or her design of the study? (p. 76)

Students often ask about the second question, 'Has the candidate slipped into "here is all I know about *x*?".' This uncertainty may be an indication of the work students have to do in order to understand the examiner's perspective.

Design of the study

- What precautions were taken against likely sources of bias?
- What are the limitations in the design? Is the candidate aware of them? . . .
- Has the candidate given an adequate justification for the design used? (pp. 76–7)

There are lists of such questions for all the key phases in the academic argument that is expected in a thesis. These will be dealt with in more detail in Chapter 10, which focuses on the viva. However, at this early stage in the process the questions can be used to generate a focus for thinking, reading and writing, and if the questions do not 'fit' your thesis, then you can write some that do.

If these questions still seem too far removed from your work it may be useful to adapt them so that they fit and provide more useful prompts for thinking and writing. It may be that a discussion with the supervisor about these expectations, questions or prompts would provide further insights into what the reader of your thesis is likely to be looking for.

These convey the type of thinking the reader of a thesis will be doing, at the point of examination, when the thesis has been completed. For those just starting a thesis, they may help to define the writing tasks yet to be done; some of these questions, if not all, can be translated into action points for early writing:

What can I write about? The design of the study

- What precautions will I take against likely sources of bias? I am most likely to be biased in . . . I am least likely to be biased in . . . Bias would reveal itself as . . . would be shown by . . .
- I will limit the design in order to make it feasible by . . . This is a positive choice – rather than weakness – because . . .
- I can justify the design I am using/going to use by . . .

These prompts provide focal points for the initial research proposal, for revisions of the proposal or for sections of early chapters in the thesis. All of the questions in the handbook can be adapted into prompts for writing in this way. This is not just to say that you are constricting your thinking right from the start in order to 'pass the exam', but that you are working on the right types of questions, right from the start.

Examiners may or may not have read this handbook. They may or may not agree with this list of questions as the 'agenda' for their reading and probing of a thesis. The point is that these questions can focus early thinking and writing. While the actual expectations of real readers remain unknown, there is no reason why you should not begin to define a core set of expectations so that you can start writing. Audience and purpose are, after all, key in any writing task, and the effective writer develops a sense of audience, even where there is to be a multiple audience.

Students are often keen to get hold of this handbook. It dissolves some of the mystique surrounding the doctorate. Because it can be difficult to get a straight answer to questions like 'What is expected?' or 'When will I have done enough?' and 'How will I know?', any hints can be very appealing. To be fair to supervisors and examiners, these are difficult questions to answer; in fact, it may not be possible, or wise, to attempt to give a definitive answer to any one of them. Yet while these insights may be demystifying and in some ways reassuring, they are only a starting point. They are not necessarily the questions that will be asked at everyone's viva. Clearly they cannot be.

Adapting these sentences so that they are relevant to your thesis is the first step, then thinking about how the questions are to be answered and then noting explicit answers. 'Explicit' is a key word here; it may be that direct answers to these questions will help you to be more explicit about some of the thinking you are doing.

More recently, further definition of criteria is provided by the British Psychological Society's *Guidelines for the Assessment of the PhD in Psychology and Related Disciplines* (BPS 2000), which includes a section on 'Criteria for assessing PhD theses in psychology'. For student and examiner alike, these shed light on a question often shrouded in mystique. The criteria provided here are refreshingly free of the heavy style often associated with the term 'criteria' in this context:

- The text should be clear and 'tell a story'.
- The submission should be 'user-friendly'. The reader should be able to find his or her way around the submission, locating tables and figures, and being able to cross-reference with ease. A numbering system for chapters, sections, and, sometimes, paragraphs can be very helpful . . .
- The submission should be no longer than necessary. Typically this will mean 75–80,000 words, with an absolute maximum of 100,000 words (p. 28).

For those who are not writing a thesis in psychology, there may be the question of how relevant these guidelines will – genuinely, in practice – be for their disciplines. At the very least, these guidelines can lead to some very important discussions with supervisors. Starting questions could be 'Have you read these?' and 'What do you think of them?' You could then discuss your reactions. You could describe – or show – the writing you have done as a result of reading the guidelines. Above all, you need to try and form your own view of the relevance of these guides for your writing.

Once you have read, and discussed, the university's Code of Practice, UCoSDA's (Universities' and Colleges' Staff Development Agency) Guidelines, the Quality Assurance Code of Practice, and so on, the key point to remember is that there is wide variation in the practice of the oral examination.

Recent research shows that there are not only variations, but inconsistencies:

> This paper examines the roles and significance of the viva in the doctoral examination process. More specifically, it addresses the following question – what purposes does the viva serve in the PhD assessment process? Discussion focuses upon (1) the roles of the viva as delineated within university policy; and (2) the purposes of the viva from the perspectives of examiners, supervisors and doctoral candidates. The findings suggest that, whether viewed in terms of institutional statements, or in terms of the perspective of academics or candidates, there is no consensus regarding the roles of the viva in the PhD examination process. Moreover, our research reveals that there are inconsistencies and contradictions concerning the purposes of the viva, both at the level of policy and practice.
>
> (Jackson and Tinkler 2001: 354)

For anyone facing a thesis examination – either in the long or short term – the 'inconsistencies and contradictions' in policy are perhaps less interesting than those in practice. If you conduct some informal, anecdotal 'research' on criteria and practices for examining theses in your department, you might find some variety. This is not to say that people in your department are inconsistent and contradictory; rather, they see each doctorate as unique, with its own set of unique parameters and criteria. However, you should not leave such matters undefined. The situation is not so complex that you cannot begin to define how your writing will be assessed. Your study is not so unique that a completely new combination of criteria will have to be drawn up. What is more likely is that the question will be deferred as long as you leave it unasked. For a fuller understanding of the whole examination process, from the examiner's perspective, see Pearce's *How to Examine a Thesis* (2005).

The outcome of reading all the codes, guides and regulations should not be that you are even more convinced that thesis writing is 'the great unknown' or 'inaccessible pinnacle' of higher education. Quite the reverse. Over the past ten years, much more work has gone into defining what is required of you – and of your supervisor and your institution – and how you can be developed in order to produce a thesis than was the case before. You have more options – more forms of study and writing to choose from – than were available as recently as ten years ago.

Any questions that remain can be treated as prompts for writing and further discussion. The more difficult the questions the better, since these will help you to refine your arguments and will prevent you from being tripped up by a tricky question at your viva, or before. These questions represent one of many pretexts for writing. Practising writing when you are genuinely uncertain, and using writing to work through uncertainty, is a key skill for writing a thesis and will have uses in other contexts, after you have completed it.

Defining 'originality'

This is a key word, a key concept and, many would say, the key criterion for doctoral, and some masters level, work. A thesis has to show that the work was in some way original. There are many different interpretations of that word; each thesis may use a different definition. Phillips and Pugh (2000) provide a range of definitions (pp. 63–4), on which the following list is based:

Originality

- You say something no one has said before.
- You do empirical work that has not been done before.
- You synthesize things that have not been put together before.
- You make a new interpretation of someone else's material/ideas.
- You do something in this country that has only been done elsewhere.
- You take an existing technique and apply it to a new area.
- You work across disciplines, using different methodologies.
- You look at topics that people in your discipline have not looked at.
- You test existing knowledge in an original way.
- You add to knowledge in a way that has not been done before.
- You write down a new piece of information for the first time.
- You give a good exposition of someone else's idea.
- You continue an original piece of work.

These should be considered random rather than 'core', since there are many more possible definitions available to thesis writers. Thesis writers are advised to rehearse several definitions of originality in discussion and in writing and, above all, to let it shape their writing. In this way you will develop your understanding of the concept, in relation to your research, and you will discard some of the definitions as you go along.

What can I write about 'originality'?

- My work is/will be original in the sense that . . .

- My work is/will not be original in the sense that . . .

Write for five minutes

This writing activity has a very practical purpose. These two prompts are intended to produce text. This text may be pretty shaky to begin with, and even revisions may be contradictory, vague or abstract, but if you did this writing, you will have made a start in defining what is, after all, a key – if not the key – long-term goal of your research.

There is little point in letting several definitions of such a crucial concept as 'originality' run around in your head for the next two or three months. This may, in fact, result in a loss of focus in your work. It may produce confusion in your writing. Ultimately, it could lead to a weakness in your thesis.

Your thesis may stand – or fall – on the strength not only of the originality factor, but on your choice of definition and how you have chosen to write about it: have you chosen the right type of 'originality' for the work you are doing? Have you made a strong enough case for that type of originality in your thesis?

The supervisor – and examiner – will be looking for a clear, explicit and valid claim for originality in your thesis. It would be as well to start working out what that means now, by doing – and repeating – the short writing activity.

What is the reader looking for?

The fact that the above selection of definitions of originality was produced by a group of supervisors gives some idea of what they are looking for. Although both the group and their collection of definitions could be considered random, and therefore limited in relevance to any individual thesis, they do provide a starting point for thesis writers who are beginning to grapple with the concept. For students with more than one supervisor, things may be more complicated, as it is unlikely that both supervisors will have the same views on everything.

Supervisors look for potential originality in the proposal, for a student's ability to grasp the scale of the work and produce writing and for a coherent argument in the emerging thesis. If these elements are expected, your writing should make them easy to find. It helps if they are explicitly – i.e. verbally – marked.

Even if you find an answer to 'what the reader is looking for', the reader being your supervisor, you cannot be sure that the other reader, the external examiner, will be looking for the same thing(s). However, in terms of writing, we can say that they are looking for appropriate style, correctly used, and strong argument. The task of the thesis writer is to work out what that means in terms of his or her own writing. More information about how these terms will be used to assess a thesis may not be available: 'The examination process for doctoral theses seems to be based on assumptions which are largely untested and on understandings which are not necessarily open for discussion' (Johnston 1997: 334).

This quotation is not here to highlight the errors of other systems and other writers in other countries, but to indicate where the lack of definition of criteria, and perhaps lack of attention to the power of writing to persuade the reader, may have led writers to weaken their theses. This is, of course, a debatable interpretation, based on assumptions about causal relationships, but it seems reasonable to assume that secrecy and lack of definition have consequences for the quality of writing. If these are not addressed by the thesis writer, they are likely to produce similar weaknesses.

Examiners' reports on the doctoral examination are not always open to scrutiny, so it is difficult to know what exactly they are looking for. However, this does not mean that you should leave the concept shrouded in mystique; instead, you should start to define it, as best you can, right away. In fact, your definition(s) may shape the work to be done, moving you away from areas that are overworked already, to newer territories.

The thesis writer has to do that universal writing task, grab the reader's attention:

> . . . examiners approach the task of reading a thesis with needs very similar to readers of any new piece of work. Enthusiasm to be engaged with new ideas in their field quickly dissipates if confronted with work which is not 'reader-friendly'.
>
> (Johnston 1997: 333)

One answer to the question of what the reader is looking for is therefore 'reader-friendly' writing.

Seeing the examiner as a 'reader' is an important reminder. While examiners clearly bring the highest standards to their reading of the thesis, we cannot let this somehow release us from the responsibility of making our writing make sense to them:

> The notion of an examiner as a reader of a thesis, like a reader of any other piece of writing, may not be obvious to many postgraduate candidates and possibly their supervisors. There is sometimes an assumption that the examiner is an expert in the field and does not have the expectations of a 'normal' reader. It is worth remembering that all readers require assistance to understand the work, that they feel distracted and irritated by poorly presented work, and that they appreciate well-written, interesting and logically presented arguments.
>
> (Johnston 1997: 340)

This notion – of the external examiner requiring 'assistance' from the thesis writer – may be new to many postgraduates. Johnston's research suggests that it will be. The implication for thesis writers is not that they should write for the examiner as if he or she were a novice, but that they should see themselves as 'assisting' readers, by way of persuading them, to see the value of their work.

Specific remarks made by examiners do include the word 'contribution', as in contribution to knowledge, but other terms are used too:

Examiners' remarks on theses

'well conceptualised'
'critically analysed review of literature'
'aims of this piece of research are achieved'
'thorough . . . study'
'problem appears . . . worthy of in-depth study'.

(Johnston 1997: 341)

To some readers, and writers, these will seem of a lower order than 'originality', yet they would appear to be equally important to examiners. The demonstration of research 'competence', rather than, say, 'excellence', the achievement of aims, rather than achieving more than the original aims, and the strength of the argument that the subject was 'worthy of in-depth study', rather than that this was the newest, most cutting-edge subject for research, do not necessarily indicate a lowering of standards. Quite the reverse. These remarks indicate the need for a raising of standards in writing about the concepts underlying the research. The conceptual links between a new study and existing studies, the justification of new work and the thoroughness of the study of existing literature are repositioned as major achievements in the thesis writing process. This takes work.

Favourable examiners' reports, Johnston (1997) found, include the terms 'complexity, originality, critical thinking, scholarly work, significant contribution to a field, novel concepts, innovative ideas and publishable outcomes' (p. 341). Each of these could be used as a prompt for writing, not only in order to enable thesis writers to begin, and continue, to grasp these concepts in relation to their work, but also to work out the specific style, the specific words, they intend to use in writing about these aspects of their work.

Some writers, for example, will be uncomfortable claiming 'originality' in their work and will choose to use some form of impersonal construction, rather than 'I'. However, while the final thesis style can be always adjusted, the early thinking can sometimes be conducted more fluently in a more direct style. For example, the prompt 'Where in my thesis will I demonstrate . . .?' uses the first person, 'I', and a direct, informal style, in order to get straight to the point, in order to make the prompt crystal clear. Similarly, writing in response to the prompt 'I will demonstrate critical thinking in/by . . .' forces a thesis writer to stay focused on that issue.

Where in my thesis will I demonstrate . . .

- Complexity?
- Originality?
- Critical thinking?
- Scholarly work?
- Significant contribution to knowledge in the field?
- Novel concepts?
- Innovative ideas?
- Publishable outcomes?

It goes without saying, as with any of the writing activities in this book, that if these terms do not seem appropriate, thesis writers can use prompts which are more relevant to their theses. Similarly, these could be talking points – both the questions and a student's answers – for peer and student–supervisor discussions.

Johnston's (1997) paper concludes that there are two types of comments examiners make: one on the 'intellectual endeavours' reported and the other on 'communication aspects' of the thesis (p. 344). The fact that both types of comments were found strengthens that old, familiar connection we often hear about, but do not always believe, between the quality of the writing and the perceived or actual quality of the work. There are those who argue that if the work is first class, then it does not matter how badly a thesis is written. There are those who argue that 'there is often a relationship between the quality of presentation and the quality of scientific results' (Johnston 1997: 340). Johnston provides one of the most useful explanations around of how this effect can occur:

> One of the problems with work that is poorly presented is that the examiner tends to lose confidence in the candidate and can become suspicious that there are deeper problems of inadequate and rushed conceptualization.
>
> (1997: 345)

We only have to think of students' presentations we have watched to recognize this attribution pattern in ourselves: what did we think when they seemed to hesitate, or repeated themselves, or failed to define a term, or used a string of long sentences that prevented us from quite grasping what they were saying? Did we think 'Oh, that's just a presentation issue'? No, we probably thought that while these were often features of work-in-progress presentations, these students did not quite seem to have worked out what they were doing and what it meant, yet.

Can a thesis be failed for poor research? Definitely. Can it be failed for poor writing? Arguably, that is less likely. However, the research suggests that an examiner may attribute weaknesses in the writing to weaknesses in the research, and that examiners are likely to be prompted to probe more by weaknesses in the writing.

The writer has to influence 'what the reader is looking for' by providing a clear pathway through the thesis. As with any piece of writing, thesis writers have to manage the readers' subjectivity, i.e. make your reader see coherence in your writing. The answer to the question 'What are readers looking for?' should therefore be 'Whatever you told them to look for.'

IT processes and needs

All students develop their own way of managing their references or bibliography. Most new researchers know about – but some have never heard of – the software tools for managing the ever-growing files that are, or should be, their bibliography and database.

It may save time to exchange views and experiences on this potentially time-consuming process. Your university may offer you guidance as part of a research methods training programme. You may learn something from how other students have set up their databases. You may pick up hints and tips from students who are further on in their research and writing. You may save yourself reinventing the wheel. You can find out which software is genuinely useful for which purposes.

Most students will have heard about the types of software available: for example, ProCite, Reference Manager and EndNote, flagged as 'three of the world's most popular reference and bibliography management products' by Marshall (2001). All three tools are helpful, though each does the job differently. (They are all produced by the same company, ISI Researchsoft.) Stephanie Marshall has concisely reviewed the differences – and perhaps indicating what you might see as their pros and cons – that might help you choose between them:

> We tend to find EndNote is the most popular package because it is the most easy-to-use, and will appeal to researchers and students working on their own. Reference Manager offers more network features with simultaneous read/write access to databases, making it easy to share libraries and references with colleagues. ProCite . . . provides flexibility to group references and create subject bibliographies, and appeals to professional information scientists.
>
> (Marshall 2001: 16)

This article included a table listing all the functions of three forms of reference managers. It might not be a bad idea to check the latest review, of the latest versions, before you invest time and money in one of these.

For those who want more detailed and up-to-date information, *Technical Computing* might be a good place to start, particularly if your institution does not have a postgraduate network, where such information can be shared informally. Is there a second- or third-year student who could tell you what these tools are like to use in your subject area? For example, one student tells me that, in his view, MS OneNote 2003 is better than Endnote because, while Endnote is good for bibliographies and summaries, OneNote is good for many different purposes and combinations with other MS programmes. You will have to make up your own mind.

Technology also gives us tools for networking. We can email others in our field – near or far – and establish connections quickly. There are sites with abstracts, indices of journal publications, lists of other links on the web, and so on. There are discussion groups in your area that you will seek out and subscribe to. Some will be more useful than others:

> Kierkegaard would surely see in the net with its interest groups, which anyone in the world can join and where one can discuss any topic endlessly without consequences, the height of irresponsibility. Without rootedness in a particular problem, all that remains for the interest group commentator is endless gossip.
>
> (Dreyfus 1999: 16)

How will you maintain 'rootedness' and avoid 'endless gossip'? There's nothing wrong with gossip, but you presumably do not want it – your doctorate or masters – to be 'endless'. The scope and scale of thesis writing can seem overwhelming enough at times, to the student in the early, and sometimes later, stages, without the constantly shifting sands of discussion. Everything may seem to be related to your research, but is it all relevant? Acknowledge the links, but test them against the focus of your work. You may have to learn how to filter out ideas which are merely 'related', but not relevant to your research project.

Will you join interest groups, listings, conference groups, etc.? Which one(s)? You don't want to spend half your morning/day going through other people's writing. While these contacts and networks can be incredibly useful – and stimulating – they still require you, as with any other source of information, to take time to filter, and not just to collect. Again, it could be useful to talk this through with your supervisor and one or two other students.

> But we still have to explain what makes this use of the web attractive. Why is there a thrill in being able to find out everything no matter how trivial? What motivates a commitment to curiosity? Kierkegaard thought that . . . people were attracted to the press, and we can now add the Web, because the anonymous spectator *takes no risks*.
>
> (Dreyfus 1999: 17)

To this we could add that the anonymous spectator *makes no decisions*. There is just the endless gathering of information, contacts and perspectives. Decision is deferred. Selection is sidelined. Procrastination is perpetuated. Great enjoyment – and stimulation – can be had from this practice, but we can also wander pretty far from the focus of our own projects.

> Until recently, educators found it sufficient to distinguish between 'data' and 'information' – interpreted data that has a directed use. Today, a

further value must be stipulated – knowledge, which is the perspective and insights that derive from the synthesis of information. Learners need to develop the capacity to search, select and synthesize vast amounts of information to create knowledge.

(Dolence and Norris 1995: 26)

To 'data' and 'information' we could add 'opinion' and 'anecdote' and all levels of input available on the web, some of which might be clearly classified as such, and some which might not be. You will have to decide which is which and how to write about, and reference, each.

It is probably not a bad idea, then, to review your reading list – and synthesis of readings – with your supervisor from time to time, i.e. regularly making a tour of the reading and searching, in print and online, that you have been doing. This conversation need not – and perhaps should not – simply be a matter of your supervisor nodding at your selection and adding more titles and sites, but a critical appraisal, by you both, over the course of an hour or two, of the usefulness and relevance of what you have read to your project and your thesis. This may be a more testing discussion than you think, since you may still be absorbing your more recent reading; all the more reason to have this probing discussion. It makes for good rehearsals for your oral examination too.

Finally, there is the practical question of managing your disks. The worst case scenario is that your computer crashes and your back-up disk is corrupted, or there is a fire and all your electronic and hard copies go up in smoke, and you have to start all over again. It has happened. The way to avoid this is, of course, never to have all your back-ups in one place.

Backing up

- Make a second set of back-up disks/memory stick.
- Put each chapter on a separate disk/memory stick.
- Put your bibliography on a separate disk/memory stick.
- Keep them in a different building from your other set or on a server.
- When you go on holiday/to a conference, take a set of back-ups with you and leave a set with a neighbour/friend.
- Update your back-up back-ups every day.
- Print out hard copy after all major revisions.

This may seem like obvious advice, and I do not want to insult anyone's intelligence, but buildings can burn down, even university buildings. Clearly, this is very unlikely to happen to you, but even if it did, you would not lose all your work. You would not have to start again. Even the thought of that is intensely demoralizing.

Having more than one back-up, in more than one place, is a simple way of avoiding this. Printing after major revisions is one way of making sure that even if you do lose all your electronic files, you still have your work on paper.

Reasons for not writing

In evaluations of writing programmes, when participants are asked about what their 'reasons for not writing' have been (and whether or not they have overcome them), the list is endless. In fact, one participant wrote 'You name it' – there are countless reasons not to write.

Many, perhaps most, writers recognize the term 'displacement activity': the cups of coffee, reading the newspaper, making or taking phone calls and other activities we place between not writing and writing.

In addition, there may be conceptual reasons for not writing. You may have developed a convincing rationale for putting writing off till later. You may have research tasks to do first. But could you not be writing about them too? Are you sure that you are not deferring writing because you are defining the task wrongly? If you modify the task, there is always writing to be done.

There is, of course, one very good, if not essential, reason for not writing: taking a break.

Peer discussion and support

All of the ideas, hints, tips and strategies in this book are subjects you should, of course, discuss with your supervisor(s). However, discussion with peers, including those who are further on in the thesis writing process, can help you to develop your understanding of what you are getting into and how to get through it. Whether you have regular or spontaneous, formal or informal meetings and relationships with your peers, remember that you can learn a lot from each other. Perhaps more importantly, you can support each other when the task seems impossible. The process of working with a 'study buddy' is developed in Chapter 5.

Your first meeting with your supervisor

Some students will have met their supervisors before the start of their pro-grammes. However, once you are formally committed to a programme of study, you may be invited to – or may have to ask for – a more formal meeting.

Once you are aware of the formal requirements and have begun to define your goals, you may have generated a list of questions that you must discuss as soon as possible with your supervisor. If you have more than one supervisor, then 'who plays what role' will be one of your first questions.

The purpose of the first formal meeting is to agree in general terms the nature of the project and the initial tasks to progress it. Your supervisor(s) may talk you through the whole research process. If not, you will have to sound them out about your views now:

- Begin to work out what you need to learn.
- Consider what training you need.
- Leave yourself time to think some of the points through.
- Arrange a follow-up discussion.
- Plan to discuss your project *as a whole* – regularly – not just the research or writing of the moment.
- Set yourself writing tasks and targets. Define them: criteria, deadlines, length, scope, etc.
- Tell your supervisor your deadlines.
- Discuss the points raised in this chapter: your motivation, your writing practices, your understanding of research and writing, the role of the postgraduate student in your department, your supervisor's role.

You will be guided at this stage by your supervisor, but you should have an understanding of why you have been set a particular task with a particular deadline. This is not to challenge your supervisor, but to prompt you to develop your understanding of the research process you are starting.

This section includes guidance on how to develop your relationship with your supervisor, but how you relate to him or her is a very individual matter. You may feel the guidance is excellent, helping you to think through how you will interact with the person who will be reading your writing first and most. Or you may feel the advice in this section is inappropriate; you will simply do what your supervisor tells you. The key point, whichever way you react to this section, is to make sure that you have a means of clarifying the terms of your discussions. If communication does break down, then you can seek help at this early stage, from the departmental Postgraduate Director (or similar title) rather than letting the situation deteriorate.

There are many key words that you and your supervisor will use often –

about your writing – that can have quite different meanings: e.g. revise, expand, review, explain. None of these words is very specific. Each of them requires further definition.

Defining feedback

- How will you know if the feedback is good or bad?
- What will constitute useful feedback?
- Do you know what feedback you are looking for, at this stage?
- Can you ask your supervisor for that?
- Do you have to go along with whatever your supervisor says?
- Do you always have to 'do what he or she tells you'?

You may need thinking time, after the feedback, before you respond or revise, particularly if you feel undermined by the feedback.

In a supervisor training workshop participants were given a piece of student writing and asked to consider how they would comment on it. One supervisor wrote two words on the student's writing: 'See me!' That supervisor's intention was to convey urgency, directness and clarity. His comment also conveyed a willingness to respond quickly to student writing and to follow up with discussion rather than 'let the feedback do the talking'. However, from the student's point of view, and this was also the view of many of the other supervisors, the comment was intimidating. The point of this anecdote is that the supervisor did not see anything wrong with the comment, even after discussion.

Comments on your writing can be mixed up with comments on your research. It is important to work out what the feedback means before you start to act on it in new writing and revising.

The code of practice may be a useful agenda for a series of early meetings where you and your supervisor work out how you are going to manage your research and writing. These early discussions will help you work out what you are dealing with and the extent to which your supervisor is willing to adjust his or her style.

This chapter has taken a close look at the whole thesis writing process through a number of different lenses, drawing on official and unofficial sources. The next chapter looks at how the whole writing process defined in this chapter can be operationalized through a range of writing routines and regimens. The question for each thesis writer will be which suits them best. The answer should probably be, a combination of several different strategies.

Questions for reflection

Leading to fruitful and fascinating discussion in postgraduate groups:

At the start of your programme

- What is the purpose of the thesis?
- What is/are my supervisor's/supervisors' role(s)?
- How do I define an effective student–supervisor relationship?
- When do I expect to complete my research?
- What is my research topic (or area)?

Prompts for discussion

- Explicit discussion of purpose of a thesis in your subject area
- The scope of each piece of work
- The form of a thesis in your area, in your department
- What your supervisor thinks about these issues
- Further questions that discussion of these topics will raise.

Finally, this chapter, and the Introduction, have introduced a proliferation of terms and raised dozens of questions that you have to think about, and perhaps answer, as you write. It is a good idea to discuss some of these terms with your peers and supervisor.

The purpose of such discussions is to test your emerging understanding of what is involved. The outcome of such discussions might initially be 'There's more to this than I thought.'

As your understanding grows, there is no reason why you cannot move on to 'I know roughly what is expected of me' – a more positive, though, in true academic fashion, 'hedged' perspective on what thesis writing involves.

Writing timetable

Thanks so much for your help on Tuesday. I have taken your advice and made a workplan and have given my supervisor a progress report, based on what we discussed. I must say I feel a lot more confident about it now and realize it's up to me to take charge of getting the thing done.

(PhD student)

- Without a timetable for writing, you will feel out of control of the project and your confidence may suffer.
- Write about the topics raised in the codes and guidelines, as they apply to your project.
- If there is no deadline, the task may be dropped. Tasks with deadlines get done before tasks with no deadlines.
- Create 'hard' deadlines, which are fixed, non-movable, and 'soft' deadlines, which are flexible, movable.
- Set yourself two or three 'hard' deadlines for the next week.
- Set yourself two or three 'soft' deadlines for the next year.

A planning tool designed for dissertation writers – that may help you to plan your thesis writing process – is available:

Planning tool

www.strath.ac.uk/Departments/CAPLE/dissertation

Checklist

Pre-planning

- Read a recent, successful thesis by a student from your department.
- Get the university guidelines and/or regulations for thesis writers. Renew this every year. Read them every year.
- Check your university's requirements on style. Buy a style manual.
- Read the QAA documents. Visit the NPC websites.
- Choose software for references/bibliography.
- Decide when – and where – to write.
- Establish when your supervisor will be most/least available to see you about your work. How often will you meet? When will you review this arrangement?
- Who will you use as your audience when you write?
- What is the purpose of your thesis? Why are you doing this?
- When will it be finished? What is your first deadline?
- Three- or six-year plan: tasks and milestones for research and writing.
- Develop 'hard' and 'soft' deadlines for your research and your writing.
- Set a short-term goal: a task for tomorrow/next week.
- Discuss all of the above with your supervisor.

2

Starting to write

Can't it wait till later? • Audiences and purposes • Primary audience
• Secondary audience • Immediate audience • The role of the supervisor
• A common language for talking about writing • Writing to prompts
• Freewriting • Generative writing • Checklist: starting to write

> *The scariest moment is always just before you start.*
>
> (King 2000: 325)

This chapter introduces techniques for overcoming the fear of the moment –
for some writers momentary, for others monumental – when we start to write.
We can use strategies for generating text quickly to silence our internal editors,
at least during initial drafting stages. We can use writing to develop our ideas,
without thinking about our writing as 'drafts' at all. The key point is to develop
an understanding of the personal processes of writing, while meeting the
external criteria covered in Chapter 1.

As thesis writers develop an understanding of terms and strategies, their
vocabulary for talking about writing can change. Prompts for discussion
with supervisors focus on the importance of developing a shared language for
talking about writing.

Strategies covered in this chapter will be new to many thesis writers. These
strategies may not appear to 'work' first time. However, they provide
opportunities for you to try different techniques and take an active role in your
development as a writer.

Can't it wait till later?

'I don't have anything to say yet.'

Many students report that they would rather not write until they were sure that they had something to say: what can you write about when you haven't even started your research yet? However, if you wait until you feel 'ready to write', then you may not write at all. If you imagine that you will feel readier later, once you have read more, for example, then you are in for a huge disappointment and a lot of panicky writing later.

You can write when you are not sure, as long as you write in 'not sure' terms. For example, the first prompt that follows, 'My project is about . . .', is very different from 'Research questions' or 'Definition of research design'. It helps, at this 'starting stage', if your prompt for writing is appropriate to the stage you are at in your thinking. Through writing you can then develop your ideas. Through regular writing you can build your confidence that you will complete a thesis. Through revising such 'uncertain' writings you can select those sentences or ideas that seem useful and reject those that do not.

You can write . . .

- My project is about . . .
- The stage I am at now is . . .
- The next step is . . .
- What I am interested in finding out is . . .
- For my doctorate, 'original' means . . .
- Since last week/month I have progressed my project by . . .
- I have identified a problem with . . .

This activity gives you something to discuss with other researchers and, now or later, with your supervisor(s). You may even want to show them your writing, as long as it is clearly labelled as 'developing ideas', or something like that. Otherwise, there is a risk that they will read it as a draft chapter or report and will wonder why you bothered to give it to them.

Audiences and purposes

Although it is early days in the thesis writing process, writing can start now. If you wait till you feel 'sure' of your subject, you may never write at all, and you will surely not write as much or as many drafts if you leave it till the end of the research process. There will simply not be time.

The first step is to consider the context – both real and theoretical – in which you are writing. This helps to focus the writing. It also does not require much actual writing, although it will shape any writing that is done.

Audience and purpose are the key in any act of communication: everything you say – and do not say – is shaped by your analysis of the audience, or reader, and your purpose in communicating with them. For a thesis writer, audience and purpose are, literally, complex; i.e. there appears to be more than one audience.

It will help if you have more than one real audience in mind and in fact:

Writers should have a range of audiences, including listeners who understand and are sympathetic with their struggle. Writers should not be confined to 'authority readers' or critics (teachers). Peer readers bring pleasure into writing. Writing can be shared as a gift and does not always require a response. Most 'real world' writing solicits no feedback and often gets none. Ally readers help separate the writing from the writer. There may be response to questions such as 'What do you hear me saying?' or 'What do you think?' but no evaluations are necessary. Writers may feel comfortable to take risks that may ultimately improve their writing.

(Elbow 1998:
http://www.tc.cc.va.us/writcent/handouts/writing/pelbow.htm)

'Pleasure' in writing? This may be a new concept for some writers, but with the right reader, and the right regular discussions of writing along the lines described by Elbow, it might just work. The two questions he identified would be a good starting point from which writers could – perhaps mutually – work together at being audiences for each other's writing.

Primary audience

The primary audience for a thesis is the scholarly community. They set the standards. To some extent they also set the research agenda.

Scholars in your area are the readers who will be most interested in your writing. Of course, they will also be the most critical. Realistically, no matter how brilliant your work is, you can expect to get both positive and negative critiques of your writing. In fact, sometimes the more innovative a piece of work, or writing, is, the more critical attention it attracts. Innovation is very much sought after, but it also challenges what has gone before. Some people do not like that. Others simply cannot cope.

In order to develop your understanding of your own scholarly community, you have to participate in the usual forums, seminars, conferences and other meetings of specialists. These give you opportunities to rehearse your ideas and arguments among your peers and future peers. In addition, you can be making connections with other researchers in your field by email. The word 'community' suggests that we are all working together in some sort of collective enterprise, but you will be well aware that your 'community' is whatever grouping of people you can build for yourself.

As far as your writing is concerned, you will internalize certain scholars in your field, imagining them reading your work. Once you find out who your external examiner is you will also imagine him or her reading your writing. This will help you shape your writing, but it can also undermine your confidence.

We also tend to internalize both supportive and hostile, or even adversarial, audiences – real and imagined. It is important to acknowledge the role they can play in shaping our thinking and writing.

How you represent your audience to yourself is important. It is worth spending some time discussing this – either with your supervisor or with other researchers – so that you externalize your thinking. You can, of course, also write about your sense of audience. You can conduct an analysis of their expectations and you can analyse your own reactions to your audience.

Secondary audience

The term 'secondary audience' is used here to refer to your external examiner. It helps to see him or her as a representative of the scholarly community, rather than a person with idiosyncratic standards, although there may be an element of truth in that. Positioning your examiner in this way, however, will help you to target him or her in your writing.

In any case, it is likely that by the time you know who your examiner will be, you will have completed a fair amount of your writing and are unlikely to revise it with one particular reader in mind. That is not the point of this discussion of audiences. The point is that you have to direct yourself to construct an audience that is not so amorphous that you cannot target them in your writing and not so individual that you skew your writing to them alone.

Immediate audience

Your immediate reader is, of course, your supervisor. Supervisors have a formal responsibility to read your work and give you feedback on it within a reasonable length of time, throughout your research. They are, naturally, likely to have the strongest influence on your sense of audience. Again, as for the external examiner, it helps if you can see your supervisor as a representative of the scholarly community. As you get to know your supervisor well, this will become more and more difficult, but it will help you to focus.

In addition to all the people who will read your writing, it might be worth thinking about finding another supportive-yet-critical reader, someone who will give you honest feedback and complete support at the same time: your 'ideal reader'.

You may, of course, find that your supervisor does this. Real, or imagined, ideal readers can keep you motivated and can even inspire you to write, as if you were writing for them, imagining what they would say, how they would respond. This person may be a knowledgeable friend, someone who's written a thesis themselves, who knows what it's like and what it takes:

> Many writing texts caution against asking friends to read your stuff, suggesting that you're not apt to get a very unbiased opinion . . . The idea has some validity, but I don't think an unbiased opinion is exactly what I'm looking for.
>
> (King 2000: 257–8)

You will have plenty of allegedly 'unbiased opinions' of your writing to contend with over the months and years of your research. Always writing to that unbiased audience can become a bit sterile. You can never expect them to get excited by your writing. They may become so objective – and corrective – as to be boring or, finally, frustrating. Your ideal reader, on the other hand, will admire your efforts while still pointing out any faults and flaws.

We do not always have to write with a sense of audience. As strategies covered later in this chapter will illustrate, there is value in writing for other purposes than to communicate with other people. However, writing a thesis is always going to be about finding the right voice and level for an expert reader in our area. From time to time, as we write, we may feel one or other of these people peering over our shoulder. It is important that we manage that peering presence.

The role of the supervisor

In the UK we use the term 'supervisor' to designate the person who is responsible for guiding the doctoral student. In other cultures they have different titles, such as 'tutor' or 'thesis advisor' in the USA.

What does this role involve? Potentially, it has many dimensions: interpersonal, managerial, psychological/motivational, editorial and, of course, they have to be experts in the field. Supervisors have to play several different roles and should be sensitive to their students' needs as they do so.

Any text on teaching and learning in higher education will, if it includes research supervision, define the roles in more detail. For example, Brown and Atkins (1988) define the roles as follows (p. 120):

The roles of the supervisor

- Director
- Facilitator
- Adviser
- Teacher
- Guide
- Critic
- Freedom giver
- Supporter
- Friend
- Manager
- Examiner

Students are often fascinated by this list, which suggests that they have not really unpacked the role in this way before or, perhaps, that they have not really thought of the range of possibilities open to supervisors.

Many ask what exactly 'freedom giver' means: it may mean giving a steer, but helping students to find their own way. Of course, any supervisor may feel able to play more than one role, but which is your supervisor's preferred, or dominant, style? Who have you got? What can you expect to get from him or her? What are you not likely to get? What are you going to do to meet that need?

'Writing developer' is not on this list. Perhaps it is to be assumed that several – or all – of these roles are to be applied to writing, as to any other activity? In which case, how would you like to see them applied: are you looking to your supervisor to 'teach' you the higher level skills required for writing a thesis (and for publication)? Are you looking for someone who will 'manage' your writing process, helping you to get it completed on schedule? Or are you looking for someone who will, first and foremost, be a 'critic' of your writing, giving you the 'hard' feedback that you need to achieve the criteria for the doctorate? Have you discussed these expectations with your supervisor?

As your needs change, and as your supervisor trusts you to get on with the work, you may want to revisit these roles. Later in your doctorate you may feel that you need your supervisor to play a completely different role. At moments of crisis – of confidence or in research – you may feel that all you want is some support, some motivation to keep going and a moment's vision that you do have the ability to finish it. Your supervisor may or may not pick up on your changing and fluctuating needs. It might be as well to establish some pattern of communication about supervision, so that when you do request something else it does not sound like a criticism of what is currently being offered.

The role your supervisor plays – either consciously or unconsciously – will no doubt affect the role you play – consciously or unconsciously. The nature of the student–supervisor relationship may not be entirely predicated on how your supervisor acts and speaks – or on how you perceive him or her to be speaking and acting – but it will be strongly influenced by it. Students' perceptions of their supervisors will also be influenced by how others see them. For example, if your supervisor is seen by many as a 'guru', you might find it difficult not to see, or to feel that you ought to be seen to see, him or her in this light. It will not take you long to realize that some supervisors are perceived differently inside the department – and perhaps in the university – from outside the department or university. This can complicate your perception management further. The roles may or may not be complementary. Brown and Atkins (1988) define 14 possibilities (p. 121):

Relationships between student and supervisor

- Director : Follower
- Master : Servant
- Guru : Disciple
- Teacher : Pupil
- Expert : Novice
- Guide : Explorer
- Project manager : Team worker
- Auditor : Client
- Editor : Author
- Counsellor : Client
- Doctor : Patient
- Senior partner : Junior professional
- Colleague : Colleague
- Friend : Friend

As with the list of potential roles, this list is excellent for prompting discussion and reflection. We immediately find ourselves identifying our 'favourites', our preferred options for how we would like to work with our supervisors. We reject those that do not suit us, or that just do not make sense in this context. Some students will be looking at this list thinking 'Well, I know which one I like best, but I am not likely to get that from my supervisor, at any time.' This is fine. The point is to know their limitations, their strengths and weaknesses, to accept that they cannot be all things to all people and to be able to discuss – if not actually 'ask for' – what you want from them. If you do not ask, you will wait a long time till they learn to read your mind. Here is an anecdote, based on a real example:

> A colleague noticed that one of her collaborators, with whom she had been working closely for several years, had recently been looking unhappy at their one-to-one meetings. My colleague wondered about this, but put it down to personal matters. Some time later the 'unhappy' colleague raised certain criticisms, adding that my colleague 'Must have known there was something wrong' because she had begun to look visibly unhappy. In other words, the collaborator had expected her visible display of unhappiness to 'tell' my colleague that something was wrong. My colleague replied that if she were to assume that everyone who worked with her, and who appeared to be unhappy, was so because of something she had done, or not done, she would be a nervous wreck.

How might the supervisor's role definition affect your writing? The role your supervisor plays – consciously or unconsciously – can affect the role you play, both in your discussions and in your writing:

1 If you are cast in the role of 'novice' you will find it difficult to write with authority.
2 If you play the role of 'disciple' you might feel the influence of your supervisor's style of thinking and writing too strongly to find your own.
3 If you are cast in the role of 'colleague' you may feel that you cannot – yet, at the start – measure up to expectations.
4 What can you do if you are cast in a role that does not suit you, e.g. cast as expert when you feel you are a novice, or as a novice when you feel you have some knowledge?
5 Will you act out the role assigned to you? Do you have the necessary acting skills?
6 How can you influence this 'casting'?

How you perceive your immediate audience can have an enormous influence on your writing. To some extent that is inevitable; but you will have to find some way of writing for the audience 'beyond' the supervisor, the research community, while not appearing not to write for your supervisor, of course.

The supervisor's many roles, as reader, editor, critic, fellow scholar, member of the research community, may require you to do a kind of triangulation of the types of reader, so that you end up with someone to whom you can direct your writing. Having said that, it is likely that your reader will not be perfectly triangulated all of the time.

Your university's Code of Practice will indicate, or spell out, what your supervisor's responsibilities are. It may also list your responsibilities. It will tell you what your rights are: i.e. not what your rights are if something goes wrong, but what you have a right to expect from your supervisor.

Specific discussion of the role you and your supervisor feel he or she should play with regard to your writing would be a useful topic of more than one conversation. Your starting point might be a core issue like feedback:

1 Are you looking for (high-level) writing instruction?
2 Do you want mentoring about writing?
3 Will you need help with motivation to write?
4 Do you want incremental feedback on your writing?

These points could provide a starting point for these discussions. You do not need to stick with my terminology, but you could start with it and develop your own.

These two sections of Brown and Atkins (1988) have been included here because they have proved very effective in stimulating students to begin to address many different issues surrounding supervision in general and their supervisors in particular. The wide-ranging character of these lists has caused discussion to be wide-ranging, with students moving beyond their own points of reference for the purposes of discussion.

Interestingly, Brown and Atkins (1988) also define common problems in their chapter on supervision (p. 123):

Common problems for research students

1 Poor planning and management of project
2 Methodological difficulties in the research
3 Writing up
4 Isolation
5 Personal problems outside the research
6 Inadequate or negligent supervision

While only number three is explicitly about writing, it should be added that the others could be identified through the writing – or lack of it – that a student does.

All of the points in this section are prime topics for discussions with supervisors. As these discussions progress, you should be looking to develop a common set of concepts about roles and writing.

A common language for talking about writing

In communicating with your supervisor about writing, it is helpful to define the terms you use, and to ask your supervisor to define terms he or she uses. Terms like 'revise' and 'expand', for example, will be more helpful if you know the scale, scope and purpose of the revisions. The criteria for good/bad writing – yours and your supervisor's – are almost bound to be diverse, even dynamic and possibly 'indeterminate' (Delamont et al. 2000: 40). Such a fluid state can lead to frustrating discussions. If terms are left undefined, there is every chance that you will end up talking at cross-purposes.

Definition should obviously be a topic for discussion, but think through your own ideas first, so that you can put them across clearly. Generating a few of your own definitions will, in itself, lead you to develop your understanding of writing. You may feel that there is an over-emphasis on what your supervisor wants to see in your writing; however, you have to clarify what you want to achieve and what you want in the way of feedback. In order to produce 'good' writing, you have to clarify what *you* want your writing to be about. Although thesis writing is always targeted at a particular audience, you also have to 'target' your own themes, ideas and standards in your writing:

- What is acceptable for early drafts?
- What constitutes 'good' and 'bad' writing at this stage?
- What is required for each revision?
- What/how much structure is expected in the early stages?

The purpose of such discussions with your supervisor is to develop a common language, i.e. with assumptions and definitions that you and your supervisor share, that you can agree on. This may take time to establish.

One of the challenges of thesis writing is getting agreement on – or discovering – what sort of feedback you want. This is complicated by the fact that you might not be sure what your supervisor's comments on your writing mean. It is better to have this conversation now than to continue in ignorance, risking infuriating your supervisor by repeating what he or she defines as 'errors'.

After your discussions, confirm what you have agreed with your supervisor. If you have more than one supervisor this is essential.

After discussions

- Consolidate your understanding of good and bad writing.
- Confirm agreed forms of feedback.
- Confirm agreed writing tasks.
- Discuss the meeting with other students.
- Write right away and often.
- Target your revisions: do what you agreed to do *first*.

Comments you get back on your writing can range far and wide. They can be of different types, requiring different kinds of revisions by the writer. Sometimes it is difficult to translate the comment into action. It is not always clear – how could it be? – what the supervisor is seeing in what you have written and what he or she thinks you should have done.

It is not clear to what extent it is true that most students simply accept the feedback they get from their supervisors. In discussions of feedback they seem more concerned about simply getting any feedback on their writing at all and not waiting too long for it. They more rarely raise issues about the content and quality of that feedback.

You do not have to have 'problems' with your supervisor's feedback in order to have such a discussion. See it as a way of enhancing communications. For that to be true, this discussion has to be a genuine dialogue, or as close to that as you can manage.

The following points are not intended to be read as a series; instead, one or two may raise important points you have not yet discussed explicitly with your supervisor.

Discussing feedback

- What feedback will be/has been provided on your writing?
- When was this discussed/agreed?
- Is/are the type(s) of feedback you are getting explicitly signalled by your supervisor, i.e. on the page when it is returned to you? For example: 'Overall comments' and 'Argument-specific points'.
- Do your supervisor's different kinds of feedback require different responses from/actions by you?
- Do different comments require different revisions? Have these links been discussed explicitly? Does your supervisor have a method of signalling them?
- When will this subject be reviewed (in future discussions)?

These questions might be a useful set of prompts for short bursts of free-writing. This could help you to work out what you think, where you are at and what you think your supervisor is doing, before you go into the discussion. You could also freewrite about the different interpretations you can make of the feedback and the different revisions they might lead to. This would also be an interesting talking, or emailing, point for dialogue with supervisors. Use freewriting to start any new piece of writing arising from their comments.

Even if you have discussed your supervisor's feedback form and norms with him or her explicitly, it cannot be assumed that thereafter there can be only one – nor that you will make the right – interpretation of what he or she wrote. It would also save you time if you do happen to misinterpret the feedback, which, being realistic, must happen now and again. It will also, simply, be more writing practice for you.

Such discussions of feedback are not simply excuses to ask for what you 'really want'. You have to be ready to make a strong case for what you think you need in your supervisor's feedback. You have to manage carefully any statements that appear to criticize what your supervisor is currently providing. Many supervisors are quite happy to be flexible; others will require more 'ego management' – by you. You are the one who is best placed to know how to approach this subject with your own supervisor. It might help, however, to discuss and rehearse your points with peers first.

Whatever the feedback you get on your writing, how do you convert it into action? If you are not entirely sure how to translate the feedback into action – or if you are not even sure of the meaning of some of the feedback – you can always write a response and email your supervisor a note of what you propose to do. This will give you – and your supervisor – a way of checking that you have understood the feedback. If, or once, you know each other well, you may think this unnecessary, a waste of time. However, a form of 'reflecting back' does provide an opportunity for further discussion and clarification. Further-more, later in the project you will indeed know each other's ways, assumptions and operation practices very well, but there will be much more going on then. It may still be a good idea to check that you have interpreted the feedback correctly. This is especially true if you receive – as is likely – more than one type of feedback. Your supervisor is likely to supply more than one form of feedback from his or her 'typology' at any one time.

You may also just get a word or phrase circled or underlined, as if supervisors expect you to know, or find out, what is 'wrong' with it or what requires revision, in their view. Again, if you have been working with them – and their feedback – for months or years, you may well not need any more than that. On the other hand, and earlier in the process, you may not know what they mean. You will have to ask.

Supervisors may also only make a non-committal mark on your writing because they do not see it as their job to be your editor. Some would argue that it is not their job to 'teach' you the skills of scholarly writing – i.e. skills required for thesis writing – but that you should know these already or will pick them up as you go along. The question of who exactly should 'teach writing' in a university is a matter of much debate in certain institutions; in others it is a matter of no debate at all. Who knows whether that is because there are no 'writing problems' or because there are few academic staff prepared to debate the issue and even fewer willing to take on the responsibility.

To be fair, some supervisors may feel that they do not have the knowledge or skills to teach writing. They recognize when something in your writing is wrong, but may not be able to explain to you why, technically, it is wrong. Then there are those who are very well informed about writing. It is impossible to predict which position your supervisor will take in this debate or how much knowledge he or she has about writing. You have to find out for yourself.

Are the comments global or detailed or both? For supervisors, there is a decision to make about what type of feedback to give. Do they want to make you focus on the 'big picture' of your whole argument, or a section of it? Or do they want you to tidy up the style? Is clarification of terms paramount? Given that these are all quite different questions, requiring different focus and action, the supervisors may recognize that one is more important, at this stage, than the others. For example, they may decide that the priority is to get you to define and use key terms with more clarity. There may be other aspects related to clarity that they want you to work on and this would make for an effective theme in their feedback. You may have been expecting more feedback on what you think of as the 'content', but they see the use of terms – and assessing whether or not you can use them properly – as a priority. You can regard this as a tension between what you expect and what you get. Or you can accept that you have work to do – and who would not have – in clarifying what you have written.

This short narrative is designed to illustrate the types of interaction that occur between writing and feedback, between writer and supervisor and between the student's expectations at different stages: your expectations will change in the course of your research.

There is another question: if you are looking for a certain type of feedback, why not ask for it? If you are frustrated that you have not had the feedback you expected, or that you need, then you should at least tell your supervisor what you think you need. There is, of course, no guarantee that you will get it, but you will at least have had your say and the ensuing discussion may clarify to you and your supervisor what you are both trying to do.

Some students are fearful that if they ask for something they 'want' the supervisor will be offended. This may be true. It may depend on how you raise the issue and how you ask for what you 'want'. You may want to think about developing your verbal – and non-verbal – skills for this type of discussion. It is, in fact, a new type of discussion for most students. It might be a good idea to work this out sooner, rather than later, as there will surely be subjects about which you 'disagree' during the course of your research. It is almost inconceivable that two researchers – you and your supervisor – should agree on everything in the course of three or six years.

If you are playing the role of the learner, aspiring to learn as much as you can during your research, and if you behave as the learner, using the word 'learn' explicitly, then there is every chance that supervisors will respond fairly to your requests. Some may even invite your feedback on their feedback.

However, writing is not your only means of demonstrating research expertise; you can use writing as a tool for learning and thinking: 'Both think-then-write strategies and think-while-you-write strategies have utility in the context of academic writing' (Caffarella and Barnett 2000: 40). The following sections of this chapter describe three strategies for thinking-as-you-write.

Writing to prompts

This strategy involves using a fragment of a sentence or a question to stimulate writing. Some people find the fragment to be a more productive stimulus; for others the reverse is true. The ideal situation is to be able to use both, since each might produce a different kind of writing and even different content.

The features of prompts – and what makes them effective – is that they are short, direct and informal in style and the writing activity is short. These features help focus the writer's mind on the topic he or she wants – or needs – to write about. The written product may be either the development of an idea, or the draft of part of a chapter or a bit of both.

For example, one of the most effective prompts is one that can be used at any point in the thesis writing process: 'What writing have you done and what do you want to do?' This prompt stimulates writers into taking stock of writing that has been done and helps them to focus on their own motivation to write. Psychologically, it has the added benefit of adjusting the writer's skewed view of the mountain of 'writing still to be done', and presenting him or her with the vista of what has already been achieved.

There are many other prompts that can have these effects. At the very least, they provide writing practice. Once you have tried them, you can write your own prompts, appropriate to your current writing demands. In order to test this strategy, you can write, now, for ten minutes on one of the following:

Writing to prompts

- What writing have I done and what would I like to do?
- Where do my ideas come from?
- How does what I read compare with my own views?
- What I want to write about next is . . .
- What do I want to write about next?

Certain prompts work particularly well: those that generate text and, simultaneously, prompt reflection on writing practices. Ten minutes' writing, followed by twenty minutes' discussion in pairs – ten minutes on each writer – not only generates text and provides writing practice, but also reorientates writers and their motives. It helps them take a strategic view of their writing.

Freewriting

Freewriting is included here because it has proved so successful in my thesis writing courses and writing for publication programmes across the UK. Although it was not developed specifically for thesis writing – and to some writers does not initially seem suited to it – it has helped thesis writers to 'force' the writing, to 'get something down on paper' and to build their confidence in their own writing. This seems paradoxical to some: how can writing that is scribbled down in one go be of any use for the draft of a thesis? The written outcomes are so different. The answer is that freewriting can serve several useful purposes in the writing process. Perhaps the key gain is that it helps people start writing more quickly and stops them procrastinating.

It may also change writing processes: instead of writing exclusively in large chunks of time – or 'binges' – as many academic writers report that they must do, in order to really achieve anything, we can also write in small 'snacks', just in case we run out of large chunks of time, and, more importantly, to keep the writing regular. Freewriting is one way of developing this approach.

Peter Elbow (1973), who developed this approach, argues that he can help writers improve their writing, not by looking at the qualities of good and bad writing, but by providing strategies to help writers 'actually generate words better – more freely, lucidly, and powerfully: not make judgements about words but generate them better' (pp. vi–vii). He has some interesting handouts on writing on his website.

The form of freewriting defined here is a variation on Elbow's definition of freewriting, adapted for audiences in UK higher education. It is different from the standard structures and styles of academic writing. Although you start with a topic related to your research, you do not need to write continuously about that one topic. You can change topics. You can approach topics from different angles. You can go back to where you started, if you want. Many writers say that this is like brainstorming in sentences. The only requirement is that you continue writing. Do not stop to revise, edit, score out. Keep going for the full five minutes and stop when five minutes are up.

What is freewriting?

- Writing for five minutes
- Without stopping
- In sentences
- Private writing: no external reader
- Topic: what you want to write about next
- No structure needed

If you can immediately discuss your reactions or responses to this activity with someone else that is helpful. You will see how different people's initial reactions can be (rather than just my summary of recurring reactions).

Why 'writing in sentences' makes a difference is not clear, but it does seem to be important in helping writers to begin the process of synthesizing ideas, even though many expect it to be a barrier. It helps them to move beyond the collection of thoughts and fragments in their heads. They begin to articulate their ideas. It also helps writers become more fluent.

However, we need to be clear of the goal. Freewriting has been shown to 'improve' our writing. But in what sense?

> The most effective way I know to improve your writing is to do freewriting exercises regularly. At least three times a week . . . simply write for ten minutes (later on, perhaps fifteen or twenty). Don't stop for anything. Go quickly without rushing. Never stop to look back, to cross something out . . . If you get stuck it's fine to write, 'I can't think what to say, I can't think what to say' as many times as you want . . . The only requirement is that you never stop.
>
> (Elbow 1973: 3)

This is the opposite of knowing what you want to say first, and writing about it second. Why would we do this? It runs counter to all that many of us have learned about writing in academic settings? It will simply produce bad writing. These are the recurring reactions of writers on hearing about this approach for the first time. Even after trying it only once, many argue – some hotly – that it could not possibly have any use. It is not how they work (although there is usually a minority who reveal that this, or something very like it, is already part of their writing practice). Others respond that it is, to them, more like letter writing or writing in a diary. Few people see any connection between the 'flow' and fluency to which so many writers aspire and freewriting, which does, in fact, lead to that effect.

Here are examples of students' responses to a session that introduced the very different freewriting and structuring approaches:

I found that it highlighted the main points of good writing skills. It makes you think that you really need to structure your writing carefully and consistently. Whether or not freewriting would be a good method to try would be on a personal basis and something which I will no doubt try.

Details of different types of writing skills of which we tried freewriting which helped me see I am more of a structured writer as I felt lost without an outline.

I suppose the most reassuring element of the session regards the free-writing. I have found this works very well for myself. When researching there tends to be a posture of sticking to the facts. The facts are then used in an argument. This should be for and against but ultimately to support one's final viewpoint. What tends to be put to the back of one's mind is how one 'feels' about certain issues, i.e. ethics, morality, conscience are seldom required to be aired. With freewriting I often find out what I actually feel about subject issues as opposed to what I know or what I need to find out. 'A brainstorming session for one' is how I would describe it. Honesty usually prevails.

The last writer quoted here prompts several interesting questions: what is your 'posture'? How are you seeing your role, in using the ideas of others in your thesis? To support your work? To challenge it? Both? How will your 'posture' shape your writing?

This writer also defines how freewriting – for him or her – is qualitatively different from other more structured forms; it prompts a different relationship to knowledge, to writing and to research. Freewriting prompts a more subjective process. While subjectivity in thinking and writing is usually denigrated in academic discussion, this writer implies that subjectivity has value: it helps writers to work out their relationship to knowledge, an important first step in mastering and assimilating knowledge generated by others. Finally, freewriting may help us test how much we have actually understood, in our reading and thinking: 'Honesty usually prevails' in freewriting.

However, the strength of some writers' negative reactions is also interesting: 'I find freewriting offends some people. They accuse it of being an invitation to write garbage' (Elbow 1973: 7). In my writing programmes I have found that people can be very hostile and very positive – in same- and mixed-discipline groups – towards freewriting. It may be that some people are more naturally, or conceptually, inclined towards writing than others. Some are 'freewriters' and others are 'structurers'. The structurers want to have an outline first and do not see any purpose in writing without one. In short introductory sessions, introducing different approaches to thesis writing, when students are asked to use both freewriting and structuring approaches in short writing activities, both types of writer usually emerge:

The freewriter

I am probably a freewriter. I find writing for academic purposes very difficult. This session has taught me that I can use my own style and develop it so that it can become suitable for academic writing. I now also know which key words and structuring I should use when writing.

The structurer

This session has helped cement my pre-talk views on the benefits of working to your own strengths and style. Freewriting once again proved to be a failure of epic proportions, instilling fear in the heart of this writer.

These two writers relate their reactions to the activities with their own styles as writers. They appear to be happy to take responsibility for their reactions. The contrast between the first writer's use of 'develop' and the second's use of 'cement' is striking: 'develop' is used to describe the writer's awareness of writing in stages, while 'cement' suggests that the writer is unwilling to change. The lesson to be learned from their experiences is that, while in theory we may all agree that we should have more than one – and not just our preferred – writing strategy in our writing 'toolkit', it is nevertheless quite difficult to put this into action. It requires us to change. We have to write in ways that are not so comfortable for us. We may even have to go against our intuitive sense of what is the 'right' approach to writing. But is that not what genuine learning is about?

Perhaps this discomfort is about the difference between what these writers think is useful written output and what they produce by freewriting. They can see no connection between the two. Nor can they see the value of adapting practice. This is more worrying: having tried the new strategy once, and having learned a little about it, they are nevertheless prepared to reject it. Are they assuming that they will not have to make any changes to their understanding of writing? Are they expecting to make no changes to their writing practice? Are they not expecting to grow as writers at all? Or do they 'know' that their supervisor would rubbish their writing in this form? They must have very successful writing practices already, to be so sure that their practices will see them through the whole thesis writing process.

Some writers do not immediately see freewriting as purposeful, and of course, in the usual sense (i.e. their sense) of purpose, it cannot be said to be purposeful. In other words, freewriting has different purposes than other kinds of writing activity. It would also be expected that before we would begin to see any effect on our writing, we would have to try freewriting over the longer term, certainly more than once, probably over several weeks. It is up to the individual to construct a purpose for freewriting, and any other practices, for that matter.

After such a trial period, what kinds of changes would we see?

> Freewriting isn't just therapeutic garbage. It's also a way to produce bits of writing that are genuinely *better* than usual: less random, more coherent, more highly organized.
>
> (Elbow 1973: 8)

Note the language: 'bits of writing'. Not 'chapters'. Not 'drafts'. Not 'fine sentences'. Not 'writing that we are satisfied with'. This may be a helpful shift: from the goal of immediately producing features of 'finished' writing to using writing to start. This is using writing differently: using it to scribble down a whole idea in one short burst, rather than working at several sentences about that idea and polishing them till we feel they work as a series.

Using this strategy does not mean we have to throw out all our other strategies, but it may mean that we use them for other purposes. Perhaps we ought to be clearer about what the purpose of writing – i.e. the writing activity – is, when we start to write. Freewriting may help us not to aim for all our writing goals at once. Why do we think we can produce sensible, coherent and integrated writing all in one go, all in one writing session?

How does freewriting help us to become better writers? It silences the internal editor. As Elbow argues, there is nothing wrong with editing our writing, but 'The problem is that editing goes on *at the same time* as producing' (Elbow 1973: 5), and this damages concentration and coherence.

How can it help us write a thesis? The potential for effect can be seen in this student's representative reaction to being introduced to freewriting in a postgraduate writers' group and then following it up with a session on her own. To clarify, this student is 'representative' of those who find freewriting initially interesting and rapidly – acting on that interest – discover other outcomes. This is the student's unsolicited report, by email, to the member of staff running the group:

Freewriting frees thinking

I realise you are busy but wanted to let you know of my own personal success story resulting from what was discussed in the postgrad writing group this afternoon.

I came back to the library and spent seven minutes writing for myself about what I wanted to achieve with this current task which has been INCREDIBLY frustrating. Writing in such an informal and personal style suddenly seemed to free me in the way I was thinking about writing for this task and indeed made me realise I had to look at the whole project in a much more personal light. I was allowing myself to be more emotionally responsive to all the texts I was looking at and I actually enjoyed doing it. I was getting very afraid that I was not cut out for this [research] but thanks simply to undertaking a bit of free writing that I believe will mutate into a very useful space for me to record my feelings as the project goes on, I feel much more confident.

Many thanks for the introduction – I hope I feel this after all the sessions!!

What can this first-hand account tell us about freewriting?

1 That it can create an experience of 'personal success' directly associated with writing – and reading – for the thesis.
2 That writing in an 'informal and personal style' can have value; it can make the writer step back and see 'the whole project' as a whole.
3 That freewriting can 'free' up writers' thinking about their research and writing tasks, freeing them to 'write for thinking' not just write for a chapter or report.
4 That bringing to the surface the thesis writer's 'personal' connection to his or her study is productive.
5 That emotions and feelings are part of research and writing; suppressing them may have negative effects.
6 That freewriting can increase confidence.
7 That the overall impact of this session has been to increase optimism about the study and about the self as writer.

What issues do these points raise for thesis writers?

• **Feelings and emotions**
  Are these to be suppressed for three or six years? Or are they an important part of the thesis writing – and learning – process? Presumably, the experience of emotions will not cease during this time, though their expression may be suppressed. Yet, if the writing is to be emotion-free, and if there is an illusion that the process – not just the text – has to be

emotion-free, then there will be a gulf between what writers feel and what they write, unless, of course, it does prove possible to separate feelings and thoughts.

- **The writers' group**
  Is it important that these effects were experienced when freewriting was done in a postgraduate writers' group, led by a senior academic with a willingness to mentor? Would the solitary writer have a similarly positive experience, with all of these effects?
- **Optimism and motivation**
  The importance of students' experience of success, in a writing session, undertaken by them alone, in the library, is not to be understated. If their enthusiasm is to be sustained throughout the long haul of the thesis, having a mechanism for seeing the big picture and reconnecting with the work will be invaluable. Whether freewriting will always be that mechanism is another question.
- **Student–supervisor discussions?**
  Given the issues this case raises, it might be an interesting talking point between student and supervisor. The supervisor might see the student as a bit naïve, in her 'hope' that she will feel just as positively after every writing session. The supervisor may point out that the student has, in fact, written very little. There is the question of whether all the effects described occur for all students, for all their writing.
- **Understanding writing**
  One of the most interesting insights in the student's writing is that her freewriting will 'mutate' into something else. This shows that she has grasped its potential to produce material that will 'seed' more writing and thinking. The student appears to have avoided the misconception that freewriting produces chapters; instead, she is aware of how useful it is in adjusting her perspective and moving her thinking forward. Even more interestingly, she removes freewriting from what we might see as the habitual 'space' of thesis writing, making freewriting an alternative, 'very useful space' for recording thoughts and feelings about the thesis. Without such a space, how are such thoughts and feelings to be addressed and progressed?
- **Personal v impersonal?**
  Academic writing, most would agree, has traditionally featured impersonal constructions and the passive voice to create what many see as the appropriate objective style. 'Hedging', as in the previous sentence, is another way of not saying directly what you think.

Subjective: bad	*Objective: good*
Feelings, emotions	Thoughts, concepts
Anecdotes	Arguments
The first person: 'I think'	Impersonal: 'It is possible that . . .'

Things are no longer so black and white now, as a glance at a selection of recent titles on academic writing will show. However, when we discuss examples of various styles on the continuum between these two extremes, there are students who think that the objective style is what is valued most and is, therefore, what they should produce. It would, they think, or argue, be too risky not to. The purpose of freewriting is not to replace an objective style with a subjective one; it is to put subjectivity in writing, and then to see if it 'mutates' into something else. Thesis writers do not have to do all their writing in the objective style; they do not have to show their free-writing to anyone else.

Freewriting can, therefore, have a number of different purposes. It is not one short, simple writing activity with one purpose. Thesis writers – and academic staff writing for publication – have found many different uses for it.

Uses of freewriting

- As a warm-up for writing
- To look for topics
- To sift through topics
- To write in short bursts
- To get into the 'writing habit'
- To develop fluency
- To clarify your thoughts
- To stop yourself editing too soon
- To find or choose between topics
- To do incremental writing, in stages
- To increase confidence in your writing
- To overcome obstacles by articulating them
- To put the 'personal' voice into impersonal research

Freewriting is, in some ways, like brainstorming in sentences: it can be open, exploratory and unpredictable. It is useful for finding topics. This does not mean looking for 'something to write about' but, as is more likely with thesis writers, choosing what to write about from an abundant supply of possible topics. There is all too much to write about all of the time; the question is, more often, how to go about writing about it.

The fact that it is in sentences does seem to make a difference: some writers say that they feel constrained by writing in sentences, feeling that it slows them down, makes them lose ideas. However, freewriting in sentences allows us to develop a thought, perhaps to bring ideas together, to push them a little further. They may be more intelligible, when we return to them, than bullet points. They may have captured more of the idea or thought that we had at the time. They may be better prompts for further writing.

Freewriting can help writers find focus. It may, and often does, produce a string of further questions, but these can help the writer by generating more topics for more writing, or, on reflection, they can be seen as digressions and discarded. It may not be till we write a little more on a topic or question that we realize how far it is taking us away from the focus of our work.

To say that freewriting is writing practice is not to diminish its usefulness. If writing is a skill, whatever theory of skills acquisition and maintenance we espouse, it should be clear that we ought to keep practising that skill in order to maintain and develop our ability to perform it well.

What can I write about now?

Write for 15 minutes, without stopping, on one of the following:

- All the questions you currently have about your study.
- The question 'What can I write about now?'
- Why I have nothing to write about . . .
- One of the prompts or questions you wrote in an earlier section of this chapter.

Write about all of these, one after the other. Pause to rest and consider what you have written for a few minutes only. Do not edit or revise. Count the number of words you wrote for each.

How many words did you write on each of the above prompts? Between 150 and 250 words in fifteen minutes, or more? If you did all four activities, and if you produced 250 words for each, then you have written 1000 in an hour.

Whatever the total number, you produced writing on demand by using particular prompts and a particular mode, on this occasion, but you can create variations of this activity. You can write your own prompts and questions. You can write for two thirty-minute sessions or for an hour. You can find out for yourself what your pace of writing is under these conditions. You can set yourself targets. Once you have an outline for a chapter or section you can carve the writing up into 250-word writing sessions. It is not the number of words that you produce that is the main point, though that too can be inspiring and reassuring, but the fact that you know how to produce words.

However, part of your brain is probably telling you that, while you may think it is fine that you wrote so much, what you wrote is actually dross . . . garbage . . . rubbish. Some people will be amazed that they wrote so much. This experience will release their writing selves. Others will be more sceptical of, even disgusted at, talk of 'numbers of words' when the goal is to work at the cutting edge of knowledge. This 'arithmetic of writing' will not seem to fit with their 'contribution to knowledge'.

Naturally, the writing produced in this way will not be well structured, nor will the grammar be perfect, and it may not 'flow'. But structure, grammar and flow were not the goals of the exercise. When does writing ever come out perfectly structured, with perfect grammar and style, the first time around anyway?

The point of this writing activity is not to write something that is good enough to go straight into a chapter of a thesis – how realistic a goal is that? – but to move your thinking forward, inch by inch, centimetre by centimetre, word by word, to the point where you know what your thesis is about. Then you can start explaining it to others.

It is also about developing confidence as you go, and those who take up freewriting and make it a routine part of their practice find that it does build their confidence. This should not be overlooked as a superficial gain. It will be the most important gain for some writers. Again, how can we know until we have tried it for at least several weeks?

Our freewriting can also be the subject of our own study: what we produce can be a prompt for study of the connections and gaps between our ideas and thoughts. These appear in the writing, and reflections on them may be fruitful subjects for further writing, discussion and thinking:

> After the exercise take a few moments or more to rest and think about what your wrote. Think, too, about the digressions you started and perhaps continued. Notice when they occurred and where they took you. Think about their connections. Consider them as paths you should explore.
>
> (Elbow 1973: 10)

Students' responses, for and against, on the basis of one try at it:

> 'I can only write if I have large chunks of time.'
>
> 'What can you possibly achieve in 30 minutes?'
>
> 'A brainstorming session for one.'

People often find that it helps them to get started on any piece of writing, not just their thesis or paper. It stops them procrastinating and agonizing. They 'just get something down on paper', and the writing is much easier after that.

There is research to show that we may all be either 'freewheelers' or 'structurers'; however, how do you know which you are? Many writers only discover what type of writer they are when they are 'made' to try different strategies. Some decide that they have no need to change:

1 Try it over the long term – not just once – before you decide for or against it.
2 Freewriting may 'unlock' your thinking and expression.
3 It is not intended for an audience, i.e. not for supervisors.
4 Read the following letter, written by someone who tried freewriting once in a workshop for research supervisors:

I was at your Staff Development Seminar on Postgraduate Supervision on January 16 at [named] university.

At the time I think I said that the most useful thing that I came away with was the ideas that there are all *sorts* of writing and all sorts of *feedback*. In my training, the usual process was Problem–Data–Analysis–Conclusions–Recommendation–Actions, or something like that. And writing was what you did at the end . . .

Since I've been here doing my PhD . . . I've found that, more than ever, I've wanted to write letters to people . . . I thought that, with moving into a role principally about reading and writing, I would be *less* inclined to read and write for pleasure. But the opposite is true.

I've begun to read Elbow's *Writing with Power*. Whilst those of his ideas you spoke of appealed at the time, reading them has made a much stronger impression. I feel unfettered and realise that lots of things that I've done make a lot of sense: writing half-baked discussion papers so that I have something on which to 'hang' subsequent reading; writing lots of letters when I feel confused or happy, not just to tell everyone else about it but to sort it out or do something about it for myself . . .

I've had a couple of days this week of very interesting reading (of articles in areas more or less related to my research subject) and have been struggling with how to *do something* with the new ideas they give me. The two options I've had open to me so far have been: write a summary of each article on a record-card or its electronic equivalent; or somehow give it a mention in the literature review bit of my (nascent) thesis. Now I feel that just collecting thoughts on a half-dozen articles and writing them down and seeing what happens is potentially a very worthwhile approach. Not just categorising them or citing them, but genuinely engaging with them.

So, I'm freewriting daily. I'm writing a lot – anything: letters, 'thinkpieces', verbal collisions, angry memos. The effect has been somewhat delayed, but I'm very glad I came to your seminar. Hopefully it won't mean that I just write a lot of rubbish instead of writing a small amount of rubbish, but at the moment it seems good . . .

I've learned a lot and hope that the momentum is sustained.

This letter suggests that there are three stages to this process: (1) 'collecting thoughts', (2) 'writing them down', (3) 'seeing what happens'. The end result is not just a list or system of literature, but this writer's genuine 'engagement' with them. In other words, he has not only represented what is in the literature, but processed it at, arguably, a deeper level, by working out what he thinks about it.

In disciplines where subjectivity is not always a recognized part of the writing product, freewriting can nevertheless bring the subjective into the writing process. The term 'nascent thesis' suggests this writer is at an early stage and that writing is proving useful, even although he is not sure what to do. The term 'unfettered' suggests that it is important not to structure too early.

This writer's responses give a very specific example of the value of free-writing at this stage in the writing of a doctoral thesis.

There are still uncertainties: what will this writing produce? Will momentum be sustained? Freewriting does not entirely resolve the uncertainties that are very much part of the writing process; however, it does help writers to move through their uncertainties, in spite of them, even, perhaps, to take an interest in them.

Over the longer term, the best approach, for most writers, is probably a combination of this type of freewriting strategy and structuring approaches. The trick is to make best use of both, rather than to see the weaknesses in both. Yes, they both have limits, but both have uses for doctoral thesis writers. Yes, one strategy will appeal to you more than another, but have you considered moving out of your 'comfort zone'? What would happen to your writing process if you adopted one of the strategies that does not – instinctively – seem to make sense to you?

Over the longer term, research shows that writers who were initially sceptical about the benefits of freewriting have, surprisingly, continued to use it and even to recommend it to their students. A group of academics who took the Academic Writing module in an accredited course on Teaching and Learning in Higher Education reported, in discussions, that they initially found freewriting to have limited relevance to the kind of writing they and their students had to do in their disciplines.

However, in interviews conducted five months after the end of the module, of all the new strategies they had learned about during the module, free-writing (and generative writing, covered in the next section) scored highest. In addition, they had started recommending freewriting to students who were, for example, getting bogged down in (undergraduate) dissertation writing. This research suggests that while initial responses to this approach are often hesitant and sometimes negative, it does prove useful over the longer term.

So many writers, in so many writing courses, academic staff and post-graduate students – and others outside the higher education sector – find free-writing counter-intuitive. They find the concept of 'snacking', rather than just 'bingeing', too different from their current concepts, learned in much earlier stages in their studies. What seems to be the most reasonable position in this debate, and in practice the most productive, is to combine both 'snack' and 'binge', to write in both large and small chunks of time, as the opportunity arises. However, perhaps the 'binge' sessions – of an hour or more? – should be structured sessions; rather than simply setting a goal for a large chunk of time, we can set smaller goals for smaller chunks of time.

Generative writing

Generative writing (Boice 1990) is similar to freewriting in that it does not have to be constrained – or supported – by the traditional features of academic writing. It works in a similar way, initially to force writing, and over the longer term to develop ease and fluency in writing.

Generative writing – same routine

What's the difference?

- Write for five minutes
- Without stopping
- In sentences
- Stick to one topic, possibly something from your freewriting
- Let someone else read it

As this checklist suggests, generative writing is more closed than freewriting, more focused on one topic. Unlike freewriting, it can be read by someone else – though this is optional – and that usually changes writers' experiences dramatically; they become much more aware of the requirements of the audience, their responsibility to make their writing make sense and, most acutely, the potential for judgement of their writing.

In writing workshops, when we do the two activities together, generative writing frequently makes an effective, focusing follow-up to the more open, exploratory freewriting. The value of having someone else read the generative writing is that it can break the ice; writers can get used to people reading their writing, even in rough draft form. However, some writers do not see any purpose in letting someone read their writing when, as they see it, it is in such a poor state.

If this prompts discussion of how the reader affects our writing then that has had some use already. If, in addition, we take time to consider the fact that all the writing we submit for scholarly scrutiny, particularly when writing a thesis, will be, if not first draft, then early rough draft, then we can begin to adjust our perceptions of what is 'good enough' to show to a reader. If we can go a step further and acknowledge that all of our writing is 'good enough' for the stage that we are at, then we may have arrived at a more realistic model of the writing process. This does not mean that we will feel completely comfortable about showing our work to readers; but it may result in our feeling less uncomfortable.

In combination, freewriting and generative writing can work together: freewriting produces a string of loosely related sentences, while generative writing about some part of the freewriting produces more focused writing. Having said that, thesis writers who have tried both strategies once often remark that they respond more readily to generative writing, since it seems more like structured writing. That may, indeed, be its strength or weakness.

There will be times in the doctoral process when your writing does not seem to find a structure, when you are still working out what you want to say and when the characteristics of academic writing do not chime with how your thinking is developing and seem, in fact, to block your writing. At such times students often find that freewriting is more helpful than generative writing. As one put it: 'Before you do anything, write for five minutes . . . It helps you to focus or consolidate.'

A key strategy for making sure that freewriting and generative writing are productive is to follow them with discussion. The combination of writing and talking often stimulates further writing. If you work with someone else on this activity you both have a real audience, both get an immediate response to your writing and can both prompt each other to write a little more or, at least, to decide what your next writing activity or task will be. This 'writing sandwich' is an effective means of bringing writing and discussion together, while ensuring that writing is not only discussed, but also performed. This sequence need take no more than 30 minutes, once or twice a week:

The 'writing sandwich'

1 Writing   10 minutes
2 Talking   10 minutes
3 Writing   10 minutes

This activity can be practised in a writers' group or between two postgraduates. It may even be useful for student–supervisor working sessions, as both try to clarify a point in the discussion or text.

These three strategies – writing to prompts, freewriting and generative writing – may prove immediately useful, or may be so unlike the writing you generally do that they seem unlikely to help. While they are worth persevering with, particularly for specific purposes early in a large project, and while they have been shown to help writers develop confidence and fluency, there is perhaps a need for consolidation:

Consolidation

How will scribbling for ten minutes help me write a thesis?

This question – a very valid one – has already been addressed in this chapter, but is raised here for individual writers to stop to consider how they assess the value of these strategies. More specifically, in addition to their general reaction to the strategies, writers should consider (1) what they produced using these strategies; (2) what they learned about writing; and (3) what they learned about themselves as writers.

The value of 'scribbling'

- For short, regular writing tasks or bursts
- To find a topic for a chapter/section/paragraph
- To find a focus in/for writing
- To get started, 'get something down on paper'

What the value of any of these strategies is – or could be – is for the individual writer to discover.

This chapter has presented strategies for getting started in writing. Starting from scratch is taken to mean that very small steps are appropriate. This is still an exploratory phase and writing is one of the tools for exploration. However, it is time to think about more structured writing.

The next chapter explores the challenge of finding structure in your writing, perhaps before you really believe it is feasible to produce structured writing.

This is not to say that you should stop freewriting and generative writing, nor that they will be replaced by structured writing. Thesis writing is not a linear process. There will be many iterations and many continuing uses for generative writing strategies. If you need a reminder of the range of uses of freewriting, go back to the checklist. The checklist on the uses of freewriting is not simply intended for the 'starting to write' phase; it also has important 'continuing to write' benefits.

Checklist

Starting to write

- Put together writing 'kit'.
- Arrange back-ups, paper, printer cartridges, etc.
- Buy style manual.
- Acquire reference software or system.
- Establish diary for research and writing: milestones, tasks, meetings, etc.
- Attend research training course(s).
- Develop common terms with supervisor for discussing your writing.
- Agree format, deadlines and criteria for early writings and drafts.
- Confirm decisions in writing to supervisor.
- Respond to feedback by 'reflecting back'.
- Check interpretations of supervisor's feedback on your writing.
- Do some writing to kick-start the process.

3

Seeking structure

Revising your proposal • Outlining • Finding a thesis • Writing a literature review • Plagiarism • Designing a thesis • 'Writing in layers' • Writing locations • Writing times • Checklist: seeking structure

> *The knack for all research students regardless of discipline is to pinpoint what is required and model your work accordingly.*
>
> (Burnham 1994: 33)

This quotation could be interpreted as a cynical 'give them what they ask for and no more' perspective on the course or degree. However, it is a useful reminder of how important it is to know what is expected of you. You not only have to know what is required, you have to adapt your thinking and writing accordingly.

This chapter moves towards thinking about constructing an argument for a thesis. A variety of writing activities involved is outlined, with an emphasis on finding and focusing on a central theme.

Paradoxically, as we move towards constructing and rehearsing outlines and arguments, freewriting and generative writing can still prove useful, as we explore options. They can help us to move beyond the fragments of a thesis by having several attempts at pulling them together. They allow us to write – briefly – about the whole thesis. They can help us to find the type of story that our thesis will tell.

For most writers, however, this phase of the thesis is more about 'seeking' than finding. Use writing to move forwards. Do not expect to pin down the full extent of your thesis in words or outline at this stage. This chapter takes you one step closer to that point. There is still a lot of work to do.

Revising your proposal

Go back to the original proposal you wrote in your application, on the basis of which you were admitted to the programme. Your thinking will surely have moved on since then. It is useful to write about how you have moved on. This will mean that you do not stray too far from your focus – unless you intend to – and will give you a sense that you have made progress, even if you feel that it is modest, as is likely, at this stage. You can then discuss your views with your supervisor.

Five minutes' freewriting

Has/how has your study changed since you wrote your proposal?

You can also do structured writing, based on your proposal: take each element and elaborate or revise it.

- Develop your provisional hypothesis.
- Revise your aims and objectives.
- Narrow down your research question(s).
- Identify priorities: consolidate and cut questions/issues.
- Define each word, in each question, further.

Revisiting your proposal is a good way to start developing an argument for your thesis. In fact, if you produce a 300–500-word outline, you can use this as a touchstone for future writing, returning to it again and again to remind you of the focus for your thesis. If you feel that you cannot write about your research because you have not done very much yet, if you are genuinely struggling to find topics to write about, write about the context of, or background to, your work. This will be useful for your introduction.

What can I write about? The context/background

- My research question is . . . (50 words)
- Researchers who have looked at this subject are . . . (50 words)
- They argue that . . . (25 words) Smith argues that . . . (25 words) Brown argues that . . . (25 words)
- Debate centres on the issue of . . . (25 words)
- There is still work to be done on . . . (25 words)
- My research is closest to that of X in that . . . (50 words)
- My contribution will be . . . (50 words)

The questions in this box have apparently been used by students to 'write a page 98 paper', since this box was on page 98 of the first edition. This activity seems to be particularly useful to students in the first year, or first phase, of a research project. It may have particular strengths at this stage:

- At an early stage in your research it can establish focus and/or direction, and it prompts you to write perhaps before you have a sense of focus or direction.
- It prompts you to associate your project with the literature.
- It also prompts you to distinguish your project from the literature.
- It can help to focus your reading and thinking.
- It is a manageable task: you only have to write 325 words.
- The word limit can help you to focus your writing.
- This activity can move you on to thinking about your thesis.
- At a later stage, this activity can help you to focus your thinking as you draft your conclusions and revise your introduction.

You may, of course, change your mind about the focus for your thesis, but that will happen over time. Each of these stages of writing, thinking and focusing will generate important discussion points with your supervisor.

This is not to say that writing now, and in this way, is a waste of your time, if you are only going to alter it later. Development of your ideas will occur *because* you write; it may not happen if you do not write at all. Moreover, the psychological boost that comes with seeing how far your ideas have progressed is also important. You may be so acutely aware of how far you still have to go that you have lost sight of how far you have come. In revising your proposal you will see how much clearer a sense of your central argument you have now.

Outlining

This is what an outline should do – allow you to order, categorize, and plan your writing ... Use the word processor to type the outline and then convert the outline to prose when you are completely satisfied with the content and the logical flow.

(Reif-Lehrer 2000)

Chapter 6 describes a process for outlining the final thesis; at this stage, the aim of outlining is to begin to develop a sense of what your thesis is going to look like, what type of thesis you are going to write and what your supervisor thinks about your ideas. Do not wait until you 'know what you want to say', 'have something to say' or 'have done some research' before you start work on an outline; an outline gives you a way of ordering your ideas. Even if you are not 'completely satisfied' with the content, you can produce something that is more organized than a collection of points. You can move beyond a list of ideas to a sequence of headings.

Start with your 300–500-word summary. This does not necessarily tie you down to one structure – there are many variations in any subject area – but it gives you, or starts you looking for, a framework on which to build your own argument. Drawing on the sentences and key words in your summary, you can begin to draft a list of headings or questions, in a way that prepares for the thesis format:

- *What work has been done in this area?* List names (dates), debates, how does your work relate to theirs? What did you intend to add to the conversation? What precisely was your research question?
- *What work did you do?* How did you go about answering your question? What was the field of your analysis? What materials/methods/approaches did you use? What is/was the match between question and approach? How did you choose to write about this?
- *What did you find?* What was the result of your analysis? Describe your analyses. Demonstrate in detail what you did. How does that add to the literature?
- *What does it mean?* Have you answered your research question? Are there new questions? Are there new theories, approaches, refinements?

While these questions rehearse many of the decisions a thesis writer has to make, and consider writing about before having made them, they do not yet define structure. The writer still has options. This is your first outline of your thesis; your final chapter outline may look quite different.

If you find that these questions do not seem to fit your work, you can either try writing about them anyway – you may surprise yourself – or adapt them so that they do fit and do prompt writing.

- You can rewrite these prompts as questions.
- You can adapt this writing activity, writing different questions or prompts, to suit your study and your vision of your thesis.
- The point is you have to find a way of beginning to sketch the key sections of your thesis, whatever they may be.
- Start to develop prompts from any headings, conventional or unconventional, i.e. using or adapting generic conventions.
- Try combining headings from outlines in this, or any other chapter. You do not have to stick with one.
- Discuss your emerging outline with others, including your supervisor.
- You may notice that your outline, as you customize it for your thesis, does not hold together perfectly; there are gaps and jumps in logic. This is something to work on, but not to worry about; your outline will not appear perfectly formed in your first attempt.

It is important that you find a way to write at this stage, but do not expect to find that all the prompts, questions and generic frameworks neatly fit your work. You will have to adapt some of your thinking about your work if a focus is to emerge.

Finding a thesis

In this section 'thesis' means an integrated argument that can stand up to critique. Every thesis makes a proposition and every proposition has to take into account a range of views, including opposing views. The form of the thesis forces writers to anticipate the debate which they enter when their work goes out for peer review. A thesis is the central idea that holds it all together.

Finding a thesis means creating links between phases of the work done, between pieces of writing already drafted or completed and, most importantly, between the main research question and the work done. All of this has to be done in writing. There have to be logical links between sections. Making the connections you see explicit can help to reveal your thesis, your main idea, in your writing.

Another way of thinking about – and looking for – a thesis is to think of it as a theme. It may be a strand in your writing or step in your thinking that recurs and seems to be emerging as a theme, only gradually, in the course of your work. A key to finding your thesis is to use the original research question as a touchstone, while rehearsing potential themes.

One word of warning: a thesis is an argument that, traditionally, had to be 'proved'. However, this is a term that, with a few exceptions, is not used in academic writing. It is understood that our research – and therefore our writing – is contextualized and even contingent. In other words, we are not 'proving' something for all time and all places; this is not an accurate use of the word 'prove'. Instead, we can 'show', 'suggest' and make reasonable and reasoned interpretations of what we find in our analyses of texts, substances, people or events. If that seems like a compromise, it might be useful to remember that in writing a thesis, we are entering a debate; there are many people who will not agree with our writing. Not only can we not ignore the work of those who are likely to disagree with us, but we must directly address it. We have to articulate the basis of such disagreements in our writing, showing where our work fits in the debate. Words like 'suggest' are the language of debate.

Writing a literature review

Not every thesis has a literature review, but every thesis writer has to write about the literature, showing how his or her work relates to others'. Even if you would rather write about the literature in several chapters – rather than just one – so that it is integrated in your argument, it might be helpful, for the moment, to think of it as a separate unit in your argument. This may help you to decide whose work you want to write about, whose work you probably have to write about and how you will represent the field as a whole in a general overview.

What is a literature review? There are many different definitions and purposes. Most reviews have more than one purpose. There are many definitions available, the following writers suggesting that a review is an interpretation, a synthesis, a project, a task and a new 'look' at new sources:

- An interpretation and synthesis of published research.

(Merriam 1988: 6)

- A research project in its own right.

(Bruce 1994 on Brent 1986: 137)

- A task that continues throughout the duration of the thesis . . . shows how the problem under investigation relates to previous research.

(Anderson et al. 1970: 17)

- [An opportunity to] look again at the literature . . . in . . . an area not necessarily identical with, but collateral to, your own area of study.

(Leedy 1989: 66)

Merriam's use of 'interpretation' and 'synthesis' makes clear the active role of the writer; it is the thesis writers' version of the literature, their selection and arrangement of their summaries and critiques. Brent rightly clarifies the research that is required for a review. Anderson et al. emphasize that reviewing the literature is a constant, running through the whole project. Leedy seems to suggest broadening the review's scope.

The review has a 'purpose' in two senses: on one level the purpose is for the writer to learn about the literature in the course of writing about it, and on another level the review has its own 'purpose' in that it plays a role in the thesis argument. Both purposes are captured by Bruce:

- Literature reviews in the context of postgraduate study may be defined in terms of process and product. The process involves the researcher in exploring the literature to establish the status quo, formulate a problem or research enquiry, to defend the value of pursuing the line of enquiry established, and to compare the findings and ideas of others with his or her own. The product involves the synthesis of the work of others in a form which demonstrates the accomplishment of the exploratory process.

(Bruce 1994: 218)

Each of these could be a prompt for writing in itself: (1) 'establish the *status quo*'; (2) 'formulate a problem'; (3) 'defend the value of pursuing the line of enquiry'; (4) 'compare the findings and ideas of others' with your own; (5) 'synthesis of the work of others'; and (6) 'demonstrates the accomplishment of the exploratory process'. This last one is interesting, in that it reminds us to demonstrate how thoroughly we researched the literature in order to hit upon our research topic. This may, of course, not be exactly or even approximately how we found our topic, but our search through the literature will have influenced our research by helping us to focus more precisely on what we did.

A helpful distinction between the review and the rest of the thesis is provided by Cooper:

- First, a literature review uses as its database reports of primary or original scholarship, and does not report new primary scholarship itself ... Second, a literature review seeks to summarise, evaluate, clarify and/or integrate the content of primary reports.

(Cooper 1988: 107)

While Bruce simplifies:

- Typically, the literature review forms an important chapter in the thesis, where its purpose is to provide the background to and justification for the research undertaken.

(Bruce 1994: 218)

For the writer, reviewing the literature can be a means of learning from others' thought processes, expanding their view of the field, becoming familiar with different theoretical perspectives and parallel developments. Your literature review can demonstrate your abilities as a researcher:

- Demonstrate that you [have] a professional command of the background theory.

(Phillips and Pugh 2000: 59)

- The review of literature involves locating, reading and evaluating reports of research as well as reports of casual observation and opinion

that are related to . . . the planned project. It is aimed at obtaining a
detailed knowledge of the topic being studied.

(Borg and Gall 1989: 114)

This is just one of the structures you have to create in a thesis: an account of
the work that has gone before. Who has worked in your area? Who thinks your
subject is important? How does your work relate to theirs? The rhetorical
purpose of this section is to show the 'gap', to show that there is a need for
your work. Your research will take the field or topic forward in some minor
or major way.

What is the purpose of your review? To give an overview of the 'big issues' in
your field? To select some of these for your study? To summarize others' work?
To evaluate others' work? To provide a context for your work? The last of these
probably applies to most theses; everyone has to create some kind of context
in their introduction. You may choose more than one of these purposes, to be
written in several sections?

Many students – even in the first phase of thesis work – have more knowledge of the literature than they realize. They are so acutely aware of what they
have not yet read that they tend to forget that they have read copious amounts
already. Yes, there is a mountain of information out there, but you can realize
your own knowledge by doing a few short bursts of writing to prompts or
questions, or freewriting or generative writing.

Prompts for initial writing about the literature

- What do I know about my research topic?
- What I am looking for in the literature is . . .
- What are the schools of thought in the literature?
- The 'great debates' in my area are . . .

This activity has a number of potential benefits: it can help you recognize
that you do have knowledge already, and you begin to define what that is. It
can help you identify gaps in your knowledge and you can then select which
ones you need to fill, and which you do not. The writing also makes you
connect your work with that of other researchers.

The specific prompts used also keep the focus at the general level, particularly if the writing activity is continuous and short (15 minutes maximum). If
these prompts do not seem appropriate – if they do not work to prompt you to
write – then you can change them to suit. Some writers find questions much
more effective for prompting their writing than the half-formed sentence; for
others the reverse is true.

Who is this writing for? It is not designed to be read by anyone else. If the purpose of the activity was to get your initial reactions down on paper, then you could be putting yourself under pressure by showing them to someone else right away. However, with a few revisions you might have some writing that you could show to your supervisor, share with peers or include in a draft of your literature review.

At the very least, this activity constitutes writing practice; you have done some writing today. This will help you to maintain the skill. You may find it easier to get started on more structured, high stakes writing. In fact, this short burst of writing may prove to be a sketch or draft for something else. You may feel that the quality of the writing is low, but achieving quality was not really the aim of the exercise.

Repeating this exercise would be useful for integrating new reading into your 'big picture', or overview, of your field. As you read new material in bulk it can become difficult to see how it all hangs together. You can begin to compare and contrast. Use writing to keep a focus on your study and to develop your understanding of the literature. These short bursts can generate a few notes for your record of your reading, but it may be even more important that you have had to articulate your response in writing.

The language used in these prompts can be quite informal, general, designed to keep it simple. You can, of course, make it more academic or formal. As your understanding grows, and as a picture of the literature begins to emerge, you may want to revert to more specialized language. However, such a change might complicate things, as you realize that you have to define your terms much more carefully and have to defend what you write. This is no bad thing, as long as you know that you can return to less formal writing for new subjects, for example, whenever it seems right. In other words, you can begin to write formally and informally about the literature at the same time, in parallel. The informal writing would be useful for developing and testing your understanding and the formal writing would be for the supervisor to read – for feedback – and, perhaps, for drafts of chapters or sections.

Why do we critique the literature? What are our objectives?

- To learn about it
- To reveal areas that are ripe for development
- To work out where our ideas come from

A key point about these processes is that they are all constructions; i.e. in writing about 'areas that are ripe for development' we are stating our view, giving an interpretation of the field.

The third of these may seem absurd: surely we know where our ideas come from, and if we have not read this literature before, how can it be said that our ideas come from the literature? Yet, the question 'Where do my ideas come from anyway?' does helpfully remind us that we are unlikely to have come up with something that is completely new. It is just that we have not yet discovered who is already working on our topic. We have not yet established a relationship between our work and theirs. Moreover, this question can be incredibly useful as a focusing device at those moments when we are swamped by other people's work: instead of trying to create tenuous links that we half-understand to people's work that we, likewise, half-understand, as if we were trying to represent the whole 'big picture' of all the work that is out there, the question forces us to start with ourselves, our ideas. It can help us to filter out all but two or three, maybe five or six at most, of the researchers who have had most direct influence on our work and our thinking.

The task of writing a literature review therefore is a means of learning about the literature; we write to learn about what we read. Initially, we write about material that we do not know or understand very well. As our understanding develops we fill in gaps and take out errors. One of the key processes is identifying different methodologies and theoretical approaches. Understanding such complex material takes time, but we have to understand it if we are to make an appropriate choice of method, approach or critical stance in our own research.

By writing regularly we can gradually become more comfortable writing about new knowledge in a knowledgeable way. However, we can continue to use the range of prompts, tentative and knowledgeable, personal and academic, inquiring and authoritative:

- What is the story of the 'literature' about?
- Where do my ideas come from anyway?
- What are the main ideas and who is responsible for them?

(Orna and Stevens 1995: 175)

Each of these is a legitimate prompt for writing the literature review. The trick is not just to let it become a summary of other people's work.

It is also important to realize that critiquing does not mean demolishing the opposition. Many students write as if they feel they have to rubbish the rest in order to justify their own study. Does the literature review bring context or conflict? The literature is a context for your work; it is not necessary to be in conflict with it. In fact, you have to create links, perhaps links that you do not currently see, between your work and others'. The writers who do that have more impact. Show what is contested in your field; you do not have to contest it all yourself. You do not have to see it all as contesting your study.

At the same time, fear of giving offence stops some students writing anything that might be termed a 'critique', with its associations of being critical, while they themselves are novices in the field.

The purpose of the literature review

- To give an overview of the 'big issues'
- To select some of these for your study
- To summarize other people's work
- To evaluate other people's work
- To provide a context for your work
- To identify gaps
- To develop an understanding of theory and method

Here are four students' comments and questions after an induction on literature reviews and their role within the broader argument that is a thesis. The comments show what they took to be the main points and the questions show areas where they need more information:

Students' thoughts and questions

1 The main point is to steer students through the mass of available literature in order to home in as effectively as possible on pertinent information. Also how best to present the information.
   Question: Can other lecturers assist at a later stage with this process?

2 The main point is to understand what is meant by a literature review and how it should tie in with your own research and ideas on your project.
   Question: How academic do your readings have to be – do all your readings have to be academic?

3 Main points:
   Pay attention to structure
   Keep it simple and explicit
   Be concise
   Question: Should all reports conform to the same model?

4 The main points for me were going through the generic structure, the need to argue/discuss points with others.

One of the issues that arises from working with students on literature reviews is the complex relationship between thinking, knowledge production and the writing process. Some commentators (Hart 1998) point out that students can expect to see their understanding outstripping their writing: their thinking, knowledge and abilities will be moving on, even if the writing has not. If this is so, it is worth considering the implications for the writing process. It may mean that we ought to be developing writing activities – not abilities – in order to help students to keep up with their growing understanding and knowledge.

Or do we have to wait until we fully understand before we can write? Is writing something we do at the end of a process? What would such non-writing involve? What would that lead to? Are there writing skills appropriate in form to phases in the research, e.g. freewriting for sorting out ideas? Freewriting is a key strategy at this point: it helps students to sort through their own ideas when they are most at risk of being swamped by other people's.

Alternating freewriting and note taking is an effective way of ensuring that understanding develops and that writing continues. Note taking is a mechanism for active engagement with your reading. Freewriting is a springboard for your own ideas. What will you write about? Writing for ten or fifteen minutes on a paper could capture the key elements:

Questions the literature review should ask

- What were the research aims and objectives?
- What were the outcomes of the research?
- What approaches/methods/strategy were used?
- In what context was the research conducted?
- What was its contribution to the field?
- Does it have any connection to my research question?

Remember that a key failing, according to the guidelines for external examiners, would be simply to write 'Here is all I know about my subject.' The literature review is not just a synthesis of other people's work; it also synthesizes your work with theirs. This is not an easy task, since your work is ongoing as you are writing about the literature. This is why it is important to do more than one form of writing as you go along, not just drafts of formal writing that you give to your supervisor, but also the writing to prompts and questions, freewriting and generative writing activities, illustrated in this section, or versions of them you write yourself to suit your study. Remember what Torrance et al. (1993) said about the importance of 'producing text'.

If your literature review should not just answer the question 'What do you know about your subject?', what will you write about?

Questions a literature review should answer

- Why is this subject important?
- Who else thinks it's important?
- Who has worked on this subject before?
- Who has done something similar to what I will be doing?
- What can be adapted to my own study?
- What are the gaps in the research?
- Who is going to use my material?
- What use will my project be?
- What will my contribution be?
- What specific questions will I answer?

The different purposes of the literature review can be illustrated in examples drawn from completed theses. The following examples show the writers' concerns to do the following:

1 Define their terms
2 Justify their selection of the literature
3 Justify omissions
4 Forecast sections of review
5 Signal structure
6 Link their work to the literature
7 Critique the literature
8 Define the gap
9 Use name + date + verb sentence structure to focus their overview.

1 Define terms

CHAPTER 2

LITERATURE REVIEW

A formation at a submerged orifice grows into the liquid by accelerating the surroundings away from the interface. Initially, the formation is rather like an expanding sphere, and as formation proceeds, it is elongated and its lower part constricts steadily forming a neck. The formation detaches from the orifice when its neck is severed. The detached formation rises and the portion of its volume remaining at the orifice becomes the nucleus for the next to form.

In the literature, the process of formation is consistently divided into a bubble régime and a jet régime. The bubble régime is described in terms of the periodic formation of single bubbles or of double bubbles . . .

Which of the purposes listed above has this writer chosen to shape the litera-ture review? This writer chose to begin the review with definitions. Definitions of key terms are important, since they dictate how the reader will interpret everything you say. Even very familiar specialist terms may require definition, since even they can be used in different ways.

What would make this opening much clearer would be to switch the two paragraphs: the second paragraph is beginning to give the overview of the field, classifying the subjects into two groups. It mentions 'the literature' explicitly, so the reader knows that summary is taking place.

What would strengthen the writing even further would be to add a statement of purpose and an outline of contents: a preview of the review.

These suggested revisions are not intended to imply that this is a poor piece of writing; instead, they are designed to show how the review can take shape over a number of drafts, although time could be saved by making the purpose of the piece explicit in the first draft: 'The purpose of this chapter is to . . .'

When students and supervisors read this example they often ask, with some impatience, 'What is this person talking about?' They want to see headings and sub-headings to guide their reading, a menu telling them what to expect in this chapter. They demand more signalling. They want to know why 'formations' are important. Who says so? They look for some kind of link with the previous chapter. All of these responses are pertinent. They can be translated into guidance for further writing and revision:

- Link this chapter with the previous one.
- Say why your topic is important.
- Situate it in a broader context.
- Tell us what you are going to say in the chapter.

Review writers also have to make clear that they are selecting certain material, and give reasons for their selection. You also have to say what you are not going to write about, and why. It is well known that the doctorate requires 'comprehensive coverage' of the field; what is less well known is that this is bound to require a selection, a well-informed selection of all the material available. For some writers, the pressure of trying to do justice to everyone is hard to balance with the necessity of leaving some work out:

2 Justify selection of literature

CHAPTER 2

REVIEW OF RESEARCH ON SECTIONS

Introduction

A review of the whole field of the development of strength testing would be a formidable task. The subject has been active in a research sense for about a hundred years.

This review will therefore mainly highlight experimental research done. Due to the large amount of studies done over the years, the author has inevitably missed some important works. The author apologizes in advance for seeming to ignore the work of some people while mentioning other contributions which, it may be felt, are of lesser importance.

This is *not* a very convincing account of selection; rather it seems more like an excuse for poor research. However, what I think has happened here is that the writer, being only too well aware of the need to select – and the need for humility – has taken the blame rather than the credit for his or her own selection of the literature. In other words, this text is, again, not held up as an example of poor thesis writing. Instead, it reveals one of the difficult balancing acts of writing this part of the thesis: how to do justice to the whole field while justifying your exclusion of certain key people because they are less than directly relevant to your research.

A better way of dealing with this stage in the literature review would be to state explicitly what type of selection had been made and why, including related literature that has been omitted, and why:

3 Justify omissions

It is important to clarify what is meant by cardiac rehabilitation, as the term encompasses many concepts. A recent report in the *British Medical Journal* (Bloomberg 2001) suggested that rehabilitation can take the form of drug therapy, surgical intervention, psychological rehabilitation and physiological rehabilitation. The literature on drugs and surgery will not be reviewed but is available from the following references: BBH Trial Group (2000), a major European trial on drug therapy; European Coronary Surgery Group (2000); Bounder (1999); and King (1998). This review will cover physiological and psychological aspects of cardiac rehabilitation, as these are the main areas of interest to this study.

The important skill here is to set boundaries – explicitly – to your literature review. This example also shows the writer working his or her way through several areas in a piece of multidisciplinary research. The boundaries that you set to your review have to be explicitly defined and perhaps defended. If readers are to follow your logical path – even if they do not agree with you – you have to provide an explicit forecast of the elements you will cover:

4 Forecast sections of review

LITERATURE REVIEW

As there is a vast amount of research and writing which is relevant to children's reading, this chapter concentrates on: 1 Selective review of research relevant to this study. This I will outline and then examine critically. 2 Comment on current views as expressed in recent government reports.

1. (a)
In 1995 Hummel et al. (1) studied the television viewing of 10–13 year olds. Reading was studied as an aspect of children's lives which might be influenced by television. At the time of this survey one in five homes had television – a different situation from today where most homes have at least one set and many children also have access to a video or DVD. Because of this, aspects of Hummel's work are probably of limited value, but her longitudinal study of viewers, non-viewers and new viewers in Nottingham is useful as she offers data on viewers and the control group and makes suggestions about the reading habits of children in homes with newly acquired sets. She makes interesting speculations about the possible long-term effects.

Similarly, if your literature review is structured chronologically, giving your version of the history of your field, the development of a philosophy or approach, signal this in your headings and sentences:

5 Signal structure

HISTORICAL CONNECTION OF HEALTH AND PHYSICAL EDUCATION

Traditionally physical educators were concerned with the maintenance and promotion of health of school children and the historical connection between physical education and health education is well documented in the literature (Muir 1968; Smart 1974; McNab 1985).

At the start of the twentieth century, concern regarding school children's health began to be expressed in education policy. In 1903 the Royal Commission on Physical Training proposed physical training as a subject in the primary school curriculum with the purpose of improving the medical, physical and hygiene conditions of children in schools.

The first syllabus to appear following the commission's report, suggested that:

> The primary objective of any course of physical exercises in schools is to maintain and, if possible, improve the health and physique of children.
>
> (Board of Education 1905: 9)

Literature reviews, therefore, include definition, background and chronology, not just a simple summary of other people's work. The main point is to link the literature to your own work, both in general terms and later in detail, but certainly explicitly.

6 Link your work to the literature

Background

Beginning in the late 1950s and throughout the following two decades, the debate on mixed-ability teaching was given a high priority. Among the more influential writers on the subject were Rudd (1), Willig (2), Jackson (3), Yates (4), Barker-Lunn (5) and Kelly (6). However, in the late 1980s there was a general view that 'The Mixed-Ability Debate' was no longer relevant; the argument was won and mixed-ability organization was accepted as normal practice, especially in the pre-certificate stages of education. Certainly there is a dearth of recent publications on the matter, and it has been ousted from staffroom discussion by other more pressing initiatives. So perhaps the stance has some validity. **The aim of this study is not to** contest this view. **Rather it is the intention to** maintain that if justification does exist it is limited to secondary and not the primary sector.

Sooner or later, you have to critique the literature:

7 Critique the literature

Review of Literature

. . . **A better design was used in** a British trial (Carson et al. 1992) in which three hundred men who had suffered a Myocardial Infarction (MI) and been admitted to hospital were randomly allocated to an exercise group or a control group. The patients were assessed at their first clinical visit, six weeks post-MI and again after five weeks, at one year and at three years. The dependent variables assessed were mortality, physical fitness, angina, return to work, heart size and smoking habits. Physical fitness was assessed on a bicycle ergometer and expressed as total cycling time. **The results showed** a highly significant ($p < 0.001$) difference in physical fitness between control and exercise groups as assessed by mean cycling time, the exercise group being the higher of the two. The exercise group returned to work no earlier than the control group. There was no significant difference in the smoking habits between the groups. Although the improvement in morale was not measured, it was stated to be obvious in the control group. **This trial would have been more interesting** if psychological parameters had been objectively measured, especially as the return to work rate was the same for both groups.

Once you have pointed out the limitations in existing work – limitations by design, in many, if not all, cases – without demolishing that work, then you can begin to define the gap that you are going to fill with your research. This is about constructing a logical link between the deficiencies in the research and the aims of your project:

8 Define the gap

To date no research on an exercise-based cardiac rehabilitation programme **appears to have been done** in Scotland, although it has the worst death rate from coronary heart disease in the world. **This study is an attempt to fill that gap.** The study only involves acute patients who have had recent Myocardial Infarction. Men and women will both be involved, as the study will investigate the first forty consecutive patients. It has also been shown (Sugar and Newt 1999) that provided women are selected onto a cardiac rehabilitation programme using the same criteria as for men, they derive the same benefits.

Use the name + date + verb structure – identify who (when) said what about your subject – to force yourself to write a quick sketch of the field, bringing a range of people together. What have they all said about your theme? For example, having chosen the theme of 'partnership', we can then be highly selective in what we choose to review: we can summarize, in one sentence or less, what researchers have said about our theme:

---

9 Name + date + verb

Dawn (1999) argues for a partnership approach in promoting reflection in the professional development of teachers, and earlier indicated the need for inter-dependent roles for researchers and teachers through 'collaboration, consult-ation, and negotiation' (Dawn 1999: 133). **Blue (1999)**, in a study of the roles of mentors and mentees, **identifies** this developmental partnership as a way of changing lecturers' behaviour. **Elliott (1991) proposes** a 'model of professional-ism' for teachers, with early involvement in a partnership to provide a gradual integration into the cultural ethos of the organization: here, too, the emphasis is on 'a process of collaborative problem solving' (p. 312).

The steps listed in this section do not have to be written in this order. Start anywhere. However, they do identify the main elements of a literature review and thus constitute your agenda for writing. Once you have read a few theses in your area you will have a better idea of exactly how this process is currently conducted in your discipline.

Your discipline will also be associated with one or other of several styles of referencing, such as Harvard, Chicago, Modern Languages Association, and so on. Each has its own style manual, telling you how to reference every conceiv-able type of source. Some style manuals appear in abbreviated form, shorter and in paperback, telling you how to reference everything in a thesis. Consider buying the relevant style manual, once you have confirmed with your super-visor which one you should use for your thesis. It may be the same one that you use for journal articles and could, therefore, be a worthwhile investment.

Plagiarism

When you are writing about other people's ideas it is easy, some argue, to confuse your ideas and theirs. However, this is not acceptable. Whenever you refer to someone else's ideas or writing you have to credit them by referencing their work. This seems quite clear, but many students say that they are unclear about what does and does not constitute plagiarism.

The first principle is that your record keeping should be as excellent as your writing will finally be. Apply the same high professional standards in recording references and labelling your notes.

The second principle is that there is no grey area: if you use someone else's writing, word-for-word in your own text, then that is plagiarism, whether you reference the writer or not.

In the interests of clarity, since students do appear to be genuinely confused, the following examples illustrate (1) summary (plus reference), (2) paraphrase (with reference), (3) quotation (with reference) and (4) plagiarism. The text used in this example is a paragraph from the introduction to this chapter.

The source text

Paradoxically, as we move towards constructing and rehearsing outlines and arguments, freewriting and generative writing can still prove useful, as we explore options. They can help us to move beyond the fragments of a thesis by having several attempts at pulling them together. They allow us to write – briefly – about the whole thesis. They can help us to find the type of story that our thesis will tell.

1 Summary (whole paragraph in one sentence, in my words)
Murray (2002) argues that we can use free and generative writing to develop a thesis.

2 Paraphrase (translating three source sentences into my own words)
It seems contradictory, but it is possible to develop a thesis using free and generative writing. These strategies allow us to synthesize our ideas. We can write our way towards a story for our thesis Murray (2002).

3 Quotation
Although free and generative writing are perceived to be strategies that belong at the start of a writing process, they can 'help us to move beyond the fragments of a thesis by having several attempts at pulling them together' (Murray 2002: 27).

4 Plagiarism
It is possible to move towards constructing and rehearsing outlines and arguments using freewriting and generative writing. We can move beyond the fragments of a thesis by having several attempts at pulling them together.

For the final example, even if the reference (Murray 2002) appears in that sentence, it is still plagiarism because it uses the source text word-for-word. Even though there are slight changes from the source text, there are strings of word-for-word sentences lifted from it. Example 4 is therefore a quotation and should be represented as a quotation. This is the simplest, clearest definition of plagiarism I know: when you use a source *word-for-word* you are plagiarizing. You should be quoting it.

Be aware that plagiarizing can get you thrown out of your university or your job. It is not just cheating; it is stealing.

Designing a thesis

The process of developing a thesis – of starting with a problem or issue, or resisting the first idea that comes along, and of changing your tentative thesis until it fits your purpose and your evidence – means you spend a little more time planning and less time throwing away text that didn't work.

(Flower 1989: 150)

A thesis focuses on a central question and is unified by that focus. In this section the word 'thesis' is used to refer to the whole text that represents a particular type of report on the research you (will have) undertaken for your programme of study; i.e. the text.

Another way of developing your thesis is to understand the place of its central argument in the context of a generic structure. A generic structure can be used as a starting point in the design of your thesis.

Generic thesis structure

- **Introduction/Background/Review of literature**
  Summarize and evaluate books, articles, theses, etc.
  Define the gap in the literature
  Define and justify your project
- **Theory/Approach/Method/Materials/Subjects**
  Define method, theoretical approach, instrument
  Method of inquiry
  Show links between your method and others
  Justify your method
- **Analysis/Results**
  Report what you did, list steps followed
  Document the analysis, showing how you carried it out
  Report what you found
  Prioritize sections for the thesis or for an appendix
- **Interpretation/Discussion**
  Interpret what you found
  Justify your interpretation
  Synthesize results in illustrations, tables, graphs, etc.
- **Conclusions/Implications/Recommendations**
  For future research
  For future practice
  Report issues which were beyond the scope of this study

Many other structures are available, both for your whole thesis and for chapters or sections:

- Thematic
- Narrative
- Case study analysis
- Recurring analysis
- Chronological
- Synthesis.

The first thing to recognize is that decisions about structure affect most other decisions in writing. Concerns about sentence structure and style should come after some basic decisions about structure and proportion. It also helps if there is an orientation towards writing by this stage, so that the thesis writer is comfortable with sketches and iterations.

Sketching – or outlining – can be based on generic templates; which template is your reader expecting? Define 'generic' for your discipline. What are the genres in current use? Visualizing, defining the genre and discussing all of these are the responsibility of the thesis writer.

In response to the generic approach students – and staff – often ask 'What about creativity?' In replicating these generic norms, are we losing our own voices? Are we compromising our own ideas, simply in order to fit in with the dominant – not the only – genres and conventions in style and structure? One answer is that you can use generic norms to generate structure and text. You can, of course, then revise it into any shape or structure you choose.

Once you have a sense of structure, you can begin to think about length: how long is your thesis to be? Whenever I ask a group of students what length their theses are going to be, they always, without exception look at me as if I am mad. 'It depends', they say. 'How long is a piece of string?', they elaborate rhetorically, in a piece of British English meaning that it can be any length at all and that they just have to wait and see. But can this be true? In most, if not all, institutions there is a recommended minimum and/or maximum in some, if not all, faculties. There may be some general or specific expectation operating currently in your department. You should ask.

If there is no word limit, neither maximum nor minimum, this leaves the thesis – yet again – somewhat undefined. This could be tricky. Deferring the decision about total length, and shape, will almost definitely be followed by deferring the shape and scope of parts of the thesis, chapters, sections and everything else. It will all remain undefined. Some argue that this is the most creative mode of all, and exactly what research is about: to force the student to make all these decisions. This is fair enough, as long as you are prompted to – and not prevented from – making your mind up soon.

Once you have started to think about the total length, you can then begin to think about – and perhaps even plan – the proportions of chapters. Once you have considered the lengths of chapters, you can think about the lengths of sections and sub-sections, and so on. This type of thinking will not be easy; there is a lot at stake in deciding what goes into each chapter. This is, in any case, just the first step in that process.

'Writing in layers'

Something I find useful . . . is to start by inputting the headings for the chapter, coding them to show the hierarchy . . . Then I draft what I want to say in note form under each heading, using the rough page sketches as a guide. The next step is to print out the chapter as it now stands, and make notes on it about how to develop the sections; then I go back into the file to develop the notes into a final draft of the text. The process is a kind of 'growing the writing from seed', or building successively more detailed layers.

(Orna and Stevens 1995: 174)

There are all sorts of ways – and software – for outlining text, but the conceptual stages of building a long text like a thesis can be defined as layers. Orna and Stevens's (1995) outline shows how you can set up a series of steps to grow your thesis from the original template:

1 Outline the structure: write a list of chapter headings.
2 Then write a sentence or two on the contents of each chapter.
3 Then write lists of headings for each section in each chapter.
4 Make notes, below the headings on how you will develop each section.
5 Write an introductory paragraph for each chapter (Orna and Stevens 1995: 173).
6 Write the word count, draft number and date at the top of the first page.

While your outline – after revision – helps you to plan and focus your writing, it is also useful for readers. It helps them to see your whole thesis as a whole and to form an impression, before they start reading, of how it all fits together. This is illustrated in the example which follows, a genuine piece of student writing. Details of the original study have been changed.

Note the use of the format of using a verb to make the function of each chapter explicit. Some of these verbs are more specific than others: some are a bit vague, but the main point is that the writer has begun to identify what he or she will deal with where. You will begin to see where there could be cuts, or, alternatively, where the links between chapters have to be made more explicit.

Thesis outline

- **Chapter 1 will discuss** the need for an analytical model in management.
- **Chapter 2 tries to define** the meaning of product models mainly in the context of a management model.
- **Chapter 3 discusses** what criteria are necessary for the development of a management model.
- **Chapter 4 deals with** the type of conceptual structures necessary to develop management models.
- **Chapter 5 covers** the abstraction of information from a model and the various methods possible to achieve this.
- **Chapter 6 explains** one of the OUP School models closely associated with MOVE, the General OUP Reference Model (GORM).
- **Chapter 7 evaluates** one of the most influential projects of recent years in Britain, the AAWAT project.
- **Chapter 8 discusses** the highly critical work of the MOVE committee.
- **Chapter 9 describes** four research prototypes designed to implement the ideas developed in management modelling.
- **Chapter 10 deals with** what is perhaps current thinking and the likely future of management models, aspect or domain models, and these will have particular reference to managers.
- **Chapter 11 concludes by making** the case for management modelling and identifying important issues for future practice.

See Ballenger (2004) for a list of 'Active Verbs for Discussing Ideas' that might help you to define the purposes of your chapters.

This example is not provided here in order to point out its, or its writer's, weaknesses. It is a draft, a first attempt to sketch out the main line of argument from chapter to chapter and the main contents of each chapter. This example demonstrates the characteristics of structure drafts. There is no reason to expect that a first draft of this important exercise will be perfect. Once it has been put down on paper, the draft will require many revisions. In addition, such drafts benefit from recurring student-supervisor discussions, as the thesis writers develops an understanding of what the thesis argument or story line is.

The purpose of this example is to prompt you to force a whole draft and then look back on it for revisions. Using informal English is not inappropriate for this task. It has specific advantages here: it helps you to concentrate on how you are going to define what you want to say, in writing, without worrying too much about how you are going to say it.

In revising the draft outline, the writer could make several types of changes:

- Make the verbs more precise (e.g. not 'deals with' but 'describes').
- Make the style less hesitant (e.g. not 'tries to define' but 'defines').

- Make vague words more precise (e.g. not 'a number of' but 'four').
- Make the logical structure clearer.
- Make explicit connections between chapters.

Now that you are aware of the ways in which a draft outline can be improved, you may be able to produce a better first draft. In any case, you will know what strengths and weaknesses to check for.

In spite of its flaws – or rather revisions yet to be done – you can use the example as a model of the kind of outline that gives your readers an overview of your whole thesis. This helps them to see your thesis as an integrated whole; they can see how the parts all join up because you have told them how they do.

Writing locations

What is the best place to write? It is clear from talking to postgraduates that there are huge differences of opinion on 'the best place to write' and that these are linked, directly or indirectly, to the student's writing routines. The following list was drawn up at one meeting of a thesis writers' group.

The best place to write

- Opinion on the library was divided: some find it too quiet, others too noisy; some cannot work without coffee, others need freedom from distraction; some want to work at home, others find this distracting.
- Specific places were identified as good environments for writing: in their room on campus; in the conservatory (at home); on or in bed – quite a few like this, but others strongly disagreed; on the sofa at home; in cafés, which some liked for their non-intensive feel, but others found too distracting; in the home office.
- At different stages in the PhD we thought we would like different locations: when we need lots of books, we need to be in the library; when reading, we could be at home; when feeling stale or isolated, we might decide to work in a café, etc.
- A state of mind: given the variations, we decided that the location itself was not what was important for productive work and writing. What mattered was the frame of mind we were in; others felt that being in their preferred location helped put them in the right frame of mind.
- Routine was another important question that came up in our discussion: all of us felt that some sort of routine was essential, including both work and non-work time (e.g. going to the gym, being with friends, taking a break).

We agreed that this was important because it helped us to take a break from work without feeling guilty.

- Good and bad times of the day for working: it was clear that we differed on this, as some prefer mornings, others evenings. We agreed that there was no point in trying to override our natural work rhythm. Some were relieved to hear that working in the evening was OK.
- Starting rituals: what do we do before we start? Freewriting, cup of tea, arranging work space, going for a run. These were activities that we found induced the right frame of mind.
- Rewards: cup of coffee, cigarette, exercise, sleep, television, etc. throughout the working day. Some of these breaks were useful for signalling, to ourselves and others, that we had stopped working.
- New students found it useful to listen to those who were further on. They could also see that the research, how we work, and the relationship to the research change over the years.

The interesting thing about these notes, taken from an actual discussion among students, organized by students, the notes written by students, is what happens when the students considered the act of writing. They reveal their own views certainly, but they are learning from each other. They can see for themselves that one place is unlikely to work for all writing and can take this realization forward into considerations of practice.

Writing times

These questions apply to writing times. Certainly thesis writing requires you to write regularly, but when?

- What are your options?
- When do you do your best writing?
- Different times for different kinds of writing?
- 'Regularly' means how often?
- How will you force your writing when you have to write at the 'wrong' times?

Students' comments suggest that the questions of time and place are linked. Note the links they see – or make – between place, time and other activities and 'rituals'. Design your own links that work for you.

Checklist

Seeking structure

- Start with your proposal.
- Experiment with your hypothesis/argument.
- Begin to develop your routines for writing.
- Sketch a structure for your thesis. Write headings.
- Consider the order of headings. Change it, if need be.
- Write a few sentences on each heading.
- Sub-divide headings; write more headings and sub-headings.
- Think about limits: the number of words per chapter.
- Create explicit links: use link words
- Keep a view of the thesis as a whole.
- Write in your own voice from time to time.
- Buy a style manual.
- Identify the best place to write.

4

The first milestone

First writing milestone • The first-year report • From notes to draft
• Dialogue • Monitoring • Pressure • What is progress? • Work-in-progress
writing • A writers' group • Checklist: the first milestone

This chapter encourages the thesis writer to move from writer-based to reader-based thinking, from thinking about what he or she wants to say to focusing on the reader's criteria. The end of the first phase, after the first year, usually brings some form of assessment. For both part-time and full-time students this is usually about one year after registration. When and how progress is assessed will vary from institution to institution. The first-year report is one example.

This shift means that the thesis writer has to finalize something in the first stage of the doctorate. It is a process that requires regular discussion of writing with supervisors and peers. What Boice (1990) calls 'exteriorizing' is an important part of writing at this point.

From this point on there is a focus on the writing of chapters. The interaction between writing for development and writing for a chapter continues.

The key point, at the end of the first stage, is to enable thesis writers to engage with the tasks of sketching structures and writing chapters or mini-arguments or stages in an argument. Since this is often the first watershed, there will be discussion of emotional processes in this chapter.

First writing milestone

Why have one? The idea is to create a pause in the thesis process:

- Take stock of work done.
- Review, possibly revise, plan of work.
- Consolidate focus for research and, possibly, thesis.

The word 'milestone' suggests that you should have a sense of how far you have travelled and how far you still have to go. Where, on your thesis journey, would you place this milestone?

This is usually done in writing, with the student producing some form of progress report.

Psychologically, this stage can be quite intimidating, if it is conducted like a formal examination. On the other hand, students who have experienced formal examination at this stage – including a mini-viva – report that they find it very useful for testing their knowledge.

What form your 'milestone' will take is something to check with your supervisor. If there is a writing task – either reports or chapters – what is the format and what are the criteria? When is it due?

The first-year report

One clearly defined milestone is the first-year report. In some departments the first report is due in less than a year. In one it is due at nine months into the first year of the doctorate. It may take the form of a 'synoptic paper' or some other form for professional doctorates. Apart from its title and timing, you should find out the details of what you are required to write:

- Format
- Content
- Balance of writing about work done, ongoing and to be done
- References

What about the style: should the report on completed work be written in the past tense, on ongoing work in the present and work to be done in the future tense? How will you link the three? Can you make the links explicit? Can you relate your achievements and your goals to your original – or revised – proposal? Finally, is it permitted to include a summary at the start, perhaps highlighting continuity, for the obvious reasons that it will help you to pull it all together and it will make your report more user-friendly?

Some departments have very specific requirements:

- 5000–10,000 words on your topic
- Revised proposal or abstract
- Outline of chapters
- Ongoing bibliography
- Diary or summary of the past year
- Timetable for the year ahead.

Whether or not you are given such specific targets as these, it might be a good idea to produce as many of these elements as you can, if not all of them.

From notes to draft

A process for moving from notes to draft is outlined in this section:

1 Warm-up
2 Prompt
3 Distil
4 Notes-to-draft writing
5 Theme
6 Framework.

The idea is to use writing to move from the stage of having piles of notes to pulling them together in a piece of continuous writing. The outcome of this process may not be – some would argue should not be – a catalogue but a selection of your notes.

There is no secret to this transformation: write a few sentences. Do some freewriting or generative writing to pull ideas together. It might help – paradoxically – not to have all your 'materials', such as papers, chapters, books, notes, photocopies, etc., around you. Clear a space to write about what you have in your notes. The purpose is to distil your notes rather than summarize them comprehensively. This step will also help you to write down your own thoughts, and prevent you from reproducing others'.

1 Warm-up

As a warm-up for writing, do five minutes' freewriting on how you feel about writing about others' work or about consolidating your work in a chapter.

Clarify the nature of your writing task:

- What is the purpose of this writing task?
- Are you writing to process your thoughts?
- Are you writing to integrate new ideas with your project?
- Are you writing part of the thesis?

At some point in your doctorate, the last item in this list will be the case, as you will be starting to write drafts of chapters. There is no need to put this off. You know what chapters look like, what they contain, how long they are, what you are likely to say in a chapter, and so on. What you do not know – yet – is the framework for each chapter.

2 Prompt

Which chapter are you writing?
I am starting to write chapter . . .

Clarify the task by writing a prompt or question that identifies the focus for the writing: what is your prompt for writing? Then there is the question of scope: how long will you write for? You can write a list of headings, prompts or questions first, as a framework for your writing, again, before you start to write many sentences or paragraphs.

3 Distil

Without looking at your notes, write for five minutes on the topic that your notes cover, the topic for the chapter you are drafting.

This produces a focus or starting point for more sustained writing. It helps you grasp the totality of the topic, see the overview, and hold the details together. If you start with the detail you may not see – or may take longer to find – the 'big picture'. Trust your brain to do the work of remembering and synthesizing – if only for five minutes – and then you can build on that.

The questions and prompts in this section are intended not only to give you something to write about but also to help you structure your writing sessions. The questions force you to define the writing moment before you start to write. For example, a twenty-minute notes-to-draft session could include four steps:

4 Notes-to-draft writing

1 Freewriting on your chapter for five minutes: content/'story'.
2 Write three or four prompts for this chapter (five minutes).
3 Outline the chapter you are drafting for five minutes.
4 Write about a prompt you wrote in Question 2 above (five minutes).

These prompts are a mixture of two types of writing: overview and more detailed. The intention is to enable you to do both, as both are important for sketching the framework for your chapter. It is all too easy to get bogged down in detail and lose sight of the theme of the chapter. On the other hand, you want to develop a relationship between your theme and your notes, so you cannot ignore the detail.

From freewriting to formal writing

• Create an outline.
• Rehearse the point you want to make 'formally' orally.
• Write for fifteen minutes on one of your outline headings.

Do not cut-and-paste all your notes into the file for this chapter. That will only make it more difficult to find a theme. If you cut-and-paste all your notes – including notes about others' writings – into your chapters, you risk shaping your thesis to incorporate these pieces. The process of moving from notes to draft is important for making you think through what might be a quite different story: your own. Your story should shape your use of your notes, rather than vice versa.

This may seem to oversimplify what is an interaction of your notes and your present moment of thinking and writing, but at this stage you have to take on a more 'shaping' role, sketching your own structure for the chapter. In sketching a chapter, you are somehow moving beyond your notes. The chapter will be more than the sum of these parts. There may also be some notes that you will not use, if your emerging argument moves beyond them. Alternatively, you could use them to outline the development of your argument, creating a narrative of the development of your thesis or argument for this chapter. Do not worry about grammar, punctuation, spelling or style as you work through this stage.

Of course, if you have an idea of how they will all hold together, then by all means start importing them from other files. However, it might be a good idea to write down that 'idea' in a sentence. You can then use it as a 'touchstone' for your selection and for your writing.

The short bursts of writing may help you refine your theme and framework and endure the lack of closure at this stage, as you gradually become more and more sure of what the chapter is about.

5 Theme

Consider your answers to the prompts: what theme emerges?

You may, of course, change your mind later, when you revise it further. At a later stage you will want to connect the chapter you are writing now to the others, but, although you may be wondering about this aspect of continuity now, just jot down your ideas, put them to one side and refocus on the task in hand: writing this chapter.

6 Framework

What did you write on the topic '3 Distil' above?
A list of headings?
Organize your notes under these headings.

What are the key – the most important – quotations from secondary sources that you feel you want to use? You can add others later. To try to include them all will only make you get bogged down in other people's ideas and will distract you from your own.

Dialogue

The most successful authors spend as much time socializing about writing as writing (and they spend only moderate amounts of time at either).

As writers gain the confidence and experience to exteriorize, they learn where best to get practical directives about whether or not they are on the right track.

(Boice 1994: 244)

Dialogue means two-way discussion. You may want to consider whether you might have any follow-up questions. You may want to rephrase a question, if it turns out you have approached the issue from the wrong direction or if your supervisor just does not understand what you want to discuss. Discussion, rather than question-and-answer, is the goal here.

You will have views of your own on all of these issues and it might be a good idea to prepare for discussion by thinking them through, clarifying them and deciding how to voice them, or whether you will voice them. Dialogue implies that you will be ready and willing to present your own views at some point.

Developing the skills of dialogue – an important professional skill – is a component of some research methods courses:

We assume that each researcher and each tutor brings to the course his or her own expectations and assumptions, along with an individual style of dialogue, and an individual level of motivation towards dialogue. Some will develop their skills of dialoguing in this course; others will enable each other.

(Murray and Lowe 1995: 103)

These prompts are intended as a starting point for dialogue, but they can also be used for writing practice:

Dialogue: expectations

1 Will the supervisory role be changing in the next phase?
2 What is expected of you at this stage?
3 What resources will be needed?

Dialogue: meetings

1 What is a useful frequency of meetings?
2 Is the monitoring process working?
3 Do we need to 'tune' our communications strategies?
4 Troubleshooting and problem solving: what can go wrong?

Dialogue: writing

1 What are our views on thesis writing produced in this department?
2 Are there examples that illustrate good practice?
3 Can we extend our common vocabulary for discussing writing?

These are quite general by design, in order to allow for a degree of openness in the dialogue. There are bound to be issues that you want to discuss that are not on these lists. You could also do some creative dialogizing: imagine what other responses would be in this conversation. You can practise asking these questions and discussing their complexities in small groups with your peers. Both student and supervisor could write – for five minutes, private writing – on, for example, their expectations of how their roles will be modified in the middle phase of the writing of the thesis. This would give both an opportunity to externalize their assumptions and give them time to consider how to voice them in the discussion.

It may be worth pointing out, since not all students appear to know, that it is legitimate for students to ask their supervisors questions, i.e. to question what they say. This is not to say that you have to challenge them directly, but that dialogue and debate should begin to replace monologue and direction, as the student becomes more expert in the area.

Without such dialogue, expectations and assumptions may not be externalized and addressed. There is always potential for a clash, for frustration as unspoken needs go unmet and for anger, as implicitly stated requests are not provided, because they were never heard.

Monitoring

If you find it difficult to take stock of your work so far, or to represent it as fully as you would like, this may be because you have not monitored your decisions, actions and discussions in enough detail. If you have not done so already, this might be a good time to develop a system – in discussion with your supervisor – for monitoring your progress as you go along. You do not have to wait until a 'milestone' comes along; you can monitor progress more regularly. If you do so in writing, this has the added advantage of keeping communications clear.

For example, you can develop a monitoring form, for ease of use, for each meeting with your supervisor. Such a monitoring form can be very simple:

Student case notes

Student: _____   Date of meeting: _____

Time: _____

1 Object of meeting

2 Material submitted

3 Key conclusions and comments

4 Future actions

5 Next meeting

You then email this brief report to your supervisor.

Some students find this too radical; they assume that their supervisors would be grossly insulted if a student appeared to try to 'monitor' their meetings. However, the reaction of your supervisor may be as much a result of how you introduce the idea as of how they see your relationship. If you can persuade them that you see the purpose of monitoring as (1) assisting you when you come to write progress reports; (2) assisting them when they come to assess your progress; and (3) assisting both you and them by maintaining a check on communications, then they are more likely to go along with it. It might help to change the name of the mechanism, from 'monitoring form' to 'Student case notes'. The latter suggests that it is about you, not about your supervisor(s). Just make sure that you confirm the agreement, the purposes and the form in writing to them as soon as possible, for the purposes of clarifying that you have interpreted their points correctly.

This type of semi-formal monitoring is part of the process of moving up a gear at this stage in your doctorate. You may also see it as formalizing or professionalizing the process. It could be argued that the doctorate should have formal monitoring processes, just like any other large, significant project. Without some form of monitoring, how will you know that you are making progress? Will you just wait till the next progress review?

Pressure

'There's still so much to be done.'

'I haven't done enough reading.'

'I haven't done enough writing.'

'I have too much stuff.'

These are common concerns. They can be used as prompts for writing: students report that they find it useful to 'dump' or 'download' their anxieties and real concerns in five minutes' freewriting. A second writing activity – another five minutes' freewriting – could be to write about the opposite:

'There are three things that need to be done: (1) . . . , (2) . . . and (3) . . .'

'I have done enough reading about X to be able to get on with . . .'

'I have made a good start on . . .'

'I have done enough writing on X, for the moment, to be able to go on to Y.'

Each of these new prompts not only looks at the positive – what has been done – but also translates the anxiety into a cue for action. At the very least, both sets of prompts provide five minutes' writing practice.

However, while that activity began to address specific anxieties, the global picture may also need a new look. This may be a good time to review planning practices and to consider changing them: to incorporate parallel tasks, parallel lines of development. The nature of the work may have become more complex and this may be what has triggered the anxieties. They may represent a warning bell rather than just a pile of irrational fears.

What is progress?

Here are a group of students' definitions of progress:

'Progress' means . . .

- Getting results, good or bad
- Being able to explain them
- Reaching your research targets (and/or department's, supervisor's)
- Feeling confident in your research, understanding it
- Getting published
- Completing a certain amount of work
- Learning new skills
- A better understanding of what's going on in the literature

This is the place to mention the need for publications (though guidance is given in the last chapter of this book, Chapter 10). There is no reason not to be preparing papers for publication at this stage in the research, and very many good reasons for doing so. It may be that you have a conference presentation, or departmental work-in-progress presentation that you can convert into a scholarly paper. Even if you have no 'research' to report on you can still contribute to the scholarly debate ongoing in journals. As someone who has recently overviewed the field, you are well placed to write a number of different types of paper:

Writing for publication: types of paper

- The 'state of the art' paper
- The 'emerging trends' paper
- The 'how did things get like this?' paper
- The 'review' paper
  Review journals are highly ranked in some fields

A method of planning and generating time and text is suggested in Chapter 10 and a full account of the process of writing a paper for publication is provided in Murray (2005). A good first step would be to discuss with your supervisor what your options are in terms of likely target journals. The journals that you read most often are, presumably, likely to be the ones most interested in your work.

Work-in-progress writing

Alongside the move to definitive writing, there continues to be a place for more tentative writing about work in progress: work that is incomplete or inconclusive, for the moment. This is the subject of writing for the considerable time that the doctorate lasts. This is recognized by the existence of work-in-progress seminars at most universities.

Work-in-progress presentations are not always comfortable, but they are important for getting feedback on your work. Make it explicit that the work you are presenting is ongoing, that you are not claiming that it is complete and that you can plot directions for future work.

The shift from definitive to tentative – and perhaps back again? – has to be signalled in the styles you use and the words you choose, otherwise your writing might seem confused or contradictory. Your writing may be more tentative; you will have less support to offer for your arguments. It might be as well to acknowledge as much, since this is to be expected. It is not a weakness still to be working out what your strongest arguments are. If you were still doing that in the last quarter of your doctorate, that would be a worry.

Closure may not be achievable, or only for a portion of the work done. Your writing may have to be open-ended. If you are giving a presentation, you may want to make sure that the opening minute is spent clarifying the scope and purpose of your talk. You should see yourself, in this opening minute, as adjusting your audience's expectations: they are used to sitting down to listen to researchers reporting on completed pieces of work. You will have to help them adjust their listening behaviours.

If some of your audience seem to be pinning you down on aspects of the research that have not yet been developed, then you can agree, yes, those aspects have not yet been developed. I have seen too many student presentations where both staff and students grilled the presenter on why Chapter 3 was not more developed, when, in fact, he or she had only got as far as Chapter 2, for example. However well you prepare, and however clearly you forecast and justify the text of your work-in-progress presentation, do not be shocked if this happens to you. Be ready to remind the audience what you did – and did not – set out to do in your presentation.

Work-in-progress 'stories'

- The story of your learning so far?
- The story of the development of the thesis?
- The story of your understanding of the literature?
- The story of your project so far?
- Your assessment of your research so far?
- The story of the extent to which you have begun to achieve your project goals/aims/objectives at this point?

If members of your audience persist in probing areas that you have not yet developed, or not yet fully worked up, you can use this as practice for the viva, when the probing of your work, even when it is completed, is inevitable.

What type of structure – or story – is appropriate for work-in-progress presentations?

Whatever you choose as the story for your presentation, you should signal that explicitly at the start, and more than once in the course of your talk and then again at the end.

Is the glass half-full or half-empty? You may be well aware of the work that remains to be done, but can you give an account of the work that you have done, so as to make it seem like reasonable progress for the time you have spent on it . . . if that is your purpose in the presentation?

What style and language are appropriate for each phase of work-in-progress speaking and writing?

Definitive	Tentative
• Work done	Work ongoing
• Past tense	Present and conditional
• Showing (analysis/outcome)	Proposing
• Outcomes	Potential outcomes
• Questions answered	Questions remaining

In most work-in-progress presentations there are features that we might expect to see, signalled by an appropriate style. You might, for example, use more tentative language. You might explicitly state what you are and are not sure about yet. You might find it useful to make more than one interpretation of your interim 'findings' – in any sense – or to make more than one statement of your next step. You could consider the pros and cons of these and ask your audience to do so also. This dialogue will help you to develop your ideas – and possibly your confidence – further.

Towards a typology of styles

Definitive	Tentative
• The analysis shows . . .	I am not sure how to interpret this, but . . .
• This suggests . . .	This seems to suggest . . .
• This confirms . . .	This appears similar to a study in which . . .
• The aims were achieved	The first aim has been achieved . . .
• Future research . . .	The next likely step would be to . . .

Your supervisor(s) may, of course, have a similar set of expectations of how your writing will look, or they may not have thought about it in this way. (Do you know?) They may even find such attention to word choice a bit superficial; they may worry about you, since they might see you as not fixed on the content, but fixating on how to present it.

However, the style you choose will shape your presentation. Your writing will be stronger and clearer if the style has been a matter of choice – your choice – rather than just left to chance. You may have seen postgraduate presentations in which the researchers had not made a conscious choice about style and address, resulting in either understating – being too modest – or overstating – being unrealistic – about progress and plans. You will have to choose what proportion of your writing is to be definitive and what proportion tentative: will it be 50:50? Or some other proportion? Why? How will you signal this in your writing? How will other aspects of your writing about your work be changed by the 'in-progress' status? Should you also brush up your presentation skills?

One way of forcing yourself to create temporary or mini-closure in your work is to give a poster presentation either in your department, if this is appropriate, or at a conference. Many conferences, not just in the sciences, have designated sections for graduate student presentations of work in progress. An advantage of presenting a poster is that you can often have more face-to-face, one-to-one discussion with participants than with a paper presentation. It is a good way of networking. The aim is to give a snapshot – no more – of your research at a certain moment in time.

This takes a bit of forward planning: identifying an appropriate conference, relating your work to the conference theme, submitting an abstract, preparing your poster and so on. Your supervisor or peers can suggest conferences, if you do not already know which ones are most relevant. For guidance on best practice in designing posters, there is a website on graphical and verbal elements:

Preparing and Presenting a Poster
http://www.strath.ac.uk/Departments/CAPLE/poster/

In the same series there is a site on best practice in slide presentations:

Slide Presentations
http://www.strath.ac.uk/Departments/CAPLE/slides/

The sites are designed to increase your skills of presenting your research in these formats.

Your writing has to change for a poster presentation. A style shift is required: the poster requires more 'visual writing' than the thesis. Specific features of style must change as the reader becomes the viewer. Your writing will be read – if it is 'read' at all – at a distance of between one and four/five metres/yards. Your writing will have to be highly 'scan-able' from this distance. The specifics of the style shift required include: .

Style shift: example

Thesis	**Poster**
1 Long sentences	Short sentences
2 42 words	8 words
3 Elaboration of points	Main point
4 Signalling links	No link words
5 Main point last	Main point first
6 Define and explain	Show
7 The 'thesis'	The message
8 To persuade	To stimulate discussion

Link words are the key to coherence – or 'flow' – in good writing. They show readers how you get from one idea to the next, or from one sentence to the next, so that they can follow your thinking rather than trying to read your mind. However, in a poster, relationships between ideas and sections are shown visually; we do not need link words. The idea is not to make readers read traditionally from line to line, but to get them to grasp the whole snapshot.

For a poster, style shift starts with the title:

Title of thesis

Style as Voice: A Reappraisal of George Mackay Brown's Prose

The change in title would depend on the conference audience and theme, but the options are likely to be shorter and more direct:

Titles of poster

1 Style as Voice
2 George Mackay Brown: Voices in the Novels
3 Style Shift: How To Do It

If the audience attending the conference were those interested in 'style', then option one would be the best choice. If the audience were those with an interest in Scottish literature – and therefore likely to tune in to the author's name, George Mackay Brown – then option two would work best to get their attention. If the audience were postgraduate students – like yourself – who wanted to know more about the specifics of style shifts, then option three would be best. The choice, as always, is shaped by audience and purpose.

What is the purpose of your work-in-progress presentation:

• To inform?
• To persuade?
• To get feedback?
• To report?
• To raise questions?

Of these options, which is your main aim? How will that aim shape your poster?

For the writing in the main body of the poster, we have to make similar adjustments: cutting, listing, bullet pointing. For example, if we take a paragraph from a thesis – my own – we can show how it would be translated into a style suitable for a poster. This is the last paragraph of the abstract. It has many features of thesis writing:

Example of thesis style

Chapter Five, 'Prose as Voice', analyses the mechanics of interactions of voice within a narrative, demonstrating how Brown's lack of transitions from one voice to another requires the reader to make connections, to perceive the implications of intersections of points of view. Voices in Brown's fiction not only convey the blends of internal and external experience which make up characters' world-view, they are also markers of characters' control over their own lives. In Brown's novel *Greenvoe* the extent to which characters are able to voice their own views reveals the extent to which they are agents in their own experience.

Features of thesis writing used here include, among others, long sentences running over several lines, link words like 'not only . . . but also', and wordy striving for precision in 'perceive the implications of intersections of . . .'. These are acceptable features of thesis writing and the efforts to write clearly, strenuously avoiding ambiguity, and coherently, strenuously articulating links in the argument, are what we would expect to see in many completed theses.

For the poster, however, this has to change. It has to be cut from 100 words to, for example, 23:

Example of poster style

1   Style shifts show a range of perspectives.
2   No transitions: the reader has to make connections.
3   Style shifts represent characters as active or passive.

These points, under the heading that is the title of the novel, *Greenvoe*, show features of the poster style. The first demonstrates the use of a short sentence, with the direct language of 'show', and words of one syllable, all of which would easily fit on one line. The second uses the technique of breaking the line – and perhaps the concept – into two stages, using a colon. Starting with the word 'No' is potentially quite dramatic in effect and is certainly stronger than, for example, 'It is less likely that . . .', which we would probably expect to see in a thesis. The third starts with the key words 'style shifts', as did the first, thus creating the impression of a series and making a visual pattern of the words. Each element of this list of three points could be rewritten in parallel, so that each had the same form. Alternatively, the variation in form could be a conscious choice for a particular purpose.

Taking this approach of using words in a visual way further, we can show what we are trying to say in an example, using the words themselves as illustrations:

Timmy's own voice

Timmy Folster emerged, as he always did since the burning, through the window. He ambled towards the pier. He bent down and picked up a cigarette end that Ivan Westray had dropped and put it in his pocket ... He spoke amiably to himself all the time. 'Timmy's a good boy' (p. 14).

The bureaucrat's image of Timmy

[Written on an index card]
FOLSTER, Timothy John. b. 21/7/17. 5'4' 104lb. Eyes blue. Hair dark brown. Bachelor. Third (only surviving) issue of John and Mary-Ann (*neé* Linklater) Folster, Greenvoe: both deceased.

These two extracts from the novel show – not just describe – the style shift that is featured in the above extract from my thesis. These extracts can be highlighted – and should be labelled – for the poster. A set of bullet points alongside each could indicate the main points.

This is particularly appropriate, of course, for a thesis on literature, where words are the subject of study. However, it should be possible to compare two short texts from other areas in the same way: to show contrast or similarity, gap or overlap, cause and effect and so on. This involves representing the key line of argument, perhaps mimicking the structure or mode of the thesis, or part of it, in the shape of text for the poster. The structure and logic of the text remain; they are simply revealed visually.

In order to achieve this effect, you have to make a careful – and difficult – selection of your material. What is your best illustration of your work at this stage? Does this fit the conference agenda and the predictable preoccupations of participants?

What can I write about now?

1 Summarize research completed (500 words in sentences).
2 Sketch of writing to do next (500 words in sentences).
3 List three problems: write 100 words on each.
4 Write 500 words on how original proposal has evolved.

Presenting a work-in-progress poster is an important interim activity in years two and three of the doctorate. It can prevent you from getting bogged down and can adjust your focus in important ways at this key point. It can keep you moving – and make you feel that you are, finally, moving – towards the final 'clarification' of the project as a whole.

A writers' group

Problematic writers . . . do not fully join the conversation about writing. They are not ready and enthusiastic participants in the discussions and problem-solving efforts of writing groups. They seem distracted and do not listen patiently to what other writers experience or to their suggestions for new strategies. They seem to persist in seemingly self-centred and isolated efforts as writers.

(Boice 1994: 77)

Boice suggests what benefit there might be for thesis writers to form a writers' group. He also indicates how you might spot people who are not likely to find them useful. Both are probably crucial: avoid 'moaning meetings'; avoid writers who seem content to talk about the writing they have not done, at least for the purposes of writers' group.

While writers' groups have a long tradition in the USA (Gere 1987), they are less established in other cultures. They have been shown to work well for academic staff (Murray and MacKay 1998a; Morss and Murray 2001), with the aim of increasing and/or improving written output for publication, but the processes can be just as effective for postgraduate writers.

Many of the goals of thesis writers can be enhanced – even accelerated – in a writers' group: writing development, getting into the writing habit, working out a thesis, networking, peer support and research training. Once postgraduates start to share information, skills and tactics for research and writing, there is a dynamic increase in productivity, and often in enjoyment.

A group is not everyone's favourite activity. Some prefer to go it alone. There may be a middle ground, where the thesis writers' group serves very specific purposes for the individual. For this reason, that students will have different needs and purposes in attending such a group, it can help to have a facilitator. This person should have some, or all, of the following: group skills, writing development knowledge, interest in running the group (even if for the first time), and a mentoring disposition towards postgraduates. Subject expertise, i.e. expertise in the subjects of all of the doctorates being written by a group, is probably not feasible. Experience suggests that it is, in any case, not essential.

The purpose of the writers' group depends on what the participants want to achieve, but this might be a starting point.

What is the purpose of a writers' group?

- To support writers
- To create a forum for discussing writing
- To stimulate prioritizing and goal setting for writing
- To prompt discussion of writing plans and drafts
- To write regularly

Regular writers' group meetings become interim deadlines for short- and medium-term goals. In the groups in which I have been involved, we usually make a plan for a six-month period.

Although each group is different, setting its own objectives and ground rules, a core of practices has emerged in our groups. The meetings last 90 minutes. We meet twice a month and use every meeting as a deadline. However modest we feel our progress is between these meetings, at least there is progress. This structure also helps people to establish the goals and sub-goals over the six-month period. We know that we will be reporting on our progress at the meeting and that acts as an incentive to have something done by then. It acts, for most writers, like any other deadline. In addition, there is the added incentive that positive feedback will be provided in the short discussion between pairs of writers. There is no public 'naming and shaming' of those who have not written what they set out to; there is, instead, small group or pairs discussion. The facilitator can offer guidance on what does, and does not, constitute a sensible writing goal.

There are three types of activity at all group meetings:

1 Taking stock of progress, setting new goals
2 Writing
3 Discussing this writing and getting feedback.

The first involves defining writing tasks and fixing times to do them between one meeting and the next. The second involves ten minutes' private writing – or writing to show a colleague – in which participants can write about any aspect of the writing process or any part of their thesis. If they bring their outline with them, they can write a section of the thesis there and then. It is important that we do not just meet to talk about writing; we actually do it. This helps, over the longer term, to make writing much easier to start, much more routine. As writing is followed by discussion, we have an immediate, live and positive response to the writing, something that is missing in the usual process of writing in solitude.

Writers can also give each other feedback on and critiques of work in progress and on drafts of chapters or papers. In order to think through how we might do this best, we read about the process of giving and receiving critiques, discuss the processes explicitly and agree how we want to work. There is research to show that giving and receiving feedback is an important dimension of research students' development, and that, according to students, peer review – not just supervisor review – is important:

> It was found that preparing and receiving critiques from professors and peers was perceived to be the most influential element in helping [students] to understand the process of scholarly writing and in producing a better written product.
>
> (Caffarella and Barnett 2000: 39)

This type of process can help students develop a better understanding of the iterative nature of scholarly writing. The iterations that go into a thesis or scholarly paper are disguised from view and are generally unspoken. Hence students' frustration at being asked for so many revisions, perhaps. In the writers' group they can see so many other writers – staff and students in our groups – going through the same process of iterations. They can share their irritations. This is one of the key lessons learned in the writers' group. It is not just that they realize 'we are all in the same boat', but that they perceive the realities of the writing process.

Receiving critiques can be just as uncomfortable as giving them. Each requires different skills and these will develop over time. However, a thesis writer's starting point, when receiving a critique, can be quite negative:

> I'm afraid of the feedback and I wonder if the person reading mine would even be interested in the topic.
>
> [I am] very disappointed about my writing.
>
> (Caffarella and Barnett 2000: 45)

These students reveal their vulnerability, as they are about to receive critiques. The emotional dimension of writing is not always a part of discussions with supervisors. Writers may be more 'needy' (King 2000: 263) when they are writing than when they are doing anything else. The writers' group discussions allow time and space for exploring these emotional processes. Such discussions can provide helpful rehearsal time for future discussions with supervisors. Students can then prompt their supervisors to provide more direction in the practice of giving and receiving critiques, for example.

For some students, the writers' group turns out to be the only space for discussion of such processes. If their supervisor directs them to 'get on with the research and worry about the writing later', but they are worried about the writing now, then not only is closure deferred for even longer, but the processes of writing, and all that it involves, may not be learned as thoroughly. There will simply not be enough time.

It may be simplistic to make a connection between those students who do not know how long their thesis is meant to be and have no conception of how to give and receive critiques, and those supervisors who do not encourage their students to engage fully with writing throughout their doctorate. But it may also be true. Those students who have not been informed or guided, from an early stage, in their writing are those who are most likely to ask questions like 'Do I have to review the literature?' and 'How well do I need to know the external's work?', because they genuinely do not know.

Elbow (1973) makes a strong case for writers' groups – or 'teacherless classes' – arguing that they can help writers to see their writing as others see it:

> To improve your writing you don't need advice about what changes to make; you don't need theories of what is good and bad writing. You need movies of people's minds while they read your words. But you need this for a sustained period of time – at least two or three months. And you need to get the experience of not just a couple of people but of at least six or seven. And you need to keep getting it from the same people so that they get better at transmitting their experience and you get better at hearing them.
>
> (Elbow 1973: 77)

This reinforces the point that giving and receiving of critiques are processes that we would do well to give ourselves time and mechanisms to learn, rather than just hope that they will evolve, for us, or find fault with ourselves when they do not.

Elbow also makes a strong case for showing writing that is incomplete, that we are not yet happy with, to others, though you have to wonder how often writers are comfortable handing over even much revised writing for peer review and how easily they take to giving and receiving critiques; i.e. does it ever really get that comfortable, just because we have revised it ten or twelve times? Or does that 'comfort' come with the development of trust and under-standing with the 'six or seven' other writers in a group? Elbow's point is that giving our writing to others, at many stages in the writing process, before it is 'finished', is an important step in learning how to write well:

> Even if you are very busy, even if you have nothing to write about, and even if you are very blocked, you must write something and try to experi-ence it through their eyes. Of course it may not be good; you may not be satisfied with it. But if you only learn how people perceive and experience words you are satisfied with, you are missing a crucial area of learning. You often learn the most from reactions to the words you loathe. Do you want to learn how to write or protect your feelings?
>
> (Elbow 1973: 77–8)

He does not mention the words 'feedback' or 'critique' here; he seems more concerned that we see our writing through others' eyes. This, he has found, is the key learning tool.

Elbow (1973), Murray (2000) and others have developed frameworks for writers' groups and guidance on how to start them up. Elbow recommends:

- A committed group of people
- Diversity: different kinds of people and writing
- Write about anything, but write
- Make regular time
- With a chair/leader/facilitator
- Taking stock at each meeting, about that meeting.

Here are examples of talking points for your writers' group:

Writing group discussion

How can I get into the writing habit?

- Write about reading, i.e. attach it to another task you already do.
- Prioritize writing.
- Decide on a particular time to write.
- Write at the same time as students.
- List things you need to start. Draw up possible action plan.
- Write for five minutes only.
- Make spaces in the diary.

How can I stay in the writing habit?

- Plan: get a reader and a deadline.
- Form a writing group.
- Get someone who knows about writing and/or research in your field to lead it.
- Network with other writers and researchers: make talking about writing habitual.
- Treat it like a habit.
- Give yourself rewards for writing: food, drink, exercise, other writing.
- Give yourself penalties for not writing: e.g. financial penalty (one group agreed to make a donation to a charity when they missed their writing practice).
- Think in terms of very small increments.

Initial reactions to the idea of a writers' group are mixed. Given a little information about it, students are uncertain about, among other things, whether they will get a good enough return on the investment of their time in this way. Here are some responses:

Would you attend a writers' group?

I probably would attend at least one session to decide on whether or not it was useful. In the programme . . . I would probably like to see more on grammar and related topics.

I would attend a writing group. I would expect a lot of practical writing exercises with a great amount of feedback to improve my writing. Also hints on how to develop writing skills I may already have.

Yes. I'd like to hear from other students experiences/strategies for writing.

This range of reactions may be because it is a new idea to most students (and staff). In any case, the student body is diverse; why would they all want the same thing? Implicit in the hesitation of some of the initial responses is the popular, yet stigmatized, misconception that the group is for those who have writing 'problems'. This is not true; the writers' group is for those who want to write and to improve their writing as they go along.

It is obviously important to clarify what a writers' group can and cannot do. The group may gel as much because of personalities as of shared goals. Having a facilitator who is responsible for group management – staff or student? – may help to make the process work for all involved, particularly if he or she knows something about writing and writers' groups.

After six or twelve months' participation in a writers' group, six postgraduate writers contemplate its impact:

Is the writers' group effective, for you?

1 I use the group as a measure of how I am progressing my project. It focuses me on deadlines and is helpful in that respect. It has certainly helped me to produce segments of my current paper 'to order' and should help me fulfil my goal of submission by 31 March. The group discussions can be helpful in suggesting ways of focusing the actual writing, ideas for areas for submission.

2 Use of the group: discussion with others: vital! Effective! Very useful even though we're not doing the same thing, not working in the same area. Talking about real live projects. Deadlines combine meetings well – it works. Makes deadlines less 'scary', more achievable. Achieving my targets probably took 2–3 months.

3 The group provides several vital supports – sheer companionship in what can otherwise be a lonely task (writing); encouragement; but in particular

a regular refocusing, remotivating, and enforced reassessing of progress. It is perhaps a measure of the group's usefulness that the time for it is snatched from an already over-stretched timetable. The goal-setting is vital – at least until it becomes 'internalised'! To what extent am I achieving the targets I set? On the whole, surprisingly, the small goals usually are achieved; and it is significant that the last one wasn't, but it was too 'big' to draft the whole outline.

4 The early sessions helped me focus on writing, in particular on the structure of chapters and organising their creation. I have also found it helpful to talk to colleagues and discuss their approaches and problems. It is useful to have the time – the group forces me to put this part of my work on the agenda. I am supposed to spend so much of my time writing for the research, but at the moment the group is the only time during office hours that I get to do this.

5 From my experience the writing group has been a key support activity in my PhD and my life. I use the group to set up my goals in a simple and easy way (schedule) and to plan my activities in advance, set up deadlines and to reach my goals. It is a kind of support that encourages me in my research. The writing group has also helped me to improve my writing skills; in discussions I address the direction of my research and become more critical. It has helped me to 'educate' my mind to structure what I want to write and to be consistent in what I express.

6 From my point of view, the writing group has helped me get into a writing discipline. The experience of sharing with other people in the same process has been highly stimulating. It has also helped me in the process of getting things done. For example: last week I needed to write an abstract for a workshop and I simply couldn't find any words to write. Then I remembered that in one of the writing group sessions I had written some sort of abstract. I took this and it helped me to start the abstract and to give it shape. Regarding the goal-setting process, I have found that my initial goals were too ambitious. The last few weeks I have been reading more than writing. However, the goals have helped me to do some writing and not focus only on reading, as I used to do.

These reactions show the range of experiences of writers in one group. They are all making their own place in the group and finding their own purpose in its activities. What they all share is that they have found a peer group for writing.

The key to this phase of the doctorate is that you have started to demonstrate, to yourself as much as to your supervisor, that you are on the road to constructing a thesis. You can express your sense of your emerging thesis, you can articulate the strengths and weaknesses of your work and you can identify where you have made distinct progress.

The next step is to find ways to write regularly, at times continuously, always with purpose, but still using writing to explore, and perhaps ignore, new directions. Writing has now acquired a number of functions in the thesis process. However, it is time to start writing chapters, or, at least, pilot chapters.

Checklist

The first milestone

- Identify your first writing milestone(s).
- Discuss criteria and format for your first-year report.
- Do freewriting on fears, pressures, anxieties, questions, prompts.
- Discuss definitions of 'progress'.
- Update and agree a new plan of work.
- Consider setting up your own writers' group, or encourage your department/faculty/university to do so.

5

Becoming a serial writer

What is a serial writer? • Scaffolding for an argument • Paragraph structure
• Introductory paragraphs • Writing about the method(s) • Study buddy
• Regular writing • Problems with writing • Writer's block • Incremental
writing • Writing binges • Developing a writing strategy • Checklist:
becoming a serial writer

This chapter aims to make writing manageable in the middle stage of the
thesis. There is a structured approach to producing text for the thesis – the
basic unit being the paragraph – and an incremental approach to the writing
process. This chapter outlines how the writing can become more frequent,
more regular and more directed.

A key issue in phase two of the research is the extent to which chapters can
be written; if no chapters are already underway, then something may be wrong
with the writing process, or with the audience (supervisor) or the feedback.
The kinds of things that can go wrong are illustrated and defined. Although
writing processes are very individual, even personal, there are strategies for
overcoming the hurdles that students experience at this stage.

Finally, it is all very well telling people that they have to write all the way
through a project – and that they can develop habits of productive writing as
they do so – but how? How do you become a 'serial writer'?

What is a serial writer?

Writers fare best when they begin before feeling fully ready. Motivation comes most reliably in the wake of regular involvement.

(Boice 1994: 236)

Although the word 'serial' is often used to refer to a particular kind of writing – a story in instalments – for the context of this chapter, 'serial' means writing a thesis in instalments.

A serial writer is someone who sees writing as a series of tasks, who progresses from one writing task to the next and connects the writing sessions with each other, to create continuity. This saves valuable time, at the start of a writing session, when we are trying to work out what we are going to write about.

Serial writing is proposed as a productive method because it means that writing occurs regularly. 'Serial' also implies that there are regular intervals between the instalments of writing; writers establish a pattern of writing, a cadence of production that suits their working environment and a social environment that sustains – or at least does not undermine – their writing.

This method applies to writing both drafts and revisions. Writers develop their own sense of what a 'series' of revisions requires. When we write regularly, we establish a pattern of revisions. Through these we not only strengthen and clarify our arguments, but frequently – though not always – our arguments only really emerge through serial revisions. Serial writing is therefore critical for the development of our thinking through writing.

How do you become a serial writer? In order to serialize our own writing we have to envisage writing as a process, with interconnected steps. Many writers have to re-engineer writing as a series of events or moments. We have to establish what the 'episodes' in that series are and what connects them to each other.

There are many factors involved in developing this skill: behavioural, psychosocial, peer group, motivation, identity and knowledge of writing practices and processes. All of these were introduced in the first four chapters of this book, and will be developed further in this and the next five chapters.

Why would you want to be a serial writer? Serial writing is more comfortable, less stressful. It is possible to fit writing into our daily working lives. We find momentum by writing regularly and can develop our ideas over several writing moments, rather than one final push. We do not feel like failures when we do not generate a 'complete' idea in one go. We can even begin to restructure the working day to include writing:

Writing and related exercises are almost always limited to brief, daily sessions that do not interfere with more important activities such as social life, professional responsibilities, and exercising. Writers ... spend less time writing than they expect and get more (and better) writing done than before. In the long run, [this] saves more time than it takes ... What began as a near-surplus of new habits turned out to be nothing more than a couple of manageable principles, balance and moderation.

(Boice 1994: xx and xxiii)

Writing regularly – and 'on demand' – is an important professional skill. We have to be able to manage our writing along with our other professional tasks.

Scaffolding for an argument

This section argues that the combination of definition and examples is a strong unit in academic argument. For any point that we want to argue, we can use four steps as the scaffolding for our argument:

Scaffolding for your argument

1 Decide on the main point.
2 Define terms, elaborate.
3 Illustrate your point.
4 Discuss illustrations, examples or evidence: show how they say what you say they say.

Many writers stop at the third step, as if to say 'See, that proves it.' However, simply presenting evidence is not enough; we have to show how we constructed our interpretation of it and how that interpretation makes our point.

Paragraph structure

While the paragraph is often thought of as a point of style, it is actually a vital compositional tool.

Make the paragraph the unit of composition: one paragraph to each topic.
(Strunk and White [1959] 1979)

This piece of advice is taken from one of the enduring classics on writing style. Every edition of Strunk's *Elements of Style* has been a standard reference point (http:www.diku/students/myth/EOS/) for novice and experienced writers alike. It is perhaps better known – a bestseller – in the USA, but, apart from one or two differences in punctuation and spelling, the contents are as relevant, and useful, in other cultures. While Strunk's intention was to help students avoid making the most common mistakes, he provided some guidelines on how to write well. This is not just a corrective text; the qualities of good writing are defined.

The 'lessons' Strunk provides are models of concise writing: 'Use the active voice . . . Omit needless words . . . In summaries, keep to one tense.' Short illustrations support the definitions and recommendations. Many postgraduates do not know the 'rules of rhetoric' and are often at a loss as to what constitutes good writing. Many supervisors, likewise, do not know all the rules, especially in areas where writing is seen merely as the means of 'summing up' the research.

Debates about style often descend into what appear to be matters of personal preference, rather than 'rules'. It is to everyone's advantage if this debate is informed by the rules learned now, rather than the rules remembered from school days. Once we have learned the rules we can correct many of our mistakes ourselves. This is an important professional skill. We can also deviate from them at will, if it makes our point clearer:

> It is an old observation that the best writers sometimes disregard the rules of rhetoric. When they do so, however, the reader will usually find in the sentence some compensating merit, attained at the cost of the violation. Unless he [sic] is certain of doing well, he will probably do better to follow the rules. After he has learned, by their guidance, to write plain English adequate for everyday uses, let him look, for the secrets of style, to the study of the masters of literature.
>
> (Strunk and White [1959] 1979)

The best writers are surely those who know the rules, whether they deviate from them or not.

There is an interesting point here about learning the rules: we learn about *writing* by following the rules. If we do not know the rules, we may be all at sea, interestingly at sea, but unable to make conscious, confident choices between one form and another. The moral of the story is that it is a good idea to learn the rules of style, their uses and abuses. This learning process should show us how style can be a tool to help us make our points clearer and stronger.

Thesis writing involves many mini-experiments in style, as we adapt the way we 'normally' write – or the ways we have written in the past, for other tasks – to the extended argument that is a thesis.

We can design a paragraph as a unit in our argument. We do not need to wait and see how long or short a paragraph will be; we can decide to write as much or as little as we think our point requires. Of course, we can change our minds as we go along, but the outline structure is there to guide us.

Paragraph structure

(1) Topic sentence... ... ...
... (2) Elaborate/define your terms... ... ...
... ... (3) Give an example/
evidence/illustrate... ... ...
... ... (4) Say how your example makes the
point in your topic sentence.

The purpose of providing this structure – apart from the fact that many postgraduates do not seem to know about the structure of a paragraph – is that it helps us order the points we want to make and strengthen the coherence at the sub-page level. The points are all connected logically.

Link words are also needed. They can make this logical structure explicit. They lead readers through your text, making them see the connections you have put there. You do not ask them to try and work out what the link is; they cannot read your mind. They are just as likely not to see the link – or to see another link – and to attribute their 'error' to a deficiency in your writing skills.

You already have a repertoire of links: moreover, therefore, nevertheless, firstly ... secondly ... thirdly, thus and so on. Repetition can also be an effective linking device, as can a synonym or pronoun, where another word stands for the key word.

Link words: illustration

For her part, the Duchess clearly stands on the side of merit; while she never challenges the concept of an ordered society, she does strive to substitute a meritocracy for her kingdom's aristocracy. For example, she approves of the relative indifference toward degree in the French court, ... Similarly, when Ferdinand argues ... the Duchess gives her quick assent. Moreover, Antonio tells us that ...

(Selzer 1981: 72)

Throughout this paragraph Selzer uses a variety of linking techniques to make sure the reader follows him through a complicated argument:

Linking

1 The semi-colon tells the reader that two points are related. While a full stop would separate the points, the semi-colon connects them.
2 The pronoun 'she' – referring to the Duchess in the first part of the sentence – tells us that the writer is still talking about the same topic.
3 'For example, . . .' tells us how to relate two sentences: there is more specific information coming, to illustrate the point.
4 'Similarly' is another example of using the link word at the start of the sentence. The reader knows, with the first word, how to link them.
5 Repetition of 'Duchess' makes it clear that while two other names are mentioned, she is the topic for this paragraph.
6 'Moreover' is another link word, linking from the start of the sentence.

The link words, taken separately, illustrate the direction of the argument: a point is made, then defined further. An example follows, backed up by another. Emphasis is added to the point in a further example.

However, there are certain forms of academic writing where links are not needed. You have the choice: to link or not to link. For example, in abstracts and summaries there may be, by convention, no link words. The logical structure underpinning the abstract may be so obvious, in such a short text, that to add links would seem unnecessary. Structured abstracts may also have headings, making link words superfluous.

In writing for the web, even about our research, we may be able to dispense with verbal links in favour of visual links. The same applies to posters, dealt with in the previous chapter. These are not meant to be read in the same way as a thesis, one paragraph after another, one sentence after another. Readers – or, perhaps more accurately, viewers – can flit about from section to section. They may read them in any order. You do not, therefore, have to write them to be read in one order. Your role as writer is to direct their attention, but not necessarily in a linear text.

We can miss out one of the steps. For example, if we feel that we do not need to elaborate on the topic sentence, we can miss out step two. That may be asking readers to make a bit of a jump, to follow our thinking by making links for themselves, instead of making those links for the readers explicitly.

Topic sentence: 'begin each paragraph with a topic sentence; end it in conformity with the beginning' (Strunk and White [1959] 1979).

You can also think of paragraphs as working in a series, a paragraph block, where you decide that you need several paragraphs to make a point, or where you see – or want to show – that several points are related. All the points may then be brought together in a final short paragraph. First outline the points you want to write about:

Outlining paragraphs

1 Write a list of the points you want to cover.
2 Look at your list: are any of these actually more than one point?
3 Can you drop any points?
4 Are they in the right order?
5 Write a paragraph on each one.

In this way, you are making a direct link between the points you want to make and the paragraphs you need to make them. Using this approach means that you put time into planning the points, their order and depth, cutting, adding and sub-dividing, as required, and only then do you start to think about writing paragraphs. The key words you have in your list go straight into your topic sentences.

This process requires you to make some decisions about content and structure before you have to start deciding about style. You already know a few of the words for the topic sentence. You know your next step is probably to elaborate or define that topic sentence. Then illustrate, provide evidence. Then back to the main point, or to the clarification of it provided by your illustration.

Introductory paragraphs

Writing introductions is one way of working out what you want to say in a section of writing. What do you want the content to be? Writing a few sentences can force you to make a few decisions.

This activity can also help you establish a commitment to one topic – for one session of writing or one section of the thesis – and help you to focus on it.

The key elements of introductions are: (1) identify the main point; (2) define the purpose in a verb; and (3) define contents.

Introduction

Write a sentence defining the main purpose of the chapter:

This chapter [verb] . . .
This chapter is about . . .
In the chapter . . . will be described . . .
This chapter argues . . .
The aim of this chapter is to . . .
This chapter is really about . . .
In this chapter I want to argue/show/make the case that . . .

The range of styles in these options is deliberate; choose the one that fits best with your thinking at this stage. Remember this is just a draft – if not a 'predraft' – and its function is to force you to write a few sentences that help you make some decisions about what the chapter will 'do'.

This may be an important shift in your thinking at this stage: from 'What goes in this chapter?', which suggests that you feel responsible for including all your – and others' – good ideas, to 'What am I trying to achieve in this chapter?', which suggests that you have a principle of selection to help you sift through all your notes.

It may be time to start using the words 'thesis' and 'argument', as in 'The thesis of this chapter is . . .' and 'The argument of this chapter is . . .'. What is your chapter really about? Can you reduce this to one key idea? Can you revise your earlier sentences about your chapter – written for the exercises above – to create a sentence that you are surer about?

If you find that you cannot do that, then you are not yet sure of your chapter. You are not yet in control of your content. You will have to stay at this point a bit longer. This may not be the best time to start converting your notes to drafts. If you are not sure of your direction you could quickly get lost in your writing. Go back to your freewriting; the essence of the chapter may be there.

On the other hand, your writing may have produced a theme for the chapter already, but you are not sure that it is the 'right' one. This may be true. Keep writing, in the ways described in this section. Alternatively, your lack of certainty may be obscuring how much progress you have made in defining the focus for your chapter. Because there is always that nagging doubt in the back of your mind – 'But is that really what I want to say in this chapter?' – you hesitate. The result is that you fail to commit yourself to writing about one theme. Paradoxically, what appears to be a search for a 'better' theme can sometimes result in a weaker theme, because you have not incorporated as many revisions. There is an element of uncertainty in many of the writing choices you make at this stage. Drafts of chapters will provoke – rather than silence – doubts. Your argument will emerge through a series of revisions.

Use the following prompts to start writing. Insert the one that suits you:.

What can I write about now?

The next section is about . . .
The next section [reviews/evaluates/defines/describes] . . .
There are three main points in this section: . . .
This is covered in three sections: . . .

The introduction that covers these or similar points is not just an aid to your reader; it is also an aid to your writing. Writing the introduction helps you to work out exactly – and explicitly – what the purpose of your chapter is.

Writing about the method(s)

While you may not have a chapter that you call 'Methods', you will have to define your method, your approach, your analytical perspective – whatever you call it – for the research questions you have posed.

The terms you use will vary according to your discipline, and according to the position you choose to occupy in the debate in your field. There is no need to delay the choice of terms; you can start with ones that you are only half-sure of. In order to progress the thesis through this stage, you need to replace reasons for not writing with ways to write, even in uncertainty.

It may help to take as your first topic how you are going to – or went about – answering your research question, i.e. to write one of the fifteen-minute pieces that should by now be a routine part of your writing practice. Get all your ideas down on paper. The purpose is simply to start with a couple of hundred words – the fifteen minutes' writing – and then build on that over the weeks and months. As usual, write in sentences, as this may help you to develop your ideas.

- The goal is to get started.
- The task is to write informally, immediately.
- The output is 15 minutes' writing – around 200 words.

The next step is to write a list of headings, and possibly subheadings. You can use words that came up in the fifteen minutes' writing, or words from your research questions, or generic headings, such as subjects, texts, analytical tools, participants, quotes, cross-references, focus groups, questionnaires, per-spectives, journals, whatever words are relevant to your study. Each of these is a potential heading for a section.

You can force further writing by going back to the research questions: how can you relate your sentences and headings to these questions? Write a few sentences in which you explicitly link your initial writings and your original questions. If you are word processing this – as you should be – you can import the research questions from the original proposal, or your revised introduction, into this file.

For the rest of the first page of your 'method' section – or chapter – you will have to forecast the points you intend to cover in your explanation of method, or of how you went about your study.

The points you listed – that you want to cover – may need to be rearranged. Some of them may sub-divide into other headings. Some could be combined into sections within a chapter.

Outlining the 'method'

1 What did you set out to do?
2 How did you set out to do it?
3 Why did you choose that approach?
4 What were your research questions?
5 How did your method fit the questions?
6 Which topics do you need to cover to explain your methods?

Once you have some headings, there is no harm in beginning to think about length and proportion. How long will your 'method' section/chapter be? What proportion of the whole thesis will it take up? Are you using a well-established approach – that is not very contested – or are you using a new approach that will require more explanation and supporting arguments?

The following example may strike you as not directly relevant to your field or your subject; however, the point of this example is that it illustrates the elements of the opening page of the method chapter/section. In an early draft, you would not have to worry about style, such as 'The method . . . used will be described as follows.' It is more important, at this stage, to think about content than about the final finessing of style.

Here is an example of the opening page of the method chapter:

Example

METHOD

The purpose of this study was to determine the effectiveness of an exercise based cardiac rehabilitation programme on patients who had recently suffered a myocardial infarction. Over a period of ten weeks the effects of the exercise programme were compared to those of a routine care control group. This routine care control group was offered the exercise programme at the end of the ten-week control period, while the exercise group moved on to a maintenance class. The design allowed the following problems to be answered:

1 Does the cardiac rehabilitation programme have physiological effects?
2 Does the cardiac rehabilitation programme have any psychological benefits?
3 Does the cardiac rehabilitation programme improve understanding of heart disease?

The method which was used will be described as follows:

(a) subjects, (b) treatment groups, (c) dependent measures, and (d) procedures.

SUBJECTS

The subjects were 40 male (n = 29) and female (n = 11) patients who had experienced a myocardial infarction and who met the criteria for participation in the cardiac rehabilitation programme. The programme selection criteria included:

1 Aged under 70 years
2 Myocardial infarction documented by clinical history, electrocardiograph and enzyme evidence
3 Minimum of six weeks post-myocardial infarction
4 No physical problems which could preclude full participation in the exercise programme, e.g. arthritis of hips and/or knees.

This example has the essential ingredients of an introduction to a chapter: the link back to the aims of the study, the rationale for the chapter to come and forecast of its contents.

Study buddy

This term is used to designate the person(s) with whom you can have regular discussions about your writing, positive discussions, not just 'moaning sessions'.

The buddy system recognizes the need for support in navigating new developmental stages or mastering new . . . skills.

(Palumbo 2000: 27)

This may be someone from your peer group, another postgraduate in your department or a colleague in another department. It does not really matter who it is, as long as you find that your discussions are supportive and productive. Meet to write and write when you meet, otherwise you could get into the bad habit of talking about writing rather than doing it.

30-minute meetings

AGENDA

Bring your outline and diary to meetings. Write in sentences.

- **Five minutes' writing**
  What writing have your done on your project since your previous meeting?
  Time spent, words/sub-themes written, etc.?
- **Ten minutes' private writing**
  Write about the topic which is next on your writing agenda.
- **Ten minutes' discussion**
  Discuss your writing with your buddy.
- **Five minutes' private writing**
  What is your next writing sub-goal?

What you discuss has no limits; it can be any aspect of the writing process, including your achievements. The best study buddy is someone who is a regular writer too, or trying to be one.

Regular writing

Many writers – students and supervisors – believe that their best writing can only be done in long writing sessions. Some believe that they can only 'really' write this way. However, this 'binge' strategy has its drawbacks:

> With bingeing comes hypomania, the near-mania of euphoria and rushing. With bingeing comes busyness – because each binged task is followed by the need to complete other, overdue tasks while emitting all the busy signs of not wanting to be disturbed. And with bingeing comes a failing to find the times for rest and renewal that could provide energy and ideas for writing. One other thing happens with bingeing: great spacings between writing episodes demand large investments in warm-up before writing can be resumed.
>
> (Boice 1994: 240)

Furthermore, how often does it happen that we have large periods of time for writing? Even doctoral students – particularly part-timers – have many other responsibilities and tasks. Is bingeing really a productive method? Whatever we think about it, need it be our *only* method? Even when we do have a long stretch of time for writing we should probably use it for structured binges. The strategies discussed in the earlier chapters of this book are intended to enable thesis writers to use a range of approaches, to fit writing into whatever period of time they have, long or short, and probably both.

For such a large writing project, it is likely that changes will have to be made, for example:

- Last minute writing will not work.
- You will have to revise your writing much more often.
- You will have to discuss your writing.
- Your writing will be scrutinized in much more detail.
- You will have responsibility for correcting errors of grammar, punctuation, spelling, etc.

You may not even like the idea of regular writing, combining structured writing and generative strategies, writing mini-arguments as well as exploring lines of thought, unpacking a subject and thinking about what the headings might be. Alternatively, you could be writing a list of questions you are writing to answer. The point here is that the thesis writer has to continue writing in different forms in parallel from this point on (if not already).

Try to make time for regular discussion with your supervisor and study buddy about writing: about how you are managing writing, where you write, when you write, how often and how much you produce. You can discuss your emerging sense of yourself as a writer. You can share your enjoyment of it. You can exchange strategies that you develop for getting into the writing habit. For example:

What can I write about now?

1 An abstract for a conference next year (200 words?)
2 A sketch of the methods chapter in outline
3 500 words (30–60 mins?) on contents of the methods chapter

Problems with writing

At this stage in the production of a thesis, towards the middle of the second year, it is common for a whole new set of 'problems' to creep in. The writing challenges you have faced so far, and the writing strategies you have developed up to this point, may not seem to match up to the next phase of your work. You may invent brand new displacement activities. You may prioritize 'research' over writing. However, the reasons you give yourself for not writing may have underlying causes worth thinking about.

Problems with writing

- Fear of supervisor's feedback, or of supervisor in general
- Fatigue: too many 'binges', binge-only writing, more 'snacks' needed, more rest? Binges can be aversive, leaving you feeling drained
- 'Boredom', often a sign of stress in this context
- Lack of momentum: redefine this not as lack of progress, but as limited relationship between writing sessions. Connect writing activities
- Not writing often enough
- Fear of the big picture: fear of success, fear of failure
- Lack of rewards
- Signalling problems: you cannot find your way in your own writing
- Lack of forecasting
- Not achieving high enough standard in writing

The cycle of writing may have broken down and, now that you have noticed that, you can get it going again. Part-time students in particular have to put their thesis 'away' so often – sometimes for long periods – that it seems impossible to pick it back up. You can use strategies for regular 'scribbling' – if you think 'writing' is too good a word for it – to keep your ideas simmering away. Above all, the short writing activities prevent you from feeling that you have lost touch completely with your work.

Whatever you feel about your writing, whatever your sense of the 'problem', it may not be as bad as you think. It is unlikely that you will be entirely satisfied with your writing at this stage. In fact, you may not experience total satisfaction till the very end of the thesis writing process, and perhaps not even then, since no one will be more aware that your work 'could have been improved' than you.

Writer's block

Writer's block has a separate section in this chapter because it is a specific problem often identified by name. Whatever meanings different writers attach to it, it is a term we recognize. Anecdotally, it seems to be the term most often used for the most acute problems with generating text. It is also the one that is most feared – by any writer – and, perhaps, the most difficult to resolve.

In fact, the term 'writer's block' may be a term that people latch on to in order to try and explain why they are not writing; in the absence of a more precise definition, they resort to this term as a kind of catch-all. It certainly identifies the problem, even if it does not account for it.

Another way of looking at this 'syndrome', if that is the right word, is to see 'blocked' moments as a common, perhaps universal, experience. These moments when we cannot produce writing may occur at particular points in the writing process. It may be one of the popular misconceptions of writing that, once started, it all 'flows', and that those who do not 'flow' must have something wrong with them: their writing, and possibly their research, is just not good enough. Lack of feedback, in other words, may undermine – more than once – a writer's confidence in his or her work or writing.

All of the strategies in this section may help blocked writers start writing again. However, there may be a fundamental reason why they are getting blocked:

Why do writers get blocked?

- They think they must work out what they think – and what they want to say – before they can write . . . and get stuck at that point . . .

  . . . instead of using writing to sort out what they want to say.

- They struggle to work a point out logically, or scientifically or objectively . . . and get stuck at that point . . .

  . . . instead of working it out in words.

- They want to be sure before they write . . .

  . . . instead of writing when they are not sure.

- There is no end to the project in sight.

Blocked writers have somehow lost the art – or perhaps never had it – of using writing as the 'engine' of their thinking. They have not integrated it into their thinking and learning. They do not use writing to solve the problem.

A writing block, may, of course, be an indicator of a flaw in the system itself, i.e. not just in the writing task but in the writing process as a whole: 'Impatience is the single most important predictor of writing blocks' (Boice 1994: 28). It may be that the writer is going about writing too soon, without the necessary planning, prewriting or freewriting. If writers do not use the range of strategies and skills to ensure that writing, once they come to do it, can 'flow', then they will experience a breakdown in their writing, as several layers of decision demand to be made at the same time. Similarly, if writing is not routine, then there is added pressure on writers to generate fluency out of the blue, when they have been working on other, quite different, tasks. The 'patience' that Boice argues we need to practise is not just a matter of waiting for the right moment to write; it is about patiently investing time in many pre-writing activities. Those who aim to produce good text on demand are setting themselves up for a disappointment and, often, a writing block.

Part of the excitement of writing is not really knowing what exactly is going to come out in the words; it may be that blocked writers are those who, at a certain time, find that uncertainty too unsettling. Perhaps there are too many other uncertainties – about the research, the thesis or life in general – for them to be able to cope with this uncertainty, and to live with it in their writing. Yet, even the most carefully planned writing can have a life of its own, throwing up new ideas, or new ways of looking at things or new connections or distinctions.

The blocked writer may have lost sight of the meaning of the project. Since there may be no immediate effect on his or her life of completing a thesis, it seems, at times, to require just too many sacrifices. It can potentially put a strain on everyone connected to the writer.

The writer may be trying to do too much: it is not easy – and often not possible – to say what you want to say in one go. Even if you have learned a lot about writing processes and feel that you have mastered the key practices, your written output will still have to be revised. This seems obvious. Yet it can be dispiriting when you submit what you think is a fine, already much revised piece of work and it comes back requiring yet more revision, and probably, you can be sure, further revisions after that. This is a process that goes on for months and years.

The long-drawn-out nature of the thesis writing process may also be a factor. Writers may feel that there is no end in sight. They may feel that far too much attention is paid to the quality of their writing; surely it is the quality and originality of the work that matters?

It may seem that writing is too much centre-stage, too much of the time. Why is so much attention given to the strategies and qualities of academic writing? Are we not guilty of over-complicating what is essentially a reporting procedure?

Is 'guilt' a factor inhibiting blocked writers? Do they feel that they should have 'more to show', in writing, for the weeks, months or years of their work to date? Many writers – in fact, almost all that I have worked with – report that they experience guilt as part of the writing process. Even when they have met their writing target, they feel that they have not done enough. Even more interesting: even those who have exceeded their targets can feel guilt that they have not done enough writing. This is a fascinatingly common occurrence.

What does it say about writers? Is this only true for novice writers? Is it only true for thesis writers? Will this feeling 'go away' once you become a successful, regularly published writer? Possibly.

What does this guilt say about writing itself? That closure is deferred, we know. That writing is potentially endless, we know. We also know how to 'get something down on paper'. There are strategies for that in the earlier chapters of this book. Supervisors will have other ideas about how to 'unblock'. Is it that writing is challenging us on so many fronts, revealing to us what we do and do not know, what we are and are not certain of, what we are and are not 'allowed' to say in academic writing? Academic writing brings what may feel like tight constraints – rather than a useful, usable framework – and these too can block writing.

Perhaps guilt and writing are associated because we are endlessly positioned as 'not quite there yet', not quite good enough, when writing a thesis. It can feel as if failure is almost part of the process: we have failed to 'pass' every time we write. Progressively, over the months and years, we may not feel that we are getting nearer and nearer to achieving the goal; we may feel quite the opposite: who are we, having been informed of our weaknesses, to persist in trying to write this thing? We may feel that we are being positioned – or have positioned ourselves – as the upstarts, resolutely ignoring our supervisors' – and others' – account of our faults. In fact, we do not know if our work is good enough yet, and still we persist in writing, as we must. Our wilful 'offence' is to continue to produce what must be excellent work in partial or complete ignorance of our ability to produce it. Paradoxically, and often painfully, this ignorance increases, for some, the further along the thesis writing road they go.

At the end of the day, and long before the end of the thesis 'road', the writer will have to persevere with guilt-edged writing. This sounds like advice to 'pull yourself together', but an active starting point to solving the problem of writer's block would be to discard some of the myths that surround writing and to accept that it is very difficult. In unexpected ways it connects with other areas of our lives and our identity. Perhaps this is why it is – or can be – such a growth experience. It helps to have a forum where we can be as honest as we like about how bad writing feels and about how bad we feel about our writing: 'Writing is torture and, practically speaking, impossible' (Bénabou 1996: xi). Bénabou, it seems, 'experiences literature like an affliction, from within, so that it becomes his only reality, and an unlivable one at that' (p. xiii). Would any of the analyses and answers in this section alleviate his condition? Is writing sometimes 'torture' for all writers, or just for Bénabou? Is he simply using the device of overstatement for effect, to get our attention, as he does with the title of his book?

While 'torture' suggests violence, perhaps 'tortuous' is a more accurate term for thesis writing: it is full of twists and turns, with no predictable pattern. For all the frameworks and structuring devices offered in this book, there is no way to predict an individual's tortuous route to writing a thesis.

There is no direct route, only the circuitous, devious path, where no two branches go the same way. It does not even seem to move in one direction. For a writer aiming at one destination, perhaps 'torture' is the right word after all.

This is not to say that we should form support groups for writers, so that they can unburden themselves of their frustrations and complain about constraints; rather, we should reposition writing in our lives. It is bound to affect our moods, feelings and thoughts.

What is it that makes writing stop? What makes it 'unlivable'? How can we make it 'livable'? Have we internalized teachers and editors who made writing 'torture'? Do we have unproductive practices? Can writing be transformed into a creative and enjoyable process? Can we change our practices?

Our experiences of writing – and of writing instruction – are bound to have influenced how we see and do writing now. That may be part of the problem and therein may lie the solution. In discussion – and this could be a writing activity too – people reveal the power wielded by one English teacher's red pen. Some can even remember their teachers' names.

On the other hand, is it our perception of that teacher that holds us back? Are we doing it to ourselves? We can block our own writing by focusing on the negative – even if well-intentioned – feedback we received in the past, as if it were bound to apply in the present:

> Our minds are powerful instruments. When we decide that something is true or beyond our reach, it's very difficult to pierce through this self-created hurdle. When we argue for our position, it's nearly impossible. Suppose, for example, you tell yourself, 'I can't write'. You'll look for examples to prove your position. You'll remember your poor essays in high school, or recall how awkward you felt the last time you sat down to write a letter. You'll fill your head with limitations that will frighten you from trying. In order to become a writer or anything else, the first step is to silence your greatest critic – you.
>
> (Carlson 1997: 119)

Can we revise that perception and create a new internal editor? Whatever our analysis of the causes of writer's block, we still have to find ways through or round it.

The next section gives suggestions and directions for moving through the block. Some involve writing; others involve graphical alternatives to writing. Both approaches could be – or could produce – topics for discussion.

Strategies for unblocking

- Freewriting
- Generative writing
- Writing with supervisor
- Mind-mapping
- Verbal rehearsal
- 'Write down all you know about X'
  'Write down all your ideas on X'
- Construct a sense of an ending; visualize the completed thesis
- No single therapy for unblocking, say free writing, works well in isolation, especially in the long run . . . a gradual combination of treatments works best in terms of inducing a lasting and comfortable level of fluency.

(Boice 1994: 100)

Each of these strategies can help you to start writing again by writing something. Writing anything might be a good enough start. We know that freewriting, for example, has the potential to silence our internal editor and many writers find that it does help them write something. Even freewriting about the writing block produces text. Similarly, generative writing can force us to engage with a topic and push it a little bit further, although even consolidating a point already made might be a start.

The key may be to move on. Rather than sticking with the writing already done and revised, we can move on to the next topic, even though we know we have not, in any sense, 'completed' the writing of previous sections. Rather than sticking at the point at which we are stuck, in other words, we can move on.

This is where the sequence of writing to prompts, followed by freewriting, followed by generative writing, followed by structured writing, may prove most useful. While in the early stages this sequence of activities can help us to work out our ideas as we go, at later stages, as we make the mistake of thinking we know where we are going, we may benefit from what might seem to be regressing to these start-up strategies. We can use them to kick-start writing at any stage in the process. Ironically, as we become more sure of the direction of our writing we may forget to do so.

Joan Bolker (1998) specializes in helping blocked writers and approaches the problem from three angles: preventive strategies, counselling, and strategies for overcoming writer's block. She encourages people to 'write scared': 'You can ask yourself what scares you so much; try writing down the answer, and pay attention to what you've written' (p. 93). Rather than trying to overcome our fear of writing, she argues, we should work to write in spite of it. The fear may not completely go away in any case, no matter how much and how well we write. Even when the thesis is finished, passed and published we may still feel fear of writing.

Some of Bolker's 'Funky Exercises for Times When You're Stuck' are similar to activities and practices covered in this book. In fact, they are well-established techniques given a little 'funky' spin. She directs us to try five preventive strategies (pp. 96–8):

Preventive strategies

- Become so addicted to writing that you get withdrawal symptoms when you don't write.
- Finish today's writing session by defining tomorrow's.
- Do writing before everything else.
- Don't worry about done or undone writing.
- Gather together all the writing you've done and notice how much there is.

'Transforming' writing blocks is another way of looking at what we might previously have seen as a problem. Palumbo (2000) argues that we can transform our psychological blocks to 'release the writer within'. What this actually means, as his argument progresses, is that we have to transform ourselves in order to write. We can, he argues, transform ourselves through writing. Obviously, if we do not like this idea, or think that it is a bit inflated – some would dismiss it as very 'American' – then we are unlikely to be willing or able to solve writing blocks in this way or to recognize where the cause lies in our current practice. We could probably agree, however, that no one and nothing is responsible for our own blocks but ourselves.

When we hit writer's block, Palumbo directs us to make a change, any change:

> Writing begets writing. If you're stuck on a difficult scene [or chapter], write it anyway. Write it badly, obviously, burdened with clichés. Write it in verse . . . Writing begets more just as worrying begets more worrying. Obsessing begets more obsessing. Pacing back and forth begets more – . . . writing doesn't just beget writing. It also begets – and reinforces – the reality that you can write. That way pages will accumulate.
>
> (Palumbo 2000: 35–6)

If we are blocked it may be that we are, in fact, doing something wrong. If we make a change, and reflect on our reactions to and the effects of that change, then we are likely to move through the block. The change prompts a necessary stock taking of our writing. By 'spring cleaning' (Palumbo 2000: 113) we may be able to change our practice. If we do not make any changes, we may remain stuck, actually stuck, not just feeling stuck.

The sheer accumulation of pages will, of course, not immediately satisfy many supervisors or students, as a concept. As a set of behaviours, however, accumulating pages will go down well with the supervisor and will change the mind set of the writer. So there may, in fact, be a point to 'bad writing' – to answer the query of more than one student.

It is yet another myth of academic writing that only students write badly, that only those who get blocked write very little: 'Believe me, we've all written manure' (Palumbo 2000: 37). It should be encouraging to thesis writers to know that we have all been there. We have all written pieces we were not happy with. We have all written for the sake of writing, in order to see if we could get to better – or more – writing. We will all do so again. We will not find it any less painful next time it happens. We may even surprise ourselves – until it becomes routine – by having to think all this through again.

The problem is that this 'manure' writing is kept secret from novice writers for so long that they think it is just them. Everyone else knows the secret of fragrant writing. In part, that may well be true: there are lots of secrets and, when they eventually find out what they are, many people choose not to share them. This does affect our writing. All the more reason to have a supportive peer group and, if possible, mentor. Use your network to support you. If you do not have a peer, mentor or network to turn to when writing gets unbearable and blocked, then that is your first indication of something that you can – and I would argue should – change. It is – surely – no secret that the biggest secret is the power of contacts and networks to facilitate and rebrand our writing as successful.

These explanations will not silence all self-doubt: what I refer to as the 'quality question' will pop up again: 'What is the point of doing bad writing?' Have we not agreed – and is it not obvious by now – that quality is what matters? However, Palumbo (2000), quoting Ben Hecht, raises the question of whether quality output requires a different – and even more difficult – writing process: 'It takes just as much effort to make a toilet seat as it does a castle window; only the view is different' (p. 189). Writing a thesis is hard, but is it necessarily harder than writing other things? Self-doubt may just be another feature of the writing process that we will have to accept. This may mean reviewing our image of ourselves as writers: 'What you believe about yourself in relation to writing can affect your writing productivity either positively or negatively' (Hiemstra and Brier 1994: 59). Hiemstra and Brier describe physical, psychological, environmental and cognitive causes of writer's block. Boice (1994) similarly brings together different types of triggers: 'self-handicapping . . . shyness, choking under pressure, learned helplessness, and ineffective bargaining strategies' (p. 241).

The underlying theme in my analysis is that blocked writers have, in some sense, created their own cage. The underlying theme in the proposed solutions is that the writers have to see, and use, writing differently. They have to set their sights on the primary goal of unblocking – *using* writing – first and foremost. They have to shift their position, from being blocked writers, stuck, standing on their blocks while everyone else has sprinted towards the finish line, to being writers on the starting blocks, but going at their own pace, not sprinting but strolling. Thesis writing is not, after all, a sprint; it is a marathon.

Incremental writing

It may be that problems with writing stem from our internalized 'binge' bias: because we see writing as requiring large chunks of time, consequently we set large goals for those large timeframes. Yet the large goals remain too big and, usually, too ill-defined to be feasible and manageable. An alternative would be to see our writing as a series of smaller, more defined tasks, performed in smaller chunks of time. Incremental writing is a term I coined to describe the process of establishing stages and tasks as increments in the writing process. Its purpose is to help thesis writers to take control of their writing:

- Set yourself binge and snack writing sessions.
- Define increments in your writing.
- Allocate tasks from your outline to time slots in your diary.

There is no mystique about this; most people know that unless something is planned and, for some, literally, in a diary, then it does not exist in real time. What does turn out to be different is the allocation of writing task to particular time slots (not just deadlines) and then monitoring your progress to assess whether or not you are setting realistic increments.

Writing binges

Having laid down so many warnings about using a 'binge' approach to writing, it may seem odd to find it here, as if it were in itself a strategy. I used to argue very strongly for the 'snack' method, until so many writers, in so many groups, at so many universities (and other institutions) put their case for 'binge' writing: it seems that there will always be people who say 'I can *only* do my best work in large chunks of time.' There must, therefore, be something so deeply ingrained, and possibly effective, about the concept and practice of 'binge' writing that we should displace it altogether. My current position in the 'binge–snack' debate is that both modes have their uses, and that we should, strategically and tactically, use both. Throughout this book I therefore argue for a combined binge-and-snack method for writing the thesis.

Having said that, it is my contention that the binge should not be open-ended. One example of effective use of the binge strategy is in the run-up to a deadline, when we use an imminent deadline to force the focus on, and in, writing. Those who regularly have large chunks of time, like postgraduate students, should be looking around for a few alternative strategies. Waiting till the submission deadline is clearly not an option.

There may be others ways in which you have used the binge mode, perhaps allocating an extended period of uninterrupted time to start and complete a piece of writing. This, according to writers who favour the binge mode, gives you time to really get into the 'flow' of writing and, if that time is, in fact, uninterrupted, then you get plenty of writing done.

The question is, how often is this mode possible? How often has it actually been possible? How many times have you started and completed a writing project in this way? Do productive, successful writers in your discipline write this way?

As you study, and develop, your writing practices, you need to start noting how you actually manage your writing process. It may also be important to concede that strategies that worked for short assignments might not work for the extended process of thesis writing, unless you break that extended process up into specific writing tasks, which perhaps brings us closer to the concept of 'snack' writing?

The key feature that 'snack' writing can bring to your writing is the process of defining your writing tasks, perhaps in more detail than you do when you have large amounts of time. This in turn can enhance your motivation. You might think that all of those who enrol for higher degrees will have plenty of motivation, all of the time, but many report that motivation has its peaks and troughs. In order to continually progress your writing, it might help to link your motivation to your writing, which takes us back to the research quoted at the start of this chapter: 'Motivation comes most reliably in the wake of regular involvement' (Boice 1994: 236).

Combining 'binge' and 'snack' modes can build a productive writing process, and you clearly need to be productive to sustain your writing as you develop your understanding and manage your research. 'Binge' writing works best when you have a clear mental picture of what you want to write, either in the form of a graphical representation or a detailed outline. This helps you to see the connections between your ideas or points as you write. Writing in that way, and writing regularly, you will find that your writing is focused and fluent. In other words, both binge and snack modes can be combined with the other strategies covered in this book and other strategies that you will learn from other writers.

Developing a writing strategy

Until you get to the point where you have an effective writing strategy, you have to try a range of different strategies. Ultimately, most thesis writers and researchers report that they want to be able to write better and more easily. How you achieve this might be by writing regularly and in different modes:

- Do regular freewriting, generative writing and/or writing to prompts
- Do a detailed outline before you start
- Alternative short and long bursts of writing
- Use each mode of writing for a specific purpose.

The last point means that you have to decide what the purpose of each writing session is:

1 Are you doing a writing warm-up, doing structured writing, writing to develop your thinking or what?
2 What is the purpose of your text? What point do you intend to make?
3 Design your writing slot accordingly.

Unless you do this, the whole process may seem quite chaotic – or at least 'organic' – and the different writing activities will seem pointless. In addition, there will be cycles of feedback and iterations of revisions that are constantly moving your research and your thesis forward. You have to build these into your own writing process.

You can start to programme these writing activities into real time. Chapter 8 covers the whole process of writing and revising a thesis in a very limited amount of time, but it is possible, and perhaps preferable, to give yourself more time.

This chapter has explored the process of becoming a serial writer, with writing chapters being one set of tasks in your series. The section on writer's block was intended to help you overcome any one of a number of barriers, so that you could keep moving forward in your writing. The next chapter goes a step further: it explores how you can pull all your chapters together.

Checklist

Becoming a serial writer

- Write regularly.
- Measure your actual output: count/calculate the number of words/ pages you write per hour/week.
- Plan and give a work-in-progress presentation.
- Plan and write chapters of your thesis.
- Structure your writing 'binges'.
- If you get blocked, try strategies for unblocking.
- Submit conference abstract.
- Set yourself writing tasks: define form, content, length of time, number of words, before you start.
- Continue freewriting to develop your ideas and build confidence.

6

Creating closure

What is closure?

> *What does it add up to? What was the most important or central thing in it? Make it add up to something.*
>
> (Elbow 1973: 20)

Closure means limiting, shutting off, confining. In writing this requires you to develop a principle of selection: what are you going to develop in your thesis and what are you going to discard (or leave till later)?

Closure brings with it the end of debate: you have to take a stand and argue for it, arguing against other views and arguing for the exclusions you make.

A metaphor for this – and the two words are related – is the clot. The blood circulates freely through the system until it meets a clot. The blood may have been thickening for some time, restricting flow, but the clot stops flow completely. Similarly, in the thesis process ideas flow freely and even the writing can usefully be free of structure at many stages. However, there is a need to block the free flow and design an endpoint to the thesis or a part of the thesis. Like a clot, closure can be dissolved. Like a time plan, it will be revised in light of events and feedback.

This metaphor brings with it appropriate undertones of pressure, tension, pain and anxiety. This is often the hardest part of the whole intellectual exercise. Many writers avoid creating closure because they are anxious about the reader's response or because they still have not sorted out their central argument, though they may not be consciously aware of their anxiety and its cause. Others rationalize their failure to create closure by claiming creativity; they argue that it is reductive to create closure. There may also be a group of writers who do not know how to create closure.

However, it is important to rehearse closure, as it is one of the ultimate goals of writing a thesis. At the end of the day, the thesis will have to have closure and the chapters will all have to move coherently towards one ending. Each chapter will have its own form of closure. Thus it might be a good idea to practise creating closure in early drafts.

Closure is an invention; the writer has to create it. Note Elbow's emphasis on 'Make' in the quotation that opens this chapter. In research, closure may mean something quite specific:

- Achieving the aims of the study
- Delivering a result
- Integrating new and existing research and theory.

Many other definitions of closure are available. These will not all seem relevant at this time. However, even those that do not seem relevant can be useful prompts for writing towards closure, i.e. they may help writers to find closure. Writing to one of these prompts may force the creation of closure through writing.

In any case, these examples illustrate the type of prompt that is needed to argue that some closure has been achieved. While there are many variations, think about how you will demonstrate closure. As you read, note which words and phrases signal closure in general and in your discipline specifically:

Signalling closure

- Narrative structure holds the whole together.
- Each chapter answers a question and progresses the thesis argument.
- Explicit links to research aims/questions show progression through the thesis.

Closure in the thesis has to be about *showing* that you have completed a phase in your study, arguing that what you have done represents a form of closure:

- Showing that you have achieved something you set out to do
- Showing that you have begun to achieve something

- Persuading the reader that you have done so
- Demonstrating your understanding of the limits of your achievement.

The key, as always, is in defining closure in a way that suits what you have done. In reality, however, the thinking and writing tasks are negotiations between what you have done and what you think you can do with it. There is a series of such negotiations to come. Closure can seem to be deferred by these seemingly endless negotiations, yet the active search for closure is the next step.

Interim closure

Some writers may feel that closure is only really realized in the very final stages of thesis writing. In a sense this is true; the whole argument of the thesis must hold together. The approach of the deadlines may also be a factor in prompting closure. For this reason many writers are more comfortable with the term interim closure.

It is therefore your job to define what closure means for parts of your study or thesis. What research tasks or steps have you completed? What writing have you done? Above all, how have you moved forward conceptually? How far have you moved towards your conclusions? What do you – speculatively – think your ultimate conclusions will sound like?

This is, in other words, not something to defer to the end of the thesis process. You can begin to think about what closure might mean for each stage or each chapter. Interim closure is a term designed to help you make tentative decisions about what constitutes closure:

- Finishing a chapter
- Writing a work-in-progress report
- Meeting a deadline.

All of these forms of closure are, of course, contingent on feedback from your supervisor(s). Even when you strenuously and clearly articulate a definition of interim closure, they are likely to ask you to revise further. Supervisors sometimes forget that their requests for constant revisions may be preventing you from creating closure. They always seem to want you to add more, when your ultimate word length is finite. If this happens, you should try to get your supervisor to help you edit and cut, as well as add.

This may or may not change the operational definition of closure. If the feedback seems to require a huge change in your definition – i.e. if a complete reworking of the study is called for – then you have to think about two questions: (1) Is my definition of closure wrong? (2) Is the requested revision too large in scope?

In fact, you may begin to see your writing as a series of 'little closures', as you define the scale and scope of pieces of writing earlier in the writing process. Bringing a bit more definition to these early stages makes the writing, clearly, less undefined, less unpredictable, less stressful. There are fewer structural decisions, for example, along the way.

At this point, someone usually asks the question: what about creativity? This question implies that structuring somehow cuts out the creative element in the writing process. Nothing could be further from the truth. In practice, you are likely to test your outline structure – however detailed your outline or plan – and even to deviate from it at every opportunity. The trick to effective writing is to have a way to get yourself back on course. In other words, you will continue to be aware of options and new ideas as they occur to you. These will not evaporate because you have an outline or structure. This is still a 'creative' process.

Having said that, there does seem to many writers, particularly those who are starting to write, to be a tension between closure and creativity. The extended period of time available to the thesis writer intensifies this.

Inherent in closure is the idea and practice of limiting, enclosing, shutting down. For writing, this means limiting the topics in some way, developing a principle of selection or prioritization and filtering out the ideas that you are not going to develop in your thesis. One way of making yourself let go is to think of how you can use your spin-off ideas elsewhere later.

Don't put it off any longer

It is important to take stock: which writing strategies have worked? Which have failed? Which have proved productive? Is there a case for revising the thrust of the thesis? Are there barriers to writing? What impact has feedback had on writing? Are you looking for different kinds of feedback at this stage – or not? It is important to continue to discuss writing products and processes with both supervisor and peers.

You should be using this chapter to turn a significant corner in your thesis writing process: creating closure in a part of your work so far does not necessarily mean finalizing a chapter, but bringing to completion a phase of work or a piece of writing. There is also an important question about the 'big picture': how does one element of closure affect the whole study and thesis?

There is also closure in process: you move on to other parts of the thesis and can start using the techniques (covered in Chapters 1 to 5) of sketching, free-writing, outlining, drafting and redrafting now.

These strategies can also help you to stop procrastinating. Many writers, in different professions, have found that freewriting and generative writing, combined with outlining, help them to get started on a writing task sooner. They no longer avoid writing, but start immediately by 'getting something down on paper'. This, they find, makes writing much less stressful, much less a 'last minute' and 'night before the deadline' ordeal.

Research journal

You can rehearse closure – in many forms and variations – in a research journal. The journal can also help you to track, looking back, the development of your ideas; you can see that you have moved forward in your thinking. This 'history' of your thesis may in itself be part of the thesis. In some disciplines you can build a thesis around this record. In others, it may function more as a space for inventing closure.

- Why would you keep a research journal?
- How will it help you with your writing?
- Is it simply more writing practice?
- Or is there more to it than that?
- Do you know anyone in your area who keeps a research journal?

Here you can begin to use the writing prompts. As you find out about the ground rules and the environment for postgraduate study and research, you can write about your ideas and uncertainties. Most importantly, you can write about your developing ideas about your study. While there are so many external agencies, potentially shaping your work, you can pull your study back into shape through regular reflective writing. You can refocus your thinking through regular writing in a research journal.

Writing a research journal lets you write without shaping what you write to meet the expectations of your audience. The more you write for your journal, the more possible that becomes. You can free yourself from your audience, from the to-ing and fro-ing in style and structure to suit them that never really seems to satisfy them anyway:

> The thing that rather gets me down is that when I write something that is tough and fast and full of mayhem and murder, I get panned for being tough and fast and full of mayhem and murder, and then when I try to tone down a bit and develop the mental and emotional side of a situation, I get panned for leaving out what I was panned for putting in the first time. The reader expects thus and thus of Chandler because he did it before, but when he did it before he was informed that it might have been much better if he hadn't. However all this is rather vain now. From now

on, if I make mistakes, as no doubt I shall, they will not be made in a futile attempt to avoid making mistakes.

(Hiney and MacShane 2000: 30–1)

The research journal can stop you from making this mistake, of moving away from what you want to say because you want to please your audience. It can help you to overcome your fear of making mistakes.

The research journal can help you to work out shifts in gear from early writing to later writing. This is not to say that you will forget to write in the standard academic ways, but that you will have more than one location for writing. Nor will you be liberated from the expectations of your audiences; there will still be many, many revisions, in light of their comments.

If you have more than one supervisor you might find it particularly useful to keep a record of their feedback and to use the journal to bring what might be quite similar or quite different – at different stages – points into some kind of alignment that lets you move forward. There are students who find that their two supervisors do not always 'sing from the same hymn sheet'; in that case, it is down to the student to take the initiative in resolving the situation and the research journal is a good way of doing this.

The Chandler quotation, however, is intended to make the point that you can go overboard in trying to meet your audience's expectations. This can be particularly damaging for thesis writers if they are still in the early stages. You are unlikely, at that stage, to satisfy yourself with your own writing, let alone expect it to satisfy anyone else.

What will you write about? Exactly what you write about may depend on how you define the purpose of your journal, but that need not be exclusive. You can use it to track developments in the research and the thesis, or you can use it for other, quite separate purposes:

Purposes of a research journal

- Systematic written record of research and writing
- A day book or diary of the project
- Structured or semi-structured reflective writing
- Random thoughts
- Mechanism for learning
- Some combination of these

The purposes can be summed up in one phrase Moon (1999) uses in describing her own practices: the journal helps us to write through the process of 'thinking on paper in one place' (p. 119). She lists the following as potential subjects for a day book:

Contents of a research journal

- Meeting notes
- Records
- 'To do'
- 'Thoughts'
- Contacts and references
- Networking list and notes

Although Moon (1999) lists eleven ways in which we can use journal writing for learning (p. 31), the key questions for thesis writers might be more focused on their output:

1 How will the journal support my writing?
2 How will it help me write chapters?

You can use journal writing to develop your voice and to develop a style that lets you write with the appropriate amount of authority about your ideas. You can experiment with styles.

What can I write about in my journal? Meeting with supervisor

- What happened?
- What was said?
- What did I think about during the meeting?
- What did I feel during it?
- What do I think and feel now?

These questions can help you develop your thinking about an important dimension of your thesis writing process. Writing about them in this way – describing what occurred and what you feel about it – are key processes in learning from the event (Bolton 2001). You can use a split page layout, as illustrated on page 187, to separate these two types of thoughts.

Regular writing about your subject can help you to learn about your subject. Some would say it can transform your thinking. Jenny Moon (1999) endorses Flynn (1986) making exactly this point as follows:

Pedagogical structures which encourage students to read and write in stages also encourage them to transform their perceptions of texts which, in turn, may encourage them to transform their perceptions of their worlds and of themselves.

(Flynn 1986: 213)

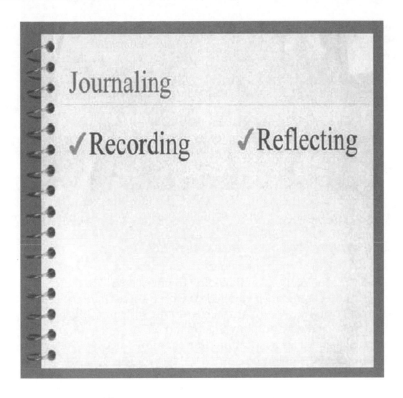

It is surely to be expected that writing a thesis will 'transform' you, but 'writing in stages' in your journal captures a different kind of effect. If you only write for the thesis, then you will only produce a certain kind of writing and, potentially, only experience a certain range of 'perceptions' of your subject and yourself. If you write in a journal, you will have a clearer idea of the shift from one stage to another, from exploratory to consolidating, for example.

This process of journaling at different stages is outlined by Moon (1999). In her description of how journaling helped her to write her book she illustrates how the journal performs different functions – and how its form may adapt to suit – at different stages:

> The origins of [my project journal] were in the notes about learning journals that began to accumulate around the time that the publishing proposal was submitted. The notes were on A5 . . . paper for portability and ring bound. Fairly soon after that I slotted in dividers for each proposed chapter heading so that stray thoughts could be entered in an appropriate 'home'. Sometimes I would focus on a particular chapter and do a personal 'brainstorm', often during some form of exercise session at the end of an evening of writing. This meant that the notes for the

chapters built up and the chapter-headed sections became the location also for writing planning notes and listing the literature to which I wanted to refer.

(Moon 1999: 118)

The sequence outlined here breaks the writing process down into stages that suit the writer's developing understanding of what he or she wants to write; i.e. the stage of writing suits the stage of thinking. In fact, the journal appears to be an engine for the development of ideas and the production of writing. The developmental power of journal writing seems to be that we can move from 'thinking on paper in one place' to thinking on paper with a way of putting our ideas in the right place. Once the idea has found its home in a chapter – even though we know it might subsequently be moved – we can relax and get on with writing about it.

The sequence involves many interacting steps:

1 starting with the proposal and moving to notes, bound together, then
2 setting chapter boundaries, filing ideas within these chapters, then
3 focused brainstorming on a chapter, with the underpinning structure bind-ing old notes and new thinking together, then
4 using the chapter files as 'locations' for planning, then
5 linking back to the literature.

This is the reverse of the 'let's master the literature and then work out what we want to do' mode. Instead, the writer develops his or her own ideas and then consults the literature for support. It is not a million miles away from the process of building up a thesis in stages.

Certainly, this may be more difficult – or impossible – for thesis writers who do not yet have the depth of knowledge and understanding that Moon must have had when she began to develop her proposal. However, her description does show the value of the journal mode in helping the writer to keep track of many different ideas and levels of thinking.

All of these points about the research journal – the theory and the practice – are potential topics for discussion with supervisors. As you struggle to achieve what Moon has suggested is possible, as your 'stages' become confused, you may feel that you want to abandon the 'Use it as an excuse for writing' strategy in favour of face-to-face contact with someone who can advise. In fact, if you do reach that point, perhaps you should ask for direction, rather than just advice.

On the other hand, if you find that your research journal is proving a great success, that is another potential talking point with your supervisor(s). You can look back on your progress, over a period of weeks or months, and see the development of an idea. This will help them to see that you are making pro-gress. It can also give them an opportunity to help you calibrate – or adjust –

your thinking and writing, if they think you are straying from the parameters of your study.

Your research journal can help you demonstrate your thinking process in, for example, the selection of research method or approach. Do not underestimate the importance of all those little notes about why you decided to write the letter to participants in your study with exactly that wording, or why you chose to send a focus group summary in that form, or why you are focusing on one text to the exclusion of another. All of these notes are rehearsals and records of important – if small – decisions in your research process. Some – perhaps all – of these should be included in your thesis.

There will, therefore, be draft material for the thesis in your research journal. This is why it is important to write down such fleeting thoughts; they influence decisions down the line. Recovering the rationale for these decisions at a later stage will be more laborious if you do not have some form of record. Save yourself some time; write it down.

The research journal provides a way of managing the parallel tasks that writing involves. It holds them together while you are developing your understanding and your ideas. The journal is at once the engine of ideas, a record of decisions and a store of fragments of future drafts. Since it does not directly create chapters, it may also work as a filter, helping you find your way in all your material. As Moon's account shows, the journal helps the writer move from journal to chapter.

If you start a research journal now, in the early stages, you might find that it serves several useful functions. Later, it might tail off, as you have less need for it, or as its supporting role gives way to the thesis itself. At that point, of course, you may want to use your research journal to jot down other ideas, such as possible topics for research bids, publications or questions at the viva.

It is your responsibility as a thesis writer to find a way to write, to be proactive in initiating these processes, to study your own practices and adapt them until you have writing habits you can rely on.

Lest we forget, since it has not yet been said, writing in these ways, in a research journal, can be fun. It can keep you in touch with who you are and why you are doing this research in the first place. It can help you to maintain your enthusiasm for your subject and for your writing.

Many professional development programmes now require – or advise – some form of portfolio, often involving a diary exercise, or some written account of work and development. They may also be required reading for the annual review panel – you need to check that. By keeping a journal you will be practising a process that could well be required of you at a later stage, by which time you will have worked out many of the practices that work in theory and work for you.

There are many uses of journals – in different forms – and many publications on the subject, such as *Personal Journaling*, and websites. There are extended uses, beyond the thesis writing process – though some would argue directly relevant to it. Some see it as a form of therapy, at no cost; others as a tool for reviewing how we think and act:

> Our lives are abundant with observations and events that have meaning for us, that when closely examined reveal to us who we are and what we truly value. We need to take the time to ask key questions so that the answers, in the form of specific details, can come readily to mind . . . If memories are the stuff our lives are made of, we should feel free to work with them consciously and creatively . . . We construct our lives through our actions and decisions, but also in the act of telling. More than we may know, we shape the circumstances of our lives into stories.
>
> (Tiberio 2000: 44)

Such articles suggest specific 'directed questions' that we might ask ourselves, questions that can be readily adapted to the thesis writer's context:

1 This is the story I would tell of how I came to do this research . . .
2 I would describe my writing process as . . .
3 I have been influenced by . . .
4 I like/hate it when my supervisor says . . .
5 My favourite writing moment was when . . .

Such accounts and narrations can help us sift through issues. They can produce a form of problem solving. A student may find, in writing about a writing problem, that isolation, rather than the writing itself, is the problem.

We can wrestle, through writing, with complexity. There may be a therapeutic effect of writing it all down, dumping it rather than analysing it. Opening up. Perhaps expressing our feelings – about the research or about anything – in full, for the first time. Moving on. It may be valuable writing practice. Once writing is started, any of these outcomes may occur, whether or not they were the intended outcomes.

Writing habits

When I face the desolate impossibility of writing five hundred pages a sick sense of failure falls on me and I know I can never do it. This happens every time. Then gradually I write one page and then another. One day's work is all I can permit myself to contemplate and I eliminate the possibility of ever finishing.

(Steinbeck 1962: 26–7)

I always begin at the ending . . . [Writers] know more about their books when

they begin them than they think they know. If a writer can't see the end, I can't
imagine how he can feel purposeful enough to begin.

(John Irving, quoted in Rekulak 2001: no page numbers)

John Steinbeck, a professional writer, clearly managed to overcome his recurring sense of failure by disregarding the endpoint. This may seem counter-
intuitive; surely we need to work towards a goal? We all know the power of
deadlines, and what happens to writing when there are not deadlines. (Tasks
that do have deadlines get done before those that don't.) Yet, what is interesting about Steinbeck's point – apart from the curiosity that a person who knew
so much success in his writing should have such a sense of failure in the
process – is that he finds a way to continue in spite of the feeling of failure. The
feeling, which he knew would recur, 'every time', is not allowed to stop him
writing. The feeling did not convince him that he would fail. For him, it was
another part of the process. He acknowledged it as such and learned to live
with it.

John Irving's way is completely the opposite: he has to know what the
ultimate goal is, where the 'destination' of his writing is, otherwise he is lost.
He explains that there is an intuitive sense of structure and continuity that will
keep us going towards the ending, once that has been fixed. This is an interesting reminder for us to rely on our brains to make sensible connections as we go
along. In the midst of writing we can discover (or should that be 'create'?)
unpredictable connections that will ultimately make sense.

The contrast between these two modes is clearly a point worth thinking
about: we have preferences for how we like to write. We have concepts about
how we think writing 'should be' done. At the start of a major piece of writing,
like a thesis, we can see it as a mountain, full of little molehills. We have to
have ways of writing through those moments – and they may be longer than
moments – when we lose sight of the purpose or of the prospect of ever
finishing.

Our understanding of how we write best clearly shapes and/or is shaped by
how we actually write. Our writing habits are directly connected to our
assumptions about writing and our experiences of it. It may be time – at the
start of a new, long writing project, to widen your range of options:

> If you have trouble writing every day, it helps to set a schedule . . . most
> authors have pretty regular work habits. Tennessee Williams and Ernest
> Hemingway began their work at dawn . . . James Baldwin started writing
> when everyone in his house went to sleep . . . Mary Gordon writes from
> 5:30 every morning until 8:00, when the rest of her family awakens . . .
> David Sedaris . . . only writes at night . . .
>
> (Rekulak 2001)

All of the writers mentioned in this quotation, for all that their practices differ,
share certain features in their writing:

- Clarity about what works for them
- Solitude
- Back-up tactics for when that fails.

> Set aside one hour every day to spend at your desk. Honor the appoint-
> ment no matter what; if the ideas aren't flowing, just try one of the other
> exercises in this book. After just three or four weeks, you should find that
> your imagination is 'primed' and ready to work when you arrive at your
> desk – and you'll be in the habit to start writing immediately.
>
> (Rekulak 2001: no page numbers)

Whatever your preference, be ready to do the opposite: if you are the kind of
person who works best when you have a goal, then you will have to submit
yourself, at some points, to floundering and to reconstructing well-laid plans
in the course of long complex processes; conversely, if you are the kind of
person who does not enjoy being driven by goals, or just does not see the point
of them, you will have to submit, at some points, to a series of deadlines and
milestones that may seem, to you, like millstones.

- Writing regularly
- In different forms
- Appropriate to the point that your thinking and research are at
- Structuring this variation over time, as a process

You can see writing problems as challenges that you can overcome, or just part
of the regular difficulty and even discomfort inherent in writing.

Halfway point

For some students the halfway point in the writing of your thesis may not
coincide with the halfway point in the three years. It may, for example, arise at
the end of your second year. By this point you are more likely to have drafts of
chapters, which you now have to revise and pull together into one unified
whole.

The idea of the halfway point in thesis writing is in itself a construction. You
may not feel or think that you are halfway towards completion, but that may
be because you have not yet conceptualized the second 'half'. If what you have
done so far is to be considered as halfway, rather than panicking or seeing
your output as inadequate, recast your plan of work and writing. At some point
soon you will, in any case, have to plan to do what you can in the time you
have.

How can the work done be seen as halfway to completion? This is a writing task. It is all very well to conceptualize – and reconceptualize – your research and writing, but we know that you have to write for the writing to develop (Torrance et al. 1993).

How can this be convincingly written up? Start with a few freewriting exercises: try and see your work from a number of points of view. Write about how you might streamline your research and writing. Think about where you can trim topics, without losing impact or coherence.

All of this – your progress and your plans – has to be discussed with your supervisor(s). You need to get a cue from them about how you will use the second half of your thesis process to finish it.

Now, or soon, you have to force yourself to think about moving from pilot chapters to draft chapters. One way of doing this is to take the initiative and define for yourself what you think you want your thesis to look like. You can define its characteristics and qualities. Unless you do this it will be difficult to progress your writing to the next stage.

> I could point to six criteria which determined the selection of . . . themes
> . . . First, I had to remember that I was working from a reasonably tight
> overall theme . . . Second, . . . there had to be scope to research them . . .
> Third, they had to be 'balanced'. Fourth, they had to be interesting. By this
> I mean that they had to provide a new slant on the existing theory, some-
> thing that would make the final document a useful resource for other
> researchers in the area. Fifth, they had to reflect issues of élite power . . .
> Sixth, I wanted there to be scope in each [chapter] to express both a
> temporal dimension – a notion of change – and a spatial dimension . . .
> (McNeill 1998: 246)

Note this writer's use of the central theme as the starting point. Then he lists six characteristics of his thesis-in-progress, while making decisions about the form of the whole thesis and of individual chapters. He also decides what he does not want to do. Whether or not you have the same criteria for your thesis, it is this kind of thinking that you need to do now, if you have not started this already. What are the criteria? What do you want to say? What is your theme? What type of writing do you want to avoid?

Note that these criteria help the writer make a selection of 'themes'. This is a crucial stage. You need to find some principle of selection for all the material, all the writing, all the plans for writing that you have been gathering over the past few months or years.

A writing exercise, beginning with the questions listed above, or using the terms that McNeill uses, or your version of them, would be a start in your decision-making process. This point in your thesis writing will only really be a 'watershed' if you make it one.

Brown's eight questions

This section describes a tool that writers find useful for outlining a piece of work. Some find that it helps them to write the summary or abstract of a paper. This involves 'writing in advance', i.e. writing when you are not quite sure of how the study will progress and conclude. It requires thinking ahead to likely, or desired, outcomes, as well as documenting the work that has been done. The trick is to connect the two in a coherent way: the work done and the work still to be done.

For those who have found it difficult to write much up to this point this approach can be used to 'jump start' the thesis. It helps the thesis writer to think about the work as a whole, including the gaps. This is a different form of writing from simply documenting work done. This is less reporting and more creatively exploring avenues down which the thesis might go.

It is crucial at this point – or at some earlier or later point, as suits you the writer – to change gear, to step back from the study and think about the story that you will tell about it. We know that a key theme is 'originality', for example; that is a constant that must be worked into your thesis somehow.

Writing at this stage is about shaping your ideas, information and intuition into a coherent whole. This shaping can be initiated by Brown's eight questions. The article on which this section draws is available at:

http://www.literaticlub.co.uk/writing/articles/write.html

Robert Brown's (1994/95) short paper focuses on action learning:

> The dream of all authors and editors is to be able to receive a steady stream of articles that are perfect to go to print just as received. The bad news is that it is just a dream. The good news is that a process called action learning can help bring the dream a little closer to reality.
>
> (Brown 1994/95: 1–8)

In the course of this short article he gives eight questions for summarizing a piece of research. Over the past eight or nine years I have introduced this to writers as a device for generating the summary or abstract of a paper they intend to write for scholarly publication. It is my experience that writers find these questions useful for outlining their work, even at a very early stage in the project. For those who are at an early stage in the research process or unsure as to where it is going, answering these questions requires a bit of imagination, projection or speculation. These should, of course, occur within the boundaries of logic and feasibility. For others, the questions are a method of generating a summary of their work so far. These questions are, therefore, designed to be used in this context, as a tool for sketching and outlining.

While they do not at first glance seem to suit all disciplines – a point that has been made many times – these questions can, nevertheless, be extremely helpful in focusing the writing. For example, writers in the humanities, social sciences, etc. find the mention of 'results' alien. They generally assume that this word refers to experimental studies. They recognize the language of research in science and engineering. However, another way of looking at this is to own up to producing some kind of 'result' in your own thesis: surely some kind of analysis is being conducted and surely some kind of established method or approach is being used in this analysis? The questions are, in fact, very difficult, requiring a fair amount of thought.

Naturally, the output will be the subject of at least one discussion with the supervisor. It may be worth noting that supervisors may not have come across this paper and are quite likely not to be using this approach for the 'shaping' stage in thesis writing. What this means is that you may have to argue the case for this task with your supervisor(s), as they will almost definitely challenge you on it, whether or not you find it a useful exercise. That is their role: to check that you have a good reason for what you are doing.

Some supervisors may think this is a bad idea: they may see it as prompting you to speculate rather than derive from what you have done. Again, you may have to argue your case. Or you may have to make the link between the stage that your work is at now and the whole story – of the thesis – that you have started to shape. This is the key point: that you have used Brown's questions (or some other device) to begin to shape the thesis; it is by no means taking its final shape as yet. This is, as with many other aspects of the writing process, just the first of many iterative steps.

It is tempting to adapt the questions to suit your subject, thesis or article. It proves more useful to adapt what you are writing about to Brown's questions. They are deceptively simple: all very short, monosyllabic, requiring short answers.

Your thesis

1 Who are the intended readers? (List 3–5 names)
2 What did you do? (50 words)
3 Why did you do it? (50 words)
4 What happened? (50 words)
5 What do the results mean in theory? (50 words)
6 What do the results mean in practice? (50 words)
7 What is the key benefit for readers? (25 words)
8 What remains unresolved? (No word limit)

This technique can be used more than once. As you progressively home in on your thesis – the whole story – you can repeat this exercise as a way of creating or checking the coherence of all the parts. It can become a device for calibrating the different elements in your complex story. It can be a touchstone for the key points. Finally, it can help you see the 'big picture' when you are engrossed in detail.

You may find it useful, in later iterations, to write your own questions, but to keep the approach of writing fifty words on each. The beauty of this is that it is easily done; the hard part is thinking it through and persisting through several drafts. As with any other successful technique, it is probably a good idea to try it as it stands and to vary it to suit later.

The power of it is that it makes us think in 'research' terms; i.e. we may not have done empirical research, but we will have to think in terms of a systematic method of analysis and will have to give an account of the 'results' of that analysis, and measure these against the aims of the research, whatever our discipline and subject area. Brown's questions, therefore, help us make an important shift from the work we are engaged in to how it can become a piece of research.

Finally, these questions can be used at a later stage to structure the abstract, or summary, of the thesis. In fact, some writers find that they can write the abstract in one draft using Brown's questions. In other words, this approach can be used not only to reveal the central argument, but also to *discover* it.

Pulling it all together

Here is a series of writing tasks that students find useful for pulling the whole thing together:

Writing activity

1 Draft an outline of your thesis – all chapters.
2 Draft an introduction to your thesis.
3 Redraft your chapter outline in light of this introduction.
4 Redraft the introduction.

These writing activities help because they force you to focus on the big picture, the whole structure. It is not a waste of your time to revise at this structural level; in fact, it will make the writing much easier.

Don't begin to write until you are 99.99% happy with your outline. You may, at first, be shocked by the suggestion that you should use 60% of your total project time to make the outline, 10% to convert it to prose, and

30% to revise. If you use 90% of the time to make a really superb outline, you will have little more work to do!

(Reif-Lehrer 2000)

Your first draft will be more focused. You will have fewer – or smaller – structural revisions to do. The style of your writing may even become clearer, as you become more confident about what you want to write, thanks to all the work you have done checking and revising your outline. Where you might – quite rightly – have questioned the above percentages at an earlier stage in your thesis writing, their sense and utility should be clearer now, at this stage.

A design for writing

You can take this approach even further. You know the maximum and minimum word lengths for a thesis in your department or university. You can allocate a word limit to each of your chapters. You can spend a higher percentage of your time – between 60 per cent and 90 per cent? – on outlining. The knock-on effect of this will be that you spend less time (for a period of between one and two weeks?) on writing paragraphs and sentences.

The output of this type of outlining should be a *very* detailed plan of your whole thesis:

Chapter 1 [title]	total words
Section 1 [title]	number of words
Section 2	
Section 3	
Section 4	

Some sections may be more detailed than others. You may want to ask your supervisor to help you plan them. You will, in any case, be looking for his or her feedback on your thesis design.

You can then design your writing process: allocate time slots for each task; note your progress towards your total word counts.

Frustration

Even as you are successfully crafting closure out of your work, there will be frustrating phases along the way. There are many causes of frustration in such an extended project:

- Iteration
- Ambiguity
- Change in status: becoming unacknowledged expert
- Getting bogged down.

The deferment of the production of the final text of your thesis may be frustrating, and you would not be the first new thesis writer to judge that your thesis was almost finished when there was still extensive work to be done.

One antidote to this frustration is presenting at conferences. This is where your thinking, research and, to some extent, writing can be tested. This can help you to get a sense of how you are progressing, since abstracts submitted to the conference are peer reviewed. You will also receive feedback on your work from peers and established experts attending your session at the conference. Of course, that feedback could create tensions between your re-conceptualization of your progress and your supervisor's conception, but this in itself can be an important student–supervisor conversation, one where you translate your 'frustration' into a focused discussion of your progress. In fact, you may have numerous discussions on this topic, but at a certain point – and only you and your supervisor can judge when – your discussion must focus on the distance between where you are at in your writing and what might constitute final closure, i.e. completion of your thesis. Your frustration may intensify as you recognize that your clear view of closure has to be revised, perhaps serially, perhaps throughout the lifetime of the project.

The definition of closure appropriate for your thesis may be dependent on methodological issues and processes, or it may depend on one step in your analysis or on your results. Even in well-designed research, this can be difficult to anticipate, and being ready to refine your definition of closure may be a helpful and fruitful approach.

Writing conclusions

In many theses, in many disciplines, the case for closure is made in the conclusion to the thesis. This is where you have to make the case for the sufficiency of your research as a 'contribution' to knowledge, or in some other sense.

When thesis writers come to draft this important chapter, they often produce writing that resembles a literature review. They foreground published research and background their own, when the reverse is what is needed: foreground your own work, by putting it first, then contextualize your work, making it explicit how you have added to the field, by mentioning links with and distinctions from the published work of others. Nor do you need to provide additional commentary on or critique of the literature – you will have done that in your literature review chapter. All that is needed in your conclusion is a clear statement of how your work relates to that of others.

Foregrounding your work

- To what extent did you achieve the aims of your study?
- Does it make sense to have a section for each aim?
- State research outcomes, drawing on earlier chapters, using the same terms.
- Start each section with a paragraph on each outcome.
- Follow this with a paragraph linking your work to the literature.
- Set an appropriate word limit: 3,000, 5,000 or 8,000 words? Or?
- Write the introduction: say what you will do in your conclusion, and why.

Another change in style that features in thesis conclusions is the use of the past tense. While you may have used both past and present tenses in previous chapters, in your conclusion you are writing about work that is completed, in the past. Using the present tense, as some thesis writers do when they draft this chapter, creates the impression that the work is ongoing. Even interpretations you made of your analysis or results – in any sense – can now appear in the past tense, since all aims, actions and interpretations are themselves the subject of a final interpretation in your conclusion.

What you have to be most careful about, at this stage in the thesis, is not to go beyond what you can evidence. In some disciplines, there may virtually be a prescribed template that you can use to prevent you overstating your results; in others, it is relatively easy to say what you think the implications of your research are before you have fully made the case for your contribution. For example, it is not unusual for a thesis writer, in a draft conclusion, to overstate an interpretation or to appear to over-generalize:

> *The 'over-generalizing present tense'*
> Each participant has its own individual characteristics in the system.
> *Revision*
> **This suggests that** each participant has its own individual characteristics in the system.

In this revision, the stated interpretation remains the same, but prefacing it with 'This suggests that' makes it clear that the statement is not a generalization about all cases – unless that is what you want to write – but an interpretation, resulting from analysis. An alternative is to add one word to the beginning of your sentences: 'Perhaps . . .'. This will radically alter the claim you make in the sentence.

Thus, when you are drafting or revising your own conclusion, you can avoid overstating or over-generalizing by signalling exactly what type of statement you are making at any given point in the chapter:

> This suggests that . . .
> One interpretation of this is . . .
> The interpretation that was made of this . . .

Look out for other symptoms of overstatement. These are terms you have to be sure are accurate. Assume that the external examiner will take them literally, or, rather, will assume that you intend them to be taken literally:

> This suggests that X is **central** to the understanding of . . .

While it is important, in a thesis conclusion, to state that you have, for example, established the role played by a factor in the mechanism of effect, you can only make that claim if you can evidence it: you have to have already shown, in an earlier chapter, that the factor 'is', or 'was', in your study or experiment, genuinely 'central' to the effect or to our understanding of the phenomenon.

If these expressions seem to you to be inappropriate or inelegant, adapt them to suit, or find your own ways to signal the final 'interpretation of your interpretations'. In fact, a thesis conclusion is not the best place to continue the process of interpretation. You should, instead, be summing up and setting your interpretations against your original aims and background literature. Of course, the question of how contested your conclusions are will affect the length, scope and complexity of your conclusion, but you should still set limits to this chapter, and, if your conclusions are controversial, then make your discussion of 'contested' or 'controversial' interpretations explicit.

It can also be useful to state explicitly what you are not arguing: 'This is not to say that . . .'. 'This cannot be taken as an indication of . . .'. 'This is not to suggest that'. This is another way of defining what you are claiming.

It is worth restating here that 'contribution' is the main criterion for the doctorate and, to a lesser extent, for masters and other research projects, where you still have to specify whether or not you have added to existing knowledge, to what extent and in what way. This is as much a test of what you know as any other part of the thesis, in the sense that you can only claim you have made a contribution if you know your field very well.

Defining contribution

- You have made a contribution – say so.
- If you use another term – not 'contribution' – define it carefully.
- What exactly is your contribution?
- In what sense can it be considered a contribution?
- To what extent, and in which contexts, can it be considered a contribution?
- On what reasonable and informed grounds might that claim be challenged?
- What is your response to that challenge?

Each of these can be subjects for writing in a conclusion chapter. It is, of course, up to you to check the appropriateness and/or relevance of each one to your thesis.

By all means draw out the 'implications' of your research, but be careful to make a strong, explicit case for contribution first:

- 'This research shows/reveals/confirms/adds/explains . . .'
- So what? State how this constitutes a 'contribution'.
- If your thesis is for a doctorate, use the word 'contribution'.
- Anticipate refutation and argue against it: 'Some would argue that . . . should have been . . .'. 'However, . . .'

A good strategy is to force yourself to start your paragraphs with 'This research shows . . .', or a variation on that, so as to foreground your contribution. This will emphasize that a contribution has been made and will make it easier for your external examiner to find your contribution.

You can strengthen your claim to contribution by stating the limitations of your claim and revealing any limitations in the design of your study. Expressions like 'In hindsight . . .' can signal that you would do things differently next time, that you are aware of weaknesses, if there are any, and there usually are, and that you know how you would avoid them in future. This is not to say that you have not made a contribution, but you might have to spell that out: in what way does the stated limitation not undermine your findings/analysis? What can you still show, on the basis of the research you did?

Some students think that they have to be categorical in their writing at this stage, in order to make a strong claim for contribution, but that may be a mistake. In fact, you can further strengthen your argument by internalizing the debate in your conclusion:

- 'Some will argue that . . .'

- 'One interpretation could be that . . .'
- 'However, this could also be taken as . . .'
- 'Alternatively, it could be an effect of . . .'
- 'This is not to say that . . .'
- 'Possible interpretations include . . .'.

Writing in this way shows that your work is still open to interpretation, and that your interpretation is one of many possible interpretations. The key point is that you acknowledge that research is open to interpretation and that you are taking responsibility for your own reading of your research. In some disciplines, this may seem to be labouring the point, but it is still your responsibility to show that you can see your work from different perspectives. What precisely that means for your discipline, and for your thesis, is for you to establish.

It is possible to overcomplicate things at this stage. Your research is completed. Even if it is still ongoing, you know roughly when and at what point, in terms of achieving your research aims, it is going to be completed. This means that the subject of your writing is much more delimited. Taking that a step further, you can, and some would argue should, match your 'aim' and your 'claim': to what extent did you achieve what you set out to achieve?

- Plan a section of your conclusion for each aim
- Establish word limits for each: all the same/different?
- Use the same words in aims/objectives for your conclusion sub-headings
- Were any aims discarded, revised, replaced? Use new terms?

When you have finally drafted your conclusion chapter, and when you have received feedback from your supervisor, you may have new revisions to do:

- Draft conclusion chapter
- Feedback-revision cycles
- Revise all chapter introductions to match.

A variation in thesis format has emerged recently that might be appropriate in your discipline and for your thesis. Looking at examples of completed, successful theses in different disciplines, I have noticed the use of a section called 'Structure of the thesis' or 'Summary of the thesis':

Structure of the thesis

- Why? – shows the structure of the whole as a whole. Of immense value to external examiners, helping them to find their way around your thesis. This is not a repeat of your abstract. The abstract shows the logical structure of the whole argument; the summary shows what's in the chapters and clarifies how they hang together, why some are short and others long, what type of sequence they are in and, in a word or two, why. In this way, it signposts the thesis argument and shows linkage.
- What? – can be 500–1,000 words, or 2–4 pages. Sentences can begin, 'Chapter one outlines . . .', 'Chapter two describes . . .'. Placed at the end of the introduction.
- How? – in words or in a one-page diagram. This works very well to show groupings of chapters: for example, if Chapters 3, 4 and 5 are all related, or similar in kind, you can display them as three boxes arranged horizontally, while all the other chapters are displayed in boxes arranged vertically on the page. Can be a handy point of reference for your external examiner.

This chapter provided strategies for pulling your thesis together. However 'interim' the resulting closure might be, you have made progress. The element of frustration that ends this phase may become even more acute as you move into the constant-revising phase of the thesis writing process. The next chapter aims to help you focus on what you have to do to polish your text to the point that it is not perfect, but acceptable: a key distinction.

Checklist

Creating closure

- Start a research journal.
- Rehearse central themes.
- Review your research journal for a central argument.
- Use Brown's eight questions to reveal/discover your central argument.
- Ask your supervisor to help you edit, cut and find closure.
- If you have not already signed up to present at a conference, do so now.

7

Fear and loathing: revising

Why 'fear and loathing?' • Repetition • Forecasting • Signalling • Signposting • Conceptualizing and reconceptualizing • Managing your editor • End of the second phase • Look back to the proposal • Checklist: revising

> *Anyone moderately familiar with the rigours of composition will not need to be told the story in detail; how he wrote and it seemed good; read it and it seemed vile; corrected and tore up; cut out; put in; was in ecstasy; in despair; had his good nights and bad mornings; snatched at ideas and lost them . . . now cried; now laughed; vacillated between this style and that; . . . and could not decide whether he was the divinest genius or the greatest fool in the world.*
>
> (Woolf [1928] 1993: 57–8)

This chapter focuses on revising processes, defining techniques and illustrating them with examples. The question of quality is addressed: how can the argument of the thesis be strengthened at the sentence and paragraph levels? Do the introductions and conclusions perform their 'signalling' function effectively? The key point here is that at the end of the second stage of thesis writing there are specific writing standards to be met. One of them, as indicated in the previous chapter, is creating closure. A key aim of revision is to reveal closure and, perhaps, through constant revisions, to discover previously obscured closure. Whether your research is just beginning to bear fruit at this stage, or whether you have completed most of your research, the trick is to keep the regular writing – and revising – going at the same time.

Why 'fear and loathing?'

That's him pushing the stone up the hill, the jerk.
I call it a stone – it's nearer the size of a kirk.
When he first started out, it just used to irk,
but now it incenses me, and him, the absolute berk.
I could do something vicious to him with a dirk.

Think of the perks, he says.
What use is a perk, I shriek,
when you haven't the time to pop open a cork
or go for so much as a walk in the park?
> ('Mrs Sisyphus', in Duffy 1999: 21)

Sisyphus . . . a king of Corinth, whose punishment in Hades was to roll
a heavy stone up a hill; as he reached the top, the stone rolled down
again . . . **Sisyphean** . . . fruitless toil . . . endless and ineffective.
> (*Shorter Oxford English Dictionary*)

Like Sisyphus, repeatedly rolling his rock up a hill for no apparent purpose,
only to roll it up again after it has duly rolled back down to the bottom of the
hill, you may feel that this is the most futile and frustrating phase of thesis
writing. You may feel that the revisions are so minute and the additions so
repetitive that they leave your latest draft very little improved on your previous draft. You may even come to loathe your own writing – and perhaps your
own study – now that it has become so familiar to you. This can be seen as a
part of the process of 'letting go'. You will soon want to be rid of your thesis.
The trick is to persevere with your revisions – and your supervisor's revisions –
until your thesis is adequate. You may find that this 'loathing' transfers to
your supervisor, or to yourself. Watch out for that. The best way of looking at
revisions is to see it as good practice – and possibly good training – for dealing
with editors and publishers.

There are many revising techniques. The ones that are covered here are
repetition, forecasting, signalling and signposting. These are the techniques
that signal connections to your main line of argument and remind you to
make more explicit the structure of your thesis and your chapters.

Repetition is particularly useful when key words are repeated, letting readers
see the connection between the section of text they are reading and your main
argument. Forecasting involves giving readers a 'menu' of what is to come.
Signalling means making links explicit. Signposting means letting readers
know where they are at any point – or at key points – in your thesis.

Revision is one of the tasks that writers dislike most. The aim of this
chapter is to identify key revision tasks. If the outlining stage has been done

well, and if introductory paragraphs have been written for each chapter, then the first full draft is likely to be more focused in any case. The revisions outlined in this chapter will help you to reveal the structure you have designed into your writing, but perhaps not yet expressed clearly enough in your draft.

Repetition

Repetition is built into the writing process, in the sense of going over the same ground again and again. The writer has to refine the text repeatedly, so that meaning and emphasis lose their potential ambiguity.

Repetition also has a role in written argument. Its purpose is to emphasize, to approach a topic from a different angle, for clarification or as a linking device. It can also be powerful rhetorically, moving the reader through a complex and perhaps contested area step by step, perhaps even making the contentious seem familiar.

This need not be word-for-word repetition (of yourself), but can be through synonyms, paraphrase, summary, pronouns and other forms, as you build up your argument point by point.

At a later stage, you may find that the writing is laboured and does seem too repetitive. You may feel that some of it needs to be cut, but it could be a waste of time and energy to try and anticipate that moment. Since it duly arrives in its own time, as you learn more about your subject and as you develop the focus of your thesis, in every chapter, it may not even be possible to predict how you will see your writing at that later stage. Repeating yourself is part of the process of academic writing.

Repetition has a real purpose as a linking device. It shows readers that you are still talking about the same subject. It helps them make connections – as you intend them to be made – between sections of your writing, between paragraphs or sentences. There is a certain amount of repetition in the process of outlining – in an introduction – what you are going to say in a chapter. You then develop your points in much more detail.

Repetition is also part of research methods: a result or outcome has to be repeatable if it is to be judged reliable. You may have to repeat observations, analyses or reflections whose repetition simply makes your point. You may, as part of your thesis, incorporate such repetition in order to strengthen your argument. This may be true for a wide range of studies, not just the experimental or 'scientific' ones.

At some points in academic writing, repeating the point seems to be the point. For many writers, this goes against the grain. Surely 'original' work should not be described in repetitive writing? However, you have to be careful that in the course of trying to find a different way of 'saying the same thing' you do not corrupt the point you want to make, or the point that your research shows it is legitimate to make.

Note the use of repetition to orchestrate a complex argument:

> Unfortunately, however, there is another **side** to Bosola, the **side** that cannot shake his age's allegiance to the concept of inherited position. This **side** of Bosola pays allegiance to the Cardinal and Ferdinand ... [my emphasis].
>
> (Selzer 1981: 75)

The word 'side' is used to show that (1) further definition follows and (2) that the second sentence is still dealing with the same point. Repetition creates unity in a text and strengthens conclusions. It is not in and of itself a 'bad thing'.

Forecasting

This is a quality of good writing: letting readers know in advance what you are going to do in the text that follows – and why – and, sometimes, what you are not going to do – and why not.

It is like giving someone a menu before their meal. Normally this would let them choose. However, for a thesis the menu gives readers an overview, along with your rationale, letting them see the whole chapter, for example, as a whole. They may choose not to agree with you, but they can see your rationale for your argument and can see, in advance, where you are going to take it. This technique maps the route through the chapter for readers, allowing them to get a grasp of what you are trying to do, rather than trying to put it all together as they go along. They cannot read your mind. If they get lost, they may well see this as your fault, not theirs.

Some writers think this is a bit constraining on them as writers and a bit patronizing on their readers. They would rather build up gradually, and logically, to their main point in the conclusion. That is what conclusions are there for, they argue. Moreover, expert readers do not need to be led by the hand in this way. They can find their own route through a mass of complex material. In fact, the writing will seem more impressive if it appears complex or difficult. This is an alternative structure for your argument.

However, I am not in complete agreement with the position rehearsed in the previous paragraph: it is too risky. Will expert readers attribute their difficulty finding their way through your text to their growing understanding of your fabulous work, or will they attribute it to your lack of writing ability? I think the latter is more likely, but you have to decide for yourself. It is another talking point for writing-oriented discussions with supervisors.

Forecasting can be in the form of a list of bullet points, like a mini-table of contents for each chapter, or it can be written as one sentence:

> I nevertheless believe that a fresh approach to the play – an approach that **investigates** the conflict between merit and degree – can contribute to a resolution of these issues. Indeed, an assessment of Webster's treatment of the tension between merit and degree not only helps to **vindicate** the Duchess's action, to **explain** the actions of Ferdinand and Bosola, and to **justify** the play's final act, but it also **establishes** Webster's play as an unblinking assertion of the primacy of personal worth over inherited position [my emphasis].
>
> (Selzer 1981: 70)

Note how the verbs not only forecast the main line of the argument – 'investigates' – but also the stages in the argument to be made in each section – 'vindicate . . . explain . . . justify . . . establishes'. This forecast tells us exactly where the argument is going and what its main point is.

Signalling

Signalling, in this context, means revealing the plan, showing the links, directing the readers' attention and thinking by the words you use. It is not enough to have constructed a fine logical plan for your writing; it must be revealed for the readers. You mark out clearly what the relationship is between the text they are reading and the ongoing 'story' of the whole thesis. Signals are there to give notice that a connection is about to be made, to warn readers that a complex section is about to start and that a shift is about to occur in the kind of information they will have to absorb.

Signalling can be achieved in one sentence, such as a transitional sentence that shows the shift from one point to another:

> The issue of the Duchess's guilt in marrying Antonio has been **debated** at length. On the one hand, Clifford Leech accuses the Duchess of . . . Muriel C. Bradbrook agrees . . . James L. Calderwood . . . condemns her marriage because . . . **On the other hand, the Duchess has not been without her champions** [my emphasis].
>
> (Selzer 1981: 70)

Note how the word 'debated' signals the structure of the paragraph that follows, while the sentence 'On the other hand . . .' performs the function of moving from one side of the debate to the other. It could be argued that this sentence has no other function; it is a transitional sentence. The author has clearly signalled where the scholars reviewed stand in this debate.

Signposting

> [Examiners] appreciate work which is logically presented, focused, succinct, summarised and in which signposts are used to help readers understand the path they are taking through the work.
>
> (Johnston 1997: 345)

This explicit reference to 'signposts' underlines why these techniques are so important: they make your writing reader-friendly. Signposting serves a similar purpose to signalling, pointing out to readers where they are at any point in the thesis. The purpose is to reassure the reader that they are still on the right path, that you – and they – have not deviated from the original path.

Headings, sub-headings and the opening words of topic sentences are useful as signposts. For example, the headings in this chapter are designed to take the reader through an emotional barrier to the specific strategies they can use: 'Fear and loathing . . . Repetition . . . Forecasting . . . Signalling . . . Signposting'. Topic sentences signpost to the reader what type of information is to come, as in the following paragraph, which signals a conclusion to this section by beginning 'All of these devices . . .'.

All of these devices have the effect of reassuring readers not only that they are following the gist of your argument but also of your ability to construct a coherent argument. It may seem like laying bare the bones of your story, but if the anatomy of your thesis is sound, then all the more reason for revealing it, rather than just hoping that readers will discover it as they go along.

While you may feel that your writing is clear enough as it is, it would do no harm to use these techniques in your revisions. How many times will your external examiner read your thesis? How long will he or she have to work out how it all fits together? How hard do you want to make him or her work to find the links and your central argument?

Conceptualizing and reconceptualizing

> *When you write a story, you're telling yourself the story . . . When you rewrite, your main job is taking out all the things that are not the story.*
>
> (King 2000: 56)

When you revise, you are, indeed, looking to create a new kind of unity in your writing. This may mean that you see it yourself for the first time; or it may mean that you have to cut, in order to reveal the main point.

For example, revisions that appear to be about clarification may, in fact, make you reconceptualize. The following paragraph could be revised to improve clarity.

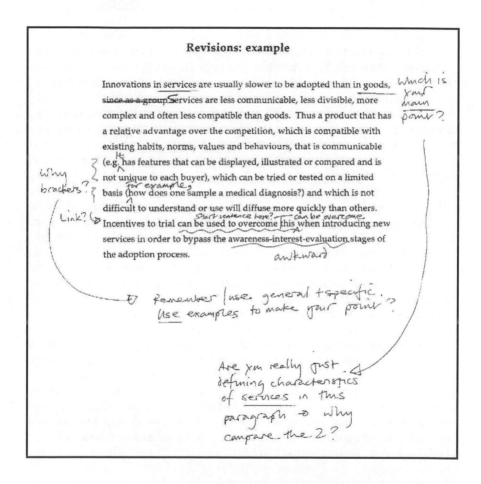

Revisions: example

Innovations in services are usually slower to be adopted than in goods, ~~since as a group~~ Services are less communicable, less divisible, more complex and often less compatible than goods. Thus a product that has a relative advantage over the competition, which is compatible with existing habits, norms, values and behaviours, that is communicable (e.g. has features that can be displayed, illustrated or compared and is not unique to each buyer), which can be tried or tested on a limited basis (how does one sample a medical diagnosis?) and which is not difficult to understand or use will diffuse more quickly than others. Incentives to trial can be used to overcome this when introducing new services in order to bypass the awareness-interest-evaluation stages of the adoption process.

Handwritten annotations:
- Which is your main point?
- why brackets?
- Link?
- For example,
- Start sentence here? — can be overcome
- awkward
- 1) Remember / use. general + specific. Use examples to make your point?
- Are you really just defining characteristics of services in this paragraph → why compare the 2?

The supervisor's comments indicate where the writer could clarify by:

1 Stating what the main point is in the first sentence. As it stands, there could be two possible main points.
2 Unpacking a point or two, such as the complexity of services.
3 Using the examples to make the point clearer, rather than 'hiding' the specifics in brackets.

4 Using repetition of the key terms – goods and services – to show links between sentences and the development of the point.

This would result in a clearer paragraph:

Innovations in services are usually slower to be adopted than in goods. Services are less communicable, less divisible, more complex and often less compatible. Thus goods that have a relative advantage over the competition, which are compatible with existing habits, norms, values and behaviours, that are communicable will diffuse more quickly. For example, they will have features that can be displayed, illustrated or compared, are not unique to each buyer and can be tried or tested on a limited basis. Services are more complex. For example, how does one sample a medical diagnosis? The barriers to adoption of services, however, can be overcome by incentives to trial.

However, a third revision could focus on services and begin to explore their complexity.

Innovations in services are usually slow to be adopted. However, if they can be made more compatible with existing habits, norms, values and behaviours that are communicable they will diffuse more quickly. Perhaps there could be an emphasis on features that can be displayed, illustrated or compared, that are not unique to each buyer and can be tried or tested on a limited basis. If services can be presented in this way, barriers to adoption can be overcome. One way of doing this is through incentives to trial.

To be perfectly honest, I have no idea whether or not this revision would stand up to scholarly scrutiny. My point is that the writing can be improved in certain specific ways. In fact, it could be improved further by, for example, making this one paragraph into two: one on goods and one on services. If the comparison was important, it might become more detailed. A third paragraph, pointing out the main differences, or the implications of differences, or making some other point that is important to the thesis argument at this stage, could be added. To demonstrate all of the possible revisions would be to take the point too far for the purposes of this chapter. However, it is important to recognize that this text could go through dozens of revisions until both writer and reader were happy with it. The final revision involved a potential reconceptualization of this stage in the argument and, perhaps, of the thinking behind this part of the thesis.

Managing your editor

The purpose of this section is to link the supervisor to the writing process. At this stage, the role of the supervisor is key.

The title of this section should not be taken to mean that the role of supervisors is to 'edit' their students' writing. Is it, in any case, editing that you want? Is it editing that they think they should be doing? Some supervisors see it as their role, covertly or overtly, to ensure the quality of written English is perfect; others see that as the student's responsibility. Most students would agree that there is more to giving feedback on writing than editing. Most students are looking for feedback on the content of the writing.

Receiving feedback may be a new skill that thesis writers have to learn:

> Data were gathered from 45 doctoral students through focus groups, observations, and written and oral reflections to ascertain their perceptions of a specific teaching process ... which was designed to assist these students in learning how to do academic writing. It was found that preparing and receiving critiques from professors and peers was perceived to be the most influential element in helping them to understand the process of scholarly writing and in producing a better written product. More specifically, these students believed that two factors integral to the critiquing process were responsible for building their confidence as academic writers: personalized face-to-face feedback; and the iterative or ongoing nature of the critiques they received.
>
> (Caffarella and Barnett 2000: 39)

Doctoral students themselves are the sources of data in this study. The words 'learning how to do academic writing' suggest that even they have to learn to receive feedback. Critiques – both given and received – are an important part of the learning process. The emphasis in critiques should be on making the writing better. Although this may not always seem to be the goal, thesis writers have to work hard to use critiques in that way. Analysing the types of critique you regularly – or intermittently – receive can be a way of developing your understanding of how writing is improved over many drafts, in the important iterative process. It can thereby also build confidence, as your understanding of the qualities of good academic writing grows. Feedback itself may become a seemingly endless and tedious, but crucial, iterative process, as your refine your argument.

Note how Caffarella and Barnett's abstract ends; it's not all easy. Managing your editor involves managing yourself:

In addition, these students emphasized that although the critiquing process was powerful and useful, it was also highly emotional and at times frustrating. The findings suggest that . . . instructors should be very clear about the purposes and benefits of a strong and sustained critiquing process, and assist students in learning how to both receive and give useful feedback.

(Caffarella and Barnett 2000: 39)

Do not be surprised if you have emotional responses to feedback, from supervisors or from peers. For you to deal with it you have to acknowledge that it may happen. Otherwise, it may interfere with your ability to receive feedback and with your supervisor's or peer's ability to give you feedback. Some problems might be avoided if you set ground rules.

The key to 'managing editors' is to remind them – every time you give them a written piece – what it is that they are reading. Starting a text with a statement of the rhetorical context is, in any case, good practice. For supervisors it helps them to focus on: (1) what you have done, rather than what you have not done; and (2) the feedback you are looking for on this draft. You can specify the kind of critique you need at this stage. Spell this out on a cover page:

Cover page for submitting writing to supervisors

- Date, draft number, word count
- Purpose of the writing
- How you have acted on their previous feedback

If you have discussed this with your supervisor(s) in advance you are more likely to get the critique you need, as long as they feel that it is appropriate to give it.

Managing your 'editor' may be about ego management – if that needs to be done, then that will be one of your tasks. Alternatively, it may just be good communication, helping your supervisors to focus when they sit down to read your writing. Moreover, if your supervisors are not specialists in exactly your area, you may have to work harder to keep them involved, informed and, perhaps, motivated.

A typology of supervisors' comments is something that any student can draw up, after a few months or years of experience of being supervised. Here are some examples, which may, or may not, help thesis writers to interpret the feedback they get from their supervisors and, for that matter, from any readers:

Towards a typology of comments on thesis writing

Argument	e.g. 'I think you have overstated this point.'
	e.g. 'You need to comment on the quote/table/graph.'
Clarity	e.g. 'The issue was raised that, for some, . . .'.
	Comment: 'For whom was the issue raised?'
	e.g. 'The final area . . . highlighted the need for . . .'.
	Comment: 'Area of what?'
Develop	Encouraging you to take your point further, say more.
Discuss	e.g. 'When we meet, can you tell me about . . . ?'
Distinguish	e.g. observation, analysis, commentary and summary.
	Often overlap in drafts. Signal more clearly which it is; signal
	shift between one and the other.
Expand	Important point; develop it.
Mechanics	Punctuation, grammar, spelling, correct style.
Praise	Of style, content, argument, paragraph structure, etc.
Probe	'Are you sure . . . ?'
	'Have you taken this too far . . . ?'
	'Don't you think you should . . . ?'
	'Do you have evidence for this . . . ?'
Prompt	e.g. 'What do you think this means?'
	'How does this relate to the work of X?'
Role switch	e.g. 'I'm not sure about . . .'. 'Can you remind me if . . . ?'
	Handing over the baton: student becoming the expert.
Style	e.g. 'Is that the right word?' 'Is that what you mean?'

If you – or your supervisors – find these completely, or moderately, irrelevant, then does that imply that you are using some other set of comments? Do you – and/or they – have another emerging typology? Is that explicit? Is it implicit? Underlying any comments is a rationale about the roles of writer and supervisor in the exchange of writing. It would be interesting to explore that rationale in discussion. In fact, if the rationale for your supervisor's comments is not explicitly discussed, how will you know what it is? How will you know when it changes? Will you be able to 'read' your supervisor's rationales as they evolve? Or will it be more constant than that?

The answers to these questions lie in discussions between you and your supervisors. The typology of comments can be a starting point. You and your supervisors can compare this typology with theirs: where do they differ, where do they overlap? Why?

End of the second phase

This is a marker in real time – perhaps the end of the second year, full-time – but in 'thesis time' is a construction, invented by the thesis writers, a point that you will have to construct for yourself. On the one hand, time is marching on, running out and – you may feel – leaving you behind. On the other, you have to invent a moment of closure, a sense of achievement of certain writing goals and a sense of direction as you look to the final phase of your work and writing.

This a good time to submit an abstract for a conference that will take place after your viva. (This assumes that you have a target date for submission.) Why? The conference will provide a useful – though perhaps still 'loathsome' – link with other researchers and can provide feedback. It is also a chance to network.

If you have not done so already, this is also a good time to think about who your external examiner will be. Get him or her signed up, approved and confirmed by the university administration well in advance. This is something to discuss with your supervisor as you move into the third and final phase of your thesis writing.

Look back to the proposal

The depressing thing about the revision stages is that you may have a full first draft but feel that you have it all to do over again. It is like snakes and ladders: you make so much progress up the ladders, only to slide back down the snake again. Some thesis writers even have to go all the way back to their proposal for a new starting point. Others have to rewrite their review of literature from scratch.

This could be a writing task for this stage:

Writing activity

- Produce a new detailed outline of your thesis in 10,000 words.
- This may take you eight to ten weeks, but it will let you revise your chapters with the new focus in mind.
- This will help you see more easily where you have to cut and where you have to expand.

None of this should be seen as a disaster; you have been using writing to learn and to develop your thinking. You have not lost your way. You are not starting over. It has not been time wasted.

You have also gleaned extensive feedback from your supervisor, and perhaps from many other experts. This is why focusing on your own goals is important at this stage. You should begin to think about how much – or how little – you have to do to finish. The next chapter demonstrates a fast-track route to the finish line. If you have already completed a fair amount of writing, then you can pick and choose the elements that suit you best. If you have done very little writing, and are needing to accelerate, urgently, then you may want to work through Chapter 8 step by step.

Checklist

Revising

- Forecasting for the thesis: check that you have referred to all your chapters in your introduction to your thesis.
- Forecasting for chapters: check that you have referred to all the sections, and/or the overall structure, in all your chapter introductions.
- Signalling: add explicit signals for the development of your argument.
- Signposting: make it impossible for your readers to lose their way while reading your text.

8

It is never too late to start

This chapter is an accurate representation of the process. I would strongly advise that supervisors and students read this chapter first, then dip into other chapters.

(Completed PhD, now university lecturer)

Ten steps to fast-track thesis writing

Step 1 Take stock
Step 2 Start writing
Step 3 Outline your thesis
Step 4 Make up a programme of writing
Step 5 Communicate with your supervisor(s)
Step 6 Outline each chapter
Step 7 Write regularly
Step 8 Revise
Step 9 Pull it all together
Step 10 Do final tasks

The aim of this chapter is to help writers who are starting the last phase of their research, but have not yet written much – or any – of their thesis. This approach is not for everyone, as it is highly intensive for writers and supervisors.

However, it will suit some writers perfectly. In fact, some may find that this is their preferred mode. Some may even find it exhilarating, as they watch the pile of pages grow, building momentum in their writing and recognizing the elements of a coherent story in their work. It need not just be a frantic headlong rush. The approaching final deadline may be frightening, but it can also be energizing. At this stage you have a clear objective in mind: finishing the full draft of your thesis. The long-drawn-out, sometimes oppressive thesis writing process is suddenly focused on one date.

Nor will this mode suit all supervisors. It has to be said, right at the start of this chapter, that you must have your supervisor(s) on board: they must be ready and willing to help you plan your writing over the remaining time period, to read lots of your writing in rough draft form and to give you regular and prompt feedback. Otherwise, this mode may not work. They must be willing to monitor your output, to seek you out when you do not produce text by your deadline and to give you encouragement when you get sick and tired of the whole thing. If you think you cannot get all of this from your supervisor(s), ask someone else to be your writing manager. There are advantages to having someone who is not in your subject area, who can focus on – and will help you to focus on – your writing.

This mode of thesis writing is based on the experiences of students who have produced their theses in one year full-time (equivalent to two years part-time): one full draft and one full revision. It has been done.

The aim is to do the best you can in the time that you have left. All we can ever do is write the best account in the time that we have. It may be that productive writers are those who can accept that 'compromise' of an ideal writing process (an ideal that is never realized). However, you may find that you have to negotiate with your supervisors to get them to see the fast-track process in this light. In any case, once you start making progress – and once you finish – they will be delighted. You may want to revisit these points at later stages.

In scientific disciplines this has always been the way: an intensive period of 'writing up' once the research has been completed, or almost completed. This is less established in the humanities and social sciences. In fact, it might be considered by some to be completely inappropriate in those disciplines. However, for the student who has one year to produce a thesis, the view that 'this is not how we do things' may be less important than 'this has been shown to work'.

If you meet with resistance – whatever your approach to writing – you may have to establish a compromise, or common ground, between the advice provided here and the advice provided by, for example, your supervisor. It is also worth noting – and perhaps discussing – that academics have to write in this intense way much of the time, forcing time for writing into busy schedules, accelerating the writing process. You could see this mode as a key skill. At the very least, it is good to know that you can produce a complete text when you have to.

As the writer quoted at the start of this chapter says, you may find that this works, for you, as a summary of the whole thesis writing process. Or you may find that it gives you a method of writing the whole thesis in less time than you would, ideally, have liked. However, if you read this chapter on its own, you will not find explanations of the approaches. You may not be sure why a proposed writing activity will work, or even that it will work. For explanations of and arguments for these approaches you will have to read the earlier chapters.

- This is more of a 'how to' chapter than the others.
- It takes a 'fast-track' approach.
- Ten steps are outlined for writing and revising your thesis in eight to twelve months.
- If you get blocked go back to Chapter 5.

Time is of the essence. Instead of explanations and illustrations, this chapter has bullet points and instructions. It is more directive in style. There are no detours, fewer references to the literature and choices and explanations are limited. (You can find those in other chapters.)

For this fast-track mode to work you must write regularly. Writing tasks are specified. They may be simply and directly stated, but this is not to say that they will not require hard thinking on your part.

You may have to take short cuts in your data collection. You may have to cut down the amount of data you collect or analysis you conduct, whatever your subject. You may have to shrink the data sets/texts/examples and, therefore, chapters that you originally intended for your thesis. You are likely to have to condense some of your material, as new material becomes more interesting.

This may be justifiable on the grounds that you can be more focused, do more detailed analysis or in some way increase the 'quality' of your research if you limit the number of analyses. It is not just a matter of limiting the words and cutting down the writing tasks; it is about sharpening the focus and trimming those elements which are not central. In some cases, if the analysis is excellent, then the thesis can even be shorter, say 60,000 words.

The best way to get through this is to have a 'writing manager'. What does a writing manager do? He or she will set you – or help you to set – hard writing goals and will act as a witness to your writing.

Who should be your writing manager? This person may or may not be one of your supervisors. That depends on whether or not they want to play this role and, perhaps, on whether or not you want them to.

What they have to do is monitor your output: they have to help you define goals, take stock of your output and keep moving forward in your writing.

What can you do if you cannot find a writing manager? It does, after all, require a considerable amount of commitment to supporting you. Of course, your supervisor may play this role, or part of this role. Those who provide study skills support at your university may be able and willing to play this role. Ask a peer or a friend. If there is no one, then use this book to help you manage your writing.

On a more realistic note, lest this introduction represent an accelerated mode as a last resort, it should be noted that this mode of thesis writing is not unusual. This 'fast-track' chapter is based on the experiences of students who wrote their theses in one year: a full draft of all chapters in six months, then a full revision in the next six months. You will not be the first, or last, to have reached this point in your research with little writing to show for it.

Fast-track thesis writing: initial tasks

- Find a 'writing manager'. Arrange a meeting. Discuss the role.
- Arrange a series of meetings with your supervisor(s).
- Conduct regular, honest appraisals of your written output with them.
- Let the accelerated mode concentrate your mind.
- Accept that you cannot put 'everything' in your thesis.
- Consider strategic cutting: what can be cut from the research and the thesis? A chapter? Overall word length? How close are you to the maximum? What is the minimum? How much do you have to write? Why write 100,000 if you can write 80,000 words?
- Cut tasks from your 'to do' list now. Keep only those you *have* to do.
- Keep moving forward.
- Ignore digressions and tangents.
- Arrange your life to write.
- Finish all your research, if you can. Close it down. Cut out any research that is not essential.
- If the writing is part of your research, define what analysis-through-writing you have to do.
- Do not expect to feel that it is 'finished'; you will always wish you had time to do more.
- Stop trying to keep up with the literature. (Update yourself later.)
- Decide on the content of your thesis. Choose a rough 'story line'.
- Join/create a writers' group.
- Tell your friends, family, partner etc. that you are working this way and need their support to finish.

List real barriers to writing; what has actually stopped you writing?

- Lack of organization?
- Stress?
- Distractions?
- Intimidating audience?
- Guilt at not having done more?
- Lack of contact with supervisor?
- Illness – you, friends, family, partner, pet?
- Loss/bereavement?

Get these out in the open. Discuss them with your supervisor and/or writing manager. Talk through changes you will make in order to overcome barriers.

Step 1 Take stock

Each of the ten steps in the fast-track mode should be discussed with your supervisors and/or writing manager. You need their advice: it is important to find out how much, or how little, your supervisors think you have done and to discuss how much writing they think you still have to do. This discussion should take a strategic view of your whole project. They may have a very clear image of how your thesis should look. Ask them how they see your thesis taking shape. Discuss possible chapter contents. Get a sense of what they think constitutes 'enough' for your thesis.

- Take a step back. Look at where you are in the thesis writing process.
- Quantify what writing you need to do to finish.
- Do the following tasks.
- Spend an hour discussing your stock taking with someone else.
- Do not keep to yourself how much you have to do, otherwise you are more likely to panic and less likely to change your practices.

Tasks

---

1 **List** the writing you have done for your thesis: i.e. in terms of chapters and/or parts of chapters.
2 **Add up** the number of words or pages you have written.
3 **List** chapters you have written partly or in full.
4 **List** barriers to writing. Anticipate barriers to writing regularly.
5 **Summarize** feedback from your supervisor(s) on your writing.
6 **Find** a writing manager.
   Why?   To focus on writing
   What?   Setting goals, discussing ways to write and what you write
   Who?   Supervisor or someone else
   When?   Meeting for an hour every two or three weeks
7 **Get organized**.
   Don't panic. Become more disciplined in your writing.
   Change your mode of working. Go up a gear. Change your habits.
   You have to churn out a lot of text this year.
   You feel pressure, a feeling that will not go away, but can be managed.

Use verbs

Instructions in this chapter are expressed as action words, verbs in the command form, such as 'List' and 'Find'.

- Use this form of expression to define your tasks.
- Choose verbs that define exactly what you have to do.
- Reject vague words like 'Consider' or 'Look at'.
- Choose precise words like 'Describe' or 'List'.
- These make you define exactly what to do and write.

The 'new you'

- Construct a new self-profile: you as regular writer.
- Become focused on your writing.
- Visualize yourself writing every day.
- Be selfish: let nothing stand between you and a writing goal.
- Use writing activities to maintain – and recapture – focus.
- Think about how good it will feel to finish.

Step 2 Start writing

Do not wait until someone tells you to start; start now. Discuss with your supervisor the types of writing you want to submit. There is not much point in submitting your freewriting; it is a mechanism for you to develop your ideas and fluency in writing away from the scrutiny of experts. However, you may want to negotiate with your supervisor(s) about reading rough drafts that are still very early drafts. Are they prepared to give you feedback that helps you progress to second and third drafts? Will they give you feedback that will not keep you revising indefinitely, but will move you towards an adequate draft in a limited number of revisions? Will they let you move forward to the next chapter when you still have revisions of the previous one to do?

1 Freewrite for 10 minutes on the subject of your thesis.
2 Force yourself to write for the whole 10 minutes. Do not stop.
3 Ignore your internal editor.
4 Do not stop to consult your sources.
5 Read over what you wrote. Write for another 10 minutes. Fill in gaps, develop ideas or continue where you left off. No revision needed yet.

Write a one-minute paper (Harwood 1996)

- Take this literally.
- Write for one minute only.
- Write down the main topic for your writing.
- Write one question that you are trying to answer in this writing.
- For example: write down the main point of your thesis, or your contribution, or write down the main point of one of your chapters. Then write a question that you need to answer.
- Repeat this exercise before you start each chapter.

Do a 'structured binge'

- You will be writing, from now on, in small and large chunks of time.
- Structure the large chunks of time.
- Define a writing task for each hour (1000 words).

Learn to live with imperfection

- A 'rough draft' is so called for a reason; do not polish your writing yet.
- Get used to handing in drafts that you know can be improved.
- You can hand in first drafts to your supervisor.
- Let feedback from your supervisor(s) be your agenda for revision.
- Label your drafts clearly, so they read each one for what it is.

Write in different ways

- Continue to freewrite.
- Do more structured writing in structured binges.
- Create a disk for each chapter.
- Revise where your supervisor says you need to.
- Do generative writing on topics you agree you have to cover.
- Hand in rough drafts of chapters or part of chapters.
- Discuss your writing goals with your supervisor.
- Write – don't just talk about it – in meetings with writing manager.

Step 3 Outline your thesis

As you develop a sense of what your thesis is about, force that 'sense' forward until it resembles an outline structure, however general your headings may be. Before you go any further, discuss this emerging thesis with your supervisor.

The tasks in all of these sections are for *you* to write. They prompt you to write in different ways throughout this fast-track period. However, while the instructions are all for writing you have to do, be sure to discuss them – and your output – with your supervisor.

Some of the activities will help you develop your thinking about your thesis. They may not produce text that you want to share with your supervisor. As soon as possible, however, you must agree a rough outline of chapters. You cannot write chapters until you have this.

Use the activities, templates and questions in this section in any order that suits you. You may want to go through them one by one, or you may want to go straight to outlining your research, then outline your thesis.

- Write an overview of your whole study, in sentences.
- Sketch your whole thesis in graphical form.
- Trust in your own overview of your study. Keep writing.
- Ignore gaps, errors and discontinuities. Expect them in a draft.
- Continue to write. Put off revision till later. Write in sentences.
- Do not worry about style. Keep moving forward.

About your research

Write for 30 minutes about your research, in sentences, on seven prompts:

State the subject of your thesis in one sentence.
List the aims of your research/analysis.
Describe what you did to achieve your aims.
Describe what you found in your analysis.
Explain what it means.
Define what is original about it.
List three subjects that remain unresolved.

Count: how many words did you write?

Add more prompts to the list

Write for 30 minutes on these additional prompts

- **State the subject of your thesis in one sentence.**
  State your hypothesis in a sentence.
- **List the aims of your research/analysis.**
  List your research questions.
  Give two reasons why your topic is important.
  Name three other people who think it is important.
  Write one sentence on what each says about the topic.
- **Describe what you did to achieve your aims.**
  List your reasons for doing that.
  Explain your reasons.
  Explain why you rejected alternatives.
- **Describe what you found in your analysis.**
  What did you find?
- **Explain what it means.**
- **Define what is original about it.**
- **List three subjects that remain unresolved.**

- Count the number of words you wrote.
- Save this writing on your 'Introduction' disk.
- Copy each sentence separately and paste it into a file. This is the start of that chapter's file, e.g. paste 'What did you find?' into the disk for the 'Results' chapter or into several analysis chapters.
- If these prompts do not suit your study, write others that do and write about them.
- Start all your prompts with writing verbs. These define the writing task and the type of writing that you do.

Outline your thesis structure in 30 minutes

Background/Context/Review of literature/Introduction
- The subject of the research is important because . . .
- Those who have worked on this subject include . . .
- What has not yet been done is . . .
- The research project aimed to . . .

Theory/Method/Approach/Materials/Subjects
- This study was based on the approach of . . .
- This approach was chosen because . . .

- It was likely to achieve the project aims by . . .
- Others have used this method to . . .

Results/Analysis
- The steps in the research involved . . .
- Analyses were conducted by . . .
- Data/information/observations were gathered as . . .
- These were organized into . . .

Discussion/Interpretation
- Analyses suggested that . . .
- This interpretation was based on . . .
- Taken together the analyses show . . .
- Research aims were achieved to the extent that . . .

Recommendations/Implications/Conclusions
- Further research is needed in order to . . .
- More information is needed on . . .
- Practice could be improved by . . .
- Proposed changes would be feasible if . . .

Adapt the generic framework to, or draw up a different one for, your thesis.

- List headings. Revise them: Adjust the order.
  Fill in any gaps.
  Reword them, if necessary.
  Try to make them into a continuous story.
  Revise them again till they do.

- Write long descriptive headings first, so that you know what is going into each chapter. Revise them, to make them more concise, later.

- Do the same for sub-headings for each chapter.
  Focus on the chapter you are writing now, or one you want to write next. Add notes for more detail.

- Write sentences on each heading.
  Write sentences on each sub-heading.
  Write introductory paragraphs for each chapter.

- Consider the function of each chapter in your whole argument.
  How important is each chapter?
  How will this 'importance' affect the length of each chapter?

- Allocate a number of words/pages for each chapter, e.g.:

Introduction	5000 words
Chapter 1	10,000 words
Chapter 2	15,000 words
Chapter 3	5000 words
Chapter 4	8000 words
Chapter 5	15,000 words
Chapter 6	15,000 words
Chapter 7	4000 words
Conclusions	3000 words
Total	80,000 words

In this plan, Chapters 2, 5 and 6 are key. They are longer, because they present more detailed, more complex or more contested material.

Step 4 Make up a programme of writing

There is not much time for reflection. What you need to be doing is defining writing goals and writing in any chunk of time you have, large or small.

You also need to get your supervisor(s) to approve your goals; if they think you are going down the wrong track, it is crucial that you know that before you write several thousand words rather than after.

Before you go through the following steps and tasks, discuss them with your supervisor(s).

- Define writing goals and be ready to write in every chunk of time, large or small.
- Draw up two programmes: long-term, for the whole year (or for the time you have), and short-term, for the next two or three weeks.
- In step 4 you defined writing tasks you have to do. Now allocate them to writing slots in your programmes.
- Set dates for 10–12 meetings with your supervisor(s) over the next 8–12 months. Define targets for these dates. Use them as deadlines.

An example of a writing programme is included here in order to demonstrate how writing tasks are allocated real time, how writing and revision overlap and, above all, how the feedback from supervisors drives revisions.

The structure of the meetings is constant:

- What writing has been done since the previous meeting?
- What writing is to be done next?
- How can this next writing task be defined in more detail?

Writing Programme Part 1

Meetings 1–5   8 weeks

Meeting 1   1 February
Written   4000 words (12 pages)
To write   Chapters 2 (review of literature), 3, 4, 5, 6 (30 pages each)
          Plus 15 pages on development of method
          Plus 15 pages on pilot study

Meeting 2   15 February
Written   Chapter 2 (10,000 words) to supervisor (feedback in a week or two)
Done   Coding and analysis, table of results
To write   Chapters 3–6 to have same structure
          Chapter 3 (30 pages by end March)
          Chapter 4 (30 pages by April 16)
          Chapter 5 (30 pages by May 14)
          Chapter 6 (30 pages by June 13)
          Plus freewriting, logging communications with supervisor
          All writing tasks allocated real time slots in diary
Revisions July, August, September

Meeting 3   15 March
Written   Memo to supervisor on writing schedule
          15 units of analysis (at rate of 3 units per day)
Revised   Coding scheme
To write   Chapter 3 by end of March: intro, 'This chapter is about . . .'
          Chapter plan: page allocation to topics
To revise More explicit connections between Chapters 1 and 2

Meeting 4   29 March
Written   Letter to supervisor, responding point-by-point
          Agreeing next steps
To write   Chapter 3 by end of March

Meeting 5   15 April
Written   Chapter 3
          Chapter 4 (25 pages, 4900 words)
To write   Chapter 5 by May 14

Writing Programme Part 2

Meetings 6–10   20 weeks

Meeting 6   8 May
Feedback 35 points from supervisor
Written   Tables half-done, statistics half-done
           Freewriting on supervisor's feedback
           Written response to supervisor
To write   Chapter 5 by May 14 (30 pages)

Meeting 7   17 May
Written   Chapter 5 (only 2 days late)
           Letter of thanks for supervisor
To write   Invited to contribute to journal
           Chapter 6 by mid-June
           5 hours per day, 5 or 6 days a week
           Redo stats for Chapter 3
           Appendices and references

Meeting 8   8 June
Written   5000 words this week
To write   Chapter 6 8 pages on text analysis
                      2–3 pages on results of analysis
                      8 pages of general discussion of results
                      10 pages of discussion/implications etc.
Revise   Chapter 1 (supervisor's feedback)
New programme Deadline for complete draft 15 August
           Chapter 1 Revisions 25 June
           Chapter 2 Revisions 9 July
           Chapter 3 Revisions 16 July
           Chapter 4 Revisions 23 July
           Chapter 5 Revisions 30 July
           Chapter 6 Revisions 6 August

Meeting 9   12 August
Writing routine 9am–12, 2–5, 7–9pm
Written   Chapters 1–6
To revise   Chapters 1–6

Meeting 10   10 October
Written   Chapter 6, intros, revision for user-friendliness, cut analysis
To write   Revise Chapters 5 and 6, Title page, Contents etc.

Step 5 Communicate with your supervisor(s)

You are about to start handing your supervisor(s) – regularly – large quantities of writing. Make sure they are prepared to – and have time to – read your drafts and get them back to you quickly. You may have to persuade them to do this. Plan the process with them. Make sure you both know and agree how it will work.

What you are *not* going to do is wait till you have one complete draft, before you hand anything in to your supervisor(s). Submit drafts of chapters – or parts of chapters – as soon as you have them. Revise, in response to their feedback, at the same time as you move on to writing your next chapter. You and your supervisor(s) will exchange drafts and revisions several times. But keep moving forward.

Prompts for discussion with your supervisor(s):

- I have set deadlines for submitting my chapters. What do you think?
- Do my deadlines for submitting chapters fit in with your schedule?
- Will you be away for any length of time in this period?
- How will we organize the exchange of drafts and written feedback?
- Are you prepared to read and give me feedback on first drafts?
- Will you be able to give me feedback within two or three weeks?
- What kind of feedback will you give me?

Do not worry if your supervisors ask you hard questions about your written drafts and writing practices; worry if they do not. Hard questions make you strengthen your argument; easy questions do not.

You may find that you are shifting into a new role. You may feel that you are managing your supervisor's reading of your writing. In some ways this is true; you have to prompt your supervisor to respond to your writing and indicate to him or her – explicitly – how and where you are acting on it.

Read the feedback from your supervisor(s) very carefully:

- Are they signalling that your work is 'good enough'?
- What exactly are they telling you to do to strengthen it?
- Do you need to reshape your thesis outline?
- Is there anything you can drop from your thesis outline?

Translate the comments of your supervisor(s) into writing and revising tasks

If you are unsure, check your interpretation of their feedback by sounding them out:

- Thank you for your feedback on chapter . . .
- This is how I have interpreted your feedback: . . . [list, bullet points].
- Have I interpreted your comments correctly?
- I am not entirely sure what you meant by . . . Do you mean . . . or . . . ?
- In response, I plan to do the following revisions: . . . [list].
- Please let me know – either way – what you think of this plan.

Step 6 Outline each chapter

You may feel that you are still quite far away from being 'ready' to write whole chapters. This section will help you force your writing before you feel really ready. If you wait till you feel ready, you may wait a very long time.

This step – designing chapters – builds on your draft outline of your thesis, which you have discussed with your supervisor(s). Once they have agreed the general outline, see if you can get them to endorse your chapter outlines too.

Rehearse these outlines in your discussions. See how your supervisor reacts. Write down any concrete suggestions for chapters, or likely headings or sub-headings, that come up in such meetings. Take your laptop with you, or borrow one, so that you do not waste time later in transcribing them.

- Take your thesis outline – step 3 – and expand on each heading.
- List headings and sub-headings for each chapter on separate pages.
- Add notes on each as you think of them.
- Do not force yourself to go through them in order, one by one.
- Do the ones that you have something to write for first.
- Then go back and force yourself to add one or two headings to the rest.
- Check that you still have your central thesis in mind.
- Check that all the headings develop your central thesis.

Step 7 Write regularly

- Write every day, no matter how short the time period.
- Use freewriting as a warm-up activity.
- Write straight on to word processor, not long hand.
- Count the number of words you write in each session.
- Work out the pace of your writing: how many words per hour?
- Write at the top right of the first page of draft chapters: the draft number, date and word count:

Draft 5
11.4.03
5,498 words

Chapter 4

This chapter outlines . . .

- Discard old drafts. If you cannot bring yourself to throw them out, put them out of sight and out of reach. Otherwise, you will mix up your supervisor's comments on different drafts and lose track of what you have and have not done. You will stop moving forward.

What you have to do in the fast-track mode is resolve – or ignore – the tension between (1) the 'quality question'; (2) the 'creativity question'; and (3) the 'productivity question'. Do not be put off by these questions:

1 *The quality question*
   If I just wrote down 'all I know about X', it would not be good writing. Isn't quality more important than the number of words?
2 *The creativity question*
   What will I do with new ideas? How will I fit them into my plan? Will I have any good ideas if it's all planned like this? There has to be room for creativity in the writing process.
3 *The productivity question*
   How can I write 80,000 words in six months?

Each of these questions can seem like a priority for your thesis, yet they can pull you in different directions. Consider these tensions as a luxury. You have no time to waste wondering whether this will work, questioning your plan of work and worrying about whether or not it will be 'good enough'. It is not possible to write productively with all of these anxieties in the front of your mind. You have to find a way to put them to the back of your mind. It may help to have someone who says this to you – often. You also have to read your supervisor's feedback very carefully.

Establish momentum in your writing

Freewriting: students report that they find freewriting immensely valuable at different stages in their thesis writing.

- It helps you to hear your own voice.
- It makes you focus on what you want to say.
- It gives you a way of saying what you really think, which you can then translate into more formal prose.
- It can help you work out a part of your argument that you have had difficulty explaining in writing.

Does the fast-track mode work?

Students have – quite rightly – questioned the feasibility of the accelerated mode for their contexts. It is all right for me, they say, to propose continuous writing, writing to a plan as if it were an agenda for writing, forcing writing. This works for me because I already know my field. I am writing about subjects I have been reading, thinking and writing about for years. They, by contrast, are still learning about their fields. They are dealing with new material and cannot be 'sure' – a direct quote – of their subject or, as a consequence, of their writing. They see me as further along a writing continuum than they are. They suggest that my strategies really work best – or only work at all – for those who are at that later stage, where they are 'sure' of what they want to say. There is, of course, an element of truth in this.

However, are we ever 'sure'? I am not always and entirely 'sure' that what I am writing is either an effective way of saying what I want to say, or an interesting or useful thing to say at all. While I have made a decision about what to say and am happy with that, there is still the great unknown of readers' reactions. If I waited – reading, thinking, planning and considering my options – until I was completely sure I would probably not write very much at all, for that day would never come.

There are always doubts: is that too obvious? ... Will that insult their intelligence? . . . Do I need to explain that a bit more? . . . Will they bother to do this writing activity? . . . and so on. I have to ignore these doubts – in fact, I see them now as interesting questions, some of which I note and write about later. Others I ignore, in order to carry on writing. At some point you have to be able to shut down the questions in order to write. I accept that writing regularly, in the way that I describe, is not possible for everyone, all the time, right away. It does take time to work out your own cadence and to set your own goals. We all have to establish our own route to regular writing.

The key point is, I think, that we need to get ourselves to what the students mentioned earlier saw as a later stage in the writing process: we have to reposition ourselves in the knowledge process. We cannot wait until this happens to us; we have to make it happen. We have to construct 'sure'. It is an invention. If we do not invent that moment it will not necessarily occur spontaneously. Occasionally – perhaps more often than that – we have to force it, even when we feel that being 'sure' is a very distant prospect. Thesis writers have to take themselves to that point. You can then move from being unsure and not writing, to being unsure and writing regularly. You have to silence the internal editor. We all have to do that.

You can check that the fast-track mode is working by getting regular feedback on your progress: check your plans and outlines with your supervisor.

Step 8 Revise

Translate your supervisor's comments into writing actions. For example, your supervisor says:

> You do not really seem to have made the connection here. It is implied, but I think you need to unpack your point and spell it out more. Otherwise, it seems more contentious than it really is. The connection is there, but I think you need to argue for it more carefully.

What kind of revision does this require?

- Expand on the connection.
- Add a paragraph defining it.
- Add two or three sentences explaining its significance.

Even very long comments – particularly long comments – have to be scrutinized carefully: what exactly are you being asked to do? Sometimes the comment is just the supervisor's response. Sometimes your writing triggers his or her thinking and you may decide that no revision is called for. However, most of your supervisor's comments, particularly at this stage, direct you to improve your argument. You may have to work carefully through what he or she has written in order to work out what you have to do in your next revision.

- Revise for continuity.
- Make links explicit.
- Use forecasting and signalling to reveal your plan. See Chapter 7.

Step 9 Pull it all together

Write sentences and short paragraphs to make your thesis coherent:

- Create explicit links between the end of each chapter and the beginning of the next.
- Link back to your research question(s)/aims in some/all chapter introductions.
- Make explicit connections between the aims of your study and your conclusions.
- Link your final statement about your 'contribution' to your earlier definition of the 'gap' in the literature.
- Write a summary for the final chapter that shows the progression of your argument through all your chapters.
- Write a shorter version of this summary for your introduction and abstract.

Step 10 Do final tasks

Check your university's regulations for all of the following. Follow them to the letter.

- Front matter:
    Title page
    Acknowledgements
    Contents
    Abstract
    List of figures/tables/illustrations
    Definitions

Which of these does your university *require*. In what order?

- Appendices
- Bibliography
- Layout: margins, headers, footers
- Consecutive page numbers for all chapters
- Give the whole final draft to your supervisor
- Submit final copies (how many?)
- Anything else to submit? Forms?

What do you need to do now?

- Do you need a Thesis Moratorium, to delay public access to your thesis?
- Rest. Even if you took regular breaks, you are probably exhausted.

9

The last 385 yards

The marathon • 'Done-ness is all' • Concentrated writing phase •
Well-being • Peer support • Discussion chapter • New goal • Style tips
• Finishing • Enough is enough • It is good enough • You have made a
contribution • Convince your reader • 'Polish' the text • Motivation
• Presentation of final copy • Timetable for writing • Checklist: polishing

This chapter focuses on the last phase before submission. It is assumed that your submission date has been set, or soon will be, or, at the very least, that you know when your submission date is likely to be. As with any deadline, however, if it is not an actual date, it may not work as a deadline. You are likely to overshoot any 'approximate' date.

It outlines what is often a more time-consuming task than thesis writers expect, the seemingly endless series of final, apparently hair-splitting revisions. The revisions suggested – or required – by supervisors at this stage become, hopefully, more and more detailed. Some students at this stage feel that this is a particularly pedantic set of revisions, but it is generally what is required to produce the final polished draft of a thesis.

Writing the final chapter may be the key task at this stage, but something as mechanical as creating tables or moving margins, in order to accommodate final revisions, can be just as time-consuming.

Living with uncertainty about the standard or quality of the thesis is a fact of thesis writing life at this stage. It can be even more difficult to deal with at this stage. On the other hand, if you have been writing all the way through your project, most of the writing will be done, leaving you with the task of producing a chapter that stitches it all together.

Moving away from an 'it can always be improved' towards a 'done-ness is all' approach is an important part of the letting go/finishing off stage.

Convincing supervisors that the argument is clear and that the thesis makes a contribution may also be part of the work of this phase; the real work may be strengthening what you think is already strong enough, or making more explicit what you thought was already explicit.

You may not agree with all the proposed revisions at this stage. How you respond to feedback you do not think is helpful will be an interesting final test. Knowing when a thesis is 'done' is a matter open to some debate generally, and it will probably lead to many discussions between you and your supervisor(s).

The marathon

The title of this chapter is taken from the marathon, a race, as most readers will know, requiring participants to run 26 miles and, what many do not know, 385 yards.

People who have written about their experiences of such a long run often talk about those last yards as the last straw. Having run all those miles, the last small section can seem just too much. Having written all those thousands of words, revising them yet again can seem just too much.

The trick is not to be surprised by this moment. It may be the psychological effect of almost being able to touch your goal, the main goal being completion itself at this point. It may be fatigue setting in, particularly if you have been working flat out for some time or jogging along at reasonably high pace for months or years. It could be that you are so familiar with your work that it has begun to seem really old – hardly 'original' – and irrelevant. It could be that you have sacrificed so much of your life to produce all this writing that, so close to the end, you would like to stop and get back to your life. Or it could be some combination of all of these facts, and there are others too.

The good news is that with all the writing and revising you have done so far, you have been, in a sense, training for this moment. You now know that it is not unique to you. You can probably follow the directions of the supervisors for these last few yards. This may feel like an adjustment in your relationship, but your supervisor may take on the role of 'editor' at this stage.

The main point is to remember that you only have 385 yards to go. The hard work is behind you. You just have to keep going and you will finish.

'Done-ness is all'

Men must endure
Their going hence even as their coming hither.
Ripeness is all.

(Shakespeare, *King Lear*, [1607] 1974: 9–11)

This quotation from Shakespeare's tragedy is designed to prompt readiness for death. What matters most about death, these lines of the play suggest, is that we are ready for it when it comes: we are 'ripe' for death. The implication for thesis writers is that they should be ready for the end of their theses when it duly arrives; they should be 'ripe' in the sense, perhaps, of having grown to a state of sufficient knowledge of their subjects and sufficient confidence in their work to present it for examination.

However, the title of this section is not 'Ripeness is all' but 'Done-ness is all', a made-up word designed to convey that the goal should be completion, not 'ripeness'. Feeling that your thesis is 'ripe' and ready for examination may not be achievable. The goal should be to reach closure, to defer new work and catalogue new ideas. This is particularly difficult given the infinite and immediate access to technology – constantly updating us and reminding us of how quickly our work can go out of date. Our understanding of the high standards required for a thesis examination also works to prevent us from cutting corners or compromising in any way in this final stage.

Yet, 'done-ness is all' provides a better prompt to practise the 'art of finishing', a better reminder of the need to stop developing the thesis and a better stimulus to writers to become finishers.

Concentrated writing phase

While Chapter 8 was about producing a whole thesis in one year, this chapter is about managing the last phase and/or chapter and many, many, many revisions. Some of the practices described in Chapter 8 may be useful here, but the process is different in every way: this chapter is about finding ways to do nothing but writing (and revising) until the thesis is finished.

Additional focus is required at this time. This is when you hope that your friends and family will step in and do the cooking, laundry and anything else that takes you away from writing. Some novice writers talk about the need to be 'selfish' in order to prioritize their own writing over other demands on their time. They observe what they think are more self-centred, or self-oriented, priorities among those who write regularly for scholarly publication. This may be something worth thinking, and talking, about with those around you. Are there any sacrifices they have to make to help you get your thesis 'done'?

The day-to-day routine for writing at this stage may involve a range of writing strategies:

Concentrated writing

1   **Outlining** what you want to write in each writing session
2   **Freewriting**: a five-minute warm up, to get from not-writing to writing without displacement activities
3   **Freewriting** to work out what you want to say
4   **Pacing** your regular writing: can you write/revise 1000 words an hour?
5   **Revising** in response to feedback from your supervisor
6   **Planning**: list of writing tasks and times in your diary/schedule
7   **Equipment**: stock up on paper, ink cartridges, disks

This stage involves writing in structured binges every day. Do the 'completion' tasks when you are tired: checking references, updating bibliography, setting up tables/figures, page numbering, etc. Make back-ups of everything, and not just when you are tired. Keep all drafts clearly labelled.

Well-being

Having said all that, in the previous section, about focus, sacrifice and selfishness, it is important to have some balance. You need to look after yourself if you are to have enough energy left for those last 385 yards. For most, if not all, of these areas, you know what to do to look after yourself; this is just a reminder:

Fit to write

- Diet
  Balanced, plus hydration
- Relaxation
  Do you know about Alpha Waves?
- Active distraction
- Exercise, Sport, Fitness, Fresh air
  Not everyone's choice, but an antidote to sitting for many hours at your computer. Go for a walk at least.
- Friends and Family
- Spiritual/Soul/Religion
  Whatever keeps you going, gives you a sense of purpose, this is the time to drop into it now and again.
- Comedy/Music/Arts
- Sleep/Time-out/Time off
- Creating regular slots, so that you feel guilty if you *do* work

There might also be some dual tasking, such as eating healthy take-out sandwiches while revising; thinking about your next writing or revising task while out walking, running or falling asleep; writing a paragraph or two in your head while at a concert, lecture or meeting with your supervisor; or recognizing a route to completing a section while relaxing and doing nothing. Have pen and paper, or keyboard, ready.

Peer support

Motivation and support are important at what can be a discouraging stage, as you feel you have made abundantly clear what you mean but your supervisor still writes in the margin, 'What exactly do you mean?' If you know someone else who is going through this stage you can reassure each other that this is par for the course. It is not just you. It is not just your supervisor. You have to find the right person, of course: not someone who is content to exchange complaints with you, but someone who, like you, is focused on finishing.

Your supervisor is not yet your 'peer', but the balance of power may have shifted between you. You may feel your relationship changing. You may feel yourself forming new responses to your supervisor's advice. It is important that you maintain good communications with your supervisor at this stage, even although his or her role in your thesis appears – only appears – to have changed from that of subject expert to that of editor. Yes, you will leave supervisors behind as your knowledge, confidence and standing grow, but you still need their advice at this stage, even if that advice strikes you as pedantic.

You may also need someone who can give you feedback on your working practices. Are you going about this final stage the right way? Should you be doing anything differently? This may seem like the phase in your research where you are learning least and benefit least from expert advice, but you may be wrong about that. You may benefit from a reminder of something you have forgotten, an adjustment to your practice or a pointer to any bad writing habits that you have rediscovered.

The point is to find someone – if you can – who helps you to keep going. Whether or not they have written a thesis themselves, this should be someone who believes you can do it and will say so, at regular intervals. If that person is your partner – often the only person willing to provide this amount of support – you may want to discuss the possibility of strain on your relationship. You might want to negotiate a change in duties, such as cooking and cleaning, with the promise that you will take over these duties when you have finished. This may seem like a trivial matter, but the last thing you want during this stressful final phase is domestic tensions. It may also help to acknowledge that you will be, from now on, completely absorbed in your writing, less responsive to any other demands, but that once it's over you will return to 'normal'. That will be your next big challenge.

Discussion chapter

Whatever your last chapter is called – for some it is the discussion, for others it has a title that marks the end of a sequence of titles of previous chapters – its main purpose is to pull your whole thesis together. As you interpret your 'findings', in any sense, you have to steer your writing in the direction of achieving – or revising? – your research aims or questions.

Freewriting: 15 minutes on each heading

- You have achieved what you set out to do to the extent that . . .
- Your argument for the originality of your work is . . .
- Your work confirms/challenges other research in that . . .
- Your contribution to knowledge is . . .

Where will these important statements – revised – appear in your thesis?

You may find that the last chapter you write is not the last chapter of your thesis. You may write the introduction and conclusion last. Whatever the order, the point is to 'join up all the dots', to make your thesis one continuous story. Connections between the start and the finish have to be explicit. You may also want to double check that you have 'signposted' your main theme along the way, in, for example, the introductions and conclusions to your chapters. This is how to achieve that much sought-after quality of 'flow' in your final draft: you have put links between the units of your argument.

New goal

The goal at this stage in the project is different from the goals in previous stages, in that it is, or should be, singular: nothing but writing. If this is so, then your interim goals are all about writing too.

Paradoxically, you will have done a fair amount of writing already. You may have a complete draft, much revised, with further revisions to do. This phase of your work may feel like 'new goal: old writing'.

However, there is a difference between revisions designed to develop a point and those aiming at completing an argument. You have to see the thesis as a whole, identify gaps in the story and fill them in. You may have to work with each chapter in the same way:

- What is the main theme of each chapter?
- How does it relate to the one before and the one after?
- Have you explained these relationships at the start and end of the chapters?
- Where and how can these links be clarified, strengthened or made more explicit?

You may also have new writing to do. For example, there may be some new literature that you decide you must include in your literature review, and you will have to check whether or not you need to make related adjustments in other chapters. You may have to write new introductions, spelling out the connections between your chapters, or linking each chapter back to the research questions or aims or clarifying how each chapter progresses your argument. You may have to write a new section in the final chapter showing how it all fits together. You may not yet know what your conclusions look like, but these steps may help you work out what you should be saying in your final pages.

Style tips

There are certain conventions that you can draw on – or adapt – as you move into the final phase of your thesis. Hedging – making non-definitive statements about your research – is an acceptable style at this stage. These examples show how to use the style that lets you claim some success without claiming too much:

- This suggests that . . .
- The findings show that . . .
- The limitations of the study were . . .
- Although there were limitations in . . . there were nevertheless interesting . . .

The last in this list makes a kind of trade-off of the weaknesses of your study. Although you may be all too aware of the limitations – or even flaws – in your study, do not feel that you have to reveal them all to your reader in those terms. Can you offset a weakness with an outcome? Whatever language I suggest is bound to provoke debate among thesis writers and researchers. Take the following lists as a starting point for your thinking and discussions. The words are arranged in two columns to make an obvious distinction and to steer your choices towards representing your work positively, even though you may not feel positive about all of it at this time.

Language to use	Language to avoid
• limitation	flaw
• focus, selection	omission
• completed, continuing, ongoing	incomplete
• success, impact, effective	inconclusive
• contributes to a resolution of	solves, proves

Every study will have limitations; these have to be addressed. Some are there by design, as part of the narrowing down and focusing of any piece of research. 'Flaws', however, is not the best word to use when you want to talk about what emerged as weaknesses in your study. Can you not, in any case, turn the negative into a positive and write about how you would propose to strengthen the study, if you had to do it again?

You can also strengthen your argument by writing about your work and published work in the same sentence. Although you may feel that your work does not measure up to published work yet, you have to make some connection with where your research has ended up and what others are doing. The effect may be as simple as reflected glory; your work is in the same company as more established researchers. Or, more significantly, searching for some connection between your research and others' may force you to strengthen your argument in a new way.

Finishing

It might help to remember that your research need not end with this project; you can continue to work on this topic. You probably have several questions that you would like to explore further. Anything that has been left out, that you cannot deal with in the time you have left or that your supervisor advised you to drop, you can pick up again later. This may be where you will find your next publication. The conclusion to the thesis is a springboard, looking ahead to future work.

Mini-proposal for future work

This should not just be a shopping list of ideas and potential projects. For example, you should consider:

- What is your selected priority?
- How would you do that?
- What resources would be needed?
- Is it feasible?
- How long would it take?
- Anticipate refutations – what are your arguments against them?
- What would be the benefits of this?
- What would be the implications for . . .?

This makes for a stronger ending; it shows that you have sufficient expert knowledge to (a) select an appropriate priority and (b) think it through.

Enough is enough

Just as the answer towards the end of a marathon is '385 yards', so the answer towards the end of a project is something that can be defined. This is not to say that there is one answer for all theses; what it means is that you have to make a few decisions, based on precedent – how much was enough for other thesis writers? – or time and money – how much do I have left? – or advice – how much does my supervisor say I should do?

To explore these further:

1   How many words are you required to write?
    Students and supervisors often respond that they find this a particularly superficial way of defining a thesis. Surely the quality of the work is more important than the number of the words?
2   Approximately, how many pages are there in recent, successful theses from your department?
    This is about defining the task. Yes, your thesis – and every thesis – is unique, but does it really have to be twice as long as the others?
3   Make a decision – not just 'it depends'.
    Many students – in discussion of this question – think that the thesis will take as long as it takes, in terms of time and pages. This is not strictly true. It may be that you are deferring your decision. A strategy for moving on would be to consider two or three answers to the question of what needs to be done.

You will also have your own ideas about what constitutes a 'finished' thesis. What do you think still needs to be done? Define this in terms of writing tasks. Use freewriting to get started. Do some outlining. Design any sections that you need to add.

You will also feel that you should keep updating your literature review. Be careful. Yes, your thesis should be up to date and you should add anything that is directly relevant to your work, but it should also be directly relevant to your thesis. Remember that this means you could have to find a way to integrate it in writing you have already revised many, many times. Be careful not to shift the line you have established for your argument too far by adding a new element. Will you have to make adjustments elsewhere in your thesis? You will have to check that. Remember that you can be justifiably explicit with your readers about where you drew the line on new research.

This is one example of the way in which you have to start shutting down new possibilities for this last phase. 'Done-ness is all' was intended to remind you that your goal is to finish, to stop writing. What this means is that you have to decide that you have done enough. The title of this section is 'Enough is enough' – it is not a question, like 'How much is enough?' At this stage you have to make some hard decisions about finishing off. Some students find that they not only have to convince themselves that they are ready to finish, but also have to convince their supervisors that they have done 'enough'.

It is good enough

'Good enough' means reaching an adequate standard for submission. This is sometimes a lower standard than students think. You may even – with your supervisor's advice – decide to chop a chapter from your plan, or even drop one that you have already written, if, for example, it raised too many new questions or disrupts your main story line. Your work is good enough when:

- your argument and conclusions are plausible, even if you are not completely happy with them;
- your argument is convincing and coherent;
- you have made a recognizable contribution to knowledge, even though you feel it is not earth-shattering;
- you have made this visible in your introduction, conclusions and abstract, using the word 'contribution' or something very like it;
- you have achieved some or all of the aims that you set out to achieve in your research and have reported this in your thesis;
- feedback from your supervisor indicates that your work is adequate;
- you have had publications – or even one – drawn from your research/thesis.

No one may actually say the words, 'Your thesis is now good enough . . . You have done enough . . . You can stop now.' Good supervisors will be looking for this turning point and will let you know when they think they see it, though perhaps not in exactly these words. There does come a time when there is 'enough' to constitute a thesis, but this point is hard to predict. You can help by trying to spot this point yourself.

This will not be easy. You may be so acutely aware of further work that you could still do to strengthen your study that you may not recognize this point. You may feel that you have to analyse more texts, run another phase of the study, include two or three more companies or subjects in your experiment. At this stage that could be a mistake. Think of all the time it would take to set that up, let alone the time for writing about it, revising, getting feedback and so on. If you are concerned that you might not have 'enough', now is the time to ask a direct question of your supervisor: 'Do you think that I have done enough?' If your supervisor says yes to this question, then put any thoughts of further work aside. Of course, if you feel your study or thesis has serious weaknesses, you should seek a second opinion.

This person may give you a less than direct answer. Do not panic. His or her indirectness is not necessarily a sign that you are failing. If you were in danger of not having 'enough', he or she would be more likely – or should be – to signal that explicitly. Your supervisor may also find it impossible to give a direct answer. He or she may even see it as unethical; your external examiner has the final decision about the standard of your work, not the supervisor. Your writing is already moving away from the supervisor towards the external.

Some would say that the question about 'how much is enough' cannot be answered before the viva. Others will argue – having supervised many theses – that they do have a sense of when a thesis is nearing completion. You will be told then that your thesis is 'good enough' to submit. Whether it is 'good enough' to pass will not be decided till the viva.

You have made a contribution

If you have not written about your work in these terms yet, you should do so now. It is crucial that you state your contribution – perhaps even in the same terms, using the same words, so as not to confuse matters – at several points in your thesis:

- Abstract/summary
- Introductions
- Conclusions.

You have to argue that your contribution *is* a contribution. You can rehearse this argument in discussions with your supervisors. Have a look at examples of how this step in the thesis argument has been conducted in other theses produced recently in your department. Once you have convinced yourself and your supervisor that you have made a contribution, you have to convince your next key reader, the external examiner.

Convince your reader

Although you know your thesis extremely well – only too well, as it may seem quite old and out of date to you now – you have to convince your external examiner that you have made a contribution. You have to try and see your thesis from his or her point of view.

Convincing your reader of what?

- That your work is original
- That you have expertise
- That you know the limits of your 'originality'
- That there are limits to the project
- How do you do this?
- Measuring the contribution: setting limits, putting it in context

- Defining what was 'beyond the scope of your study' and what you learned in the course of your study, what you would do differently next time.
- Convincing the reader that you have an expert overview: where is the field going in the next five to ten years? What will be the big issues? Where will your own work be situated?

The key at this stage is not to feel that you have to fill in what you now see as glaring gaps in the work, thinking or research design. It is too late for that. You will have limited time, perhaps no time, in which to 'redo' pieces of work. Doing so might unbalance the rest of the thesis and leave you with even more work and writing to do. In any case, the thesis is the type of document which can incorporate a report of what you have learned, what you would do differently and better next time, and so on. Such improvements are part of any research process and you have to show that you recognize that. You have to write about that. You may have more to write about that than you think. These points too must be communicated in your abstract/summary, introductions and conclusions.

The focus of your attention must switch now from making the work better to making the writing better. Your writing has to make the best case possible for your work as it stands. This is why so much attention is paid to the detail of writing at this stage.

'Polish' the text

This is the time for revisions so fine that they do not seem worth making. It all begins to seem a bit pedantic, with more attention to the correctness of grammar and punctuation than to the research and your contribution.

This is as it should be. Consider it good practice for doing the final edit for a journal paper or submitting your first book manuscript to a publisher. If you have already done that, note the similarities; it is about producing a text of the highest standard.

Polishing

- How does your text read for style? Read it aloud to a friend.
- Are your quotations accurate? All with page numbers?
- Are your points well illustrated by examples?
- Are your references complete? Cross-check.
- Is every paragraph clear and coherent?
- Is every chapter clear, coherent and unified?
- Are all signals and signposts in place?

As you revise – and revise again, and again – be sure to let your supervisor read the final copy (unless it is the procedure at your university that your supervisor does not see the final copy). This may seem like an obvious point, but it does happen that students think that their supervisor will not need to see yet another version. It sometimes happens that while the supervisor has seen many drafts of all the chapters, he or she has not seen them all together. It goes without saying that it is your job to make sure that your supervisor (1) sees all the chapters together and (2) sees the final draft of them all, together.

Motivation

Remember those 385 yards. You have come so far, and given up so much, that you cannot stop now. However much it hurts, or however meaningless it seems, it will hurt even more to leave it incomplete, or, as they say in the USA, 'ABD', meaning 'All but dissertation', i.e. all the requirements have been met except that. In many, perhaps most, cases this means that the thesis, or dissertation, is work-in-progress, submission pending, but for others it can be something that hangs over them for years.

This is quite a negative approach to motivation. Besides, running the last 385 yards of a marathon is simply a matter of putting one foot in front of the other. You could even walk it. The last phase of thesis writing is much more complex. However, the point is that you may be over-complicating it. You may not have as far to go as you think. You may just have convinced yourself, like the marathon runner, that the last stage is impossibly difficult.

A more positive perspective is not possible without more definition of what is actually required.

Presentation of final copy

Now is the time to combine all your files into one complete text, double spaced, with continuous page numbering. Find out from your university:

- What is the required page layout?
- What size should margins be? Where do page numbers go? How should tables/figures/illustrations be labelled?
- How should references and quotations appear in the text?
- What paper quality and size are required?
- Where can you get the regulation soft (later hard) binding done?
- How long will that take? (Can take 3–4 days.)

- How many copies must you submit?
- To whom do you submit them? Exactly where is their office?
- Are there any forms to fill in before you go?

Remember that it is your responsibility to make sure that your thesis is presented in the regulation format, exactly, with no errors. Even when you get the copies back from the photocopier or print service it is up to you to check that all the pages are the right way up, *before binding*.

What is your submission date? This should be an actual date, confirmed by the relevant committee, board or some other feature of department or university administration. Until the date is set, it is not really a deadline, and the risk is that you will use what appears to be extra time to do more work. This is fine, if this is what is needed. However, it may result in your failing to complete your thesis by then. Now, or very soon, you must have a fixed deadline for submission.

Questions for reflection

- Definition: are you clear about what you have to do?
- Motivation: do you really have the end in sight?
- Is there anything you can drop to make more time for your thesis?
- What lies between you and completion?
- What will be your reward – to yourself – for submitting your thesis?
- How do you think you will feel when it is finally submitted?

Prompts for discussion

- What will the final story look like?
- What is the thread of continuity that ties your thesis together?
- Should you be making that more explicit now, checking that it appears throughout the thesis?

Timetable for writing

Now that your submission date has been fixed, you can work out how you are going to finish your thesis. How many writing sessions can you fit in before the date? How many one-hour, two-hour, three-hour or four-hour sessions?

You can plan each day's work. Use different time slots for different purposes. For example, new writing could be done in shorter, one-hour sessions, while revising, in response to your supervisor's comments, could be a longer, two- or three-hour session. Plot your work on timelines, so that you develop an overview of what you have to do.

100 yards	200 yards	385 yards
New writing	**Revising**	**Proof-reading** **Photocopying**
Today Week ?	Week ? Week ?	Week ? Submission

For each week, define writing and revising tasks and slots. Allocate specific times on each day for these tasks.

Week 1: Revise Chapters 1 and 2

Monday

9–10.30	Reread Chapter 1
10.30–11	Break
11–1	Read supervisor's latest comments: revise
1–2	Lunch, exercise
2–3	Library: check journals, web-search, references
3–5	Revisions
5–7	Break, dinner, exercise
7–8	Revisions
8	Decide tomorrow's first task

You can plan for the whole week's work at one time, but it is a good idea to end the last session on one day with a definition of the first task for the next day. It helps you get a flying start, since you know exactly where that start is.

Look forward to the time when you can stop writing, if only temporarily. If you have a date for submission, that is the date of your holiday from writing.

This chapter started with the burden of the last 385 yards of the marathon that is the thesis. It ends with the recognition that you have now developed a sense of an ending, both to your thesis and to your experience of research. The last chapter is concerned with the very last step: the examination of your thesis.

Checklist

Polishing

You will have done these tasks many, many times, but they must be done once more before you submit your final draft.

- Check you are using the university-approved format.
- Cross-check: match chapter headings (and sub-headings) on the contents page to headings (and sub-headings) in each chapter. Exactly.
- Turn the grammar check (programme of your word processor) back on – it can be annoying if it is on all the time – and run it one more time. It picks up the knock-on effects of our revisions, that we sometimes miss, such as subject–verb agreement.
- Check you have consecutive page numbers, for every page, with no errors.
- Do the spell check again.
- Check the bibliography line-by-line.
- Check that the dates of all references match those in your bibliography.
- Locate a thesis binding service. Find out how much time they need to produce the number of copies you need (may be 3–4 days).
- Show the final draft of all chapters – all together – to your supervisor.

10

After the thesis examination: more writing?

More writing? • What is a viva? • Pre-viva • Defining tasks • Talking about your writing • Practice • Anticipate the questions • Mock viva • Fear • The external examiner • During the viva • Post-viva • Endurance • Revisions and corrections • Anti-climax • Is there life after a thesis? • Was it really worth it? • Recovering • Getting your thesis published • Audience and purpose (again) • Looking for topics • The end • Checklist: before and after the viva

Before you read any further, it should be pointed out that many students and supervisors have fixed views about the viva. They may take one look at the headings for this chapter and wonder why I am going into it in such detail. It is not my intention to challenge people's practice; students will have to weigh in the balance both my advice and their supervisors' guidance. Even if you agree with something I say, they may not. Naturally, it would be sensible for supervisors' views to carry more weight. This is not to say that you have to 'cave in' to whatever they say. You may, in fact, choose to ask them to elaborate on their views, to provide you with specific guidance.

However, if there do appear to be contradictions, it might be worthwhile exploring them further. Most supervisors – surely – will be willing to discuss your questions about your viva, whether you come by those questions yourself or whether they are raised in the reading of this chapter?

The viva is a subject surrounded by mystique and some would argue that that is how it should be: if each thesis is 'unique' and 'original', then surely the viva must be unique and original too? There is an element of truth in this: it would be dangerous to assume that you had anticipated all the questions the examiners were going to ask and knew exactly how to answer them. There must be an element of unpredictability. You will have to live with an element of unpredictability.

However, as for any other examination, there are certain conventions that operate in the viva, with particular local variations at your institution. Even if you know what these conventions are – and in my experience many students do not – that may not mean that you are ready for your viva yet. My priority in this chapter is to provide as many definitions of terms and prompts for practice as I can. I assume that any readers – students or supervisors – will then adapt my material to their specific context.

This introduction may seem to be full of obvious points, but the viva can be such a heated topic that I must clarify: what you find in this chapter is not – cannot be – specific to your institution. If, on reading it, you think that it is, then that may mean that you do not have enough information about exactly what passes for standard practice in vivas at your institution. The information in the chapter should, instead, strike you as more relevant in some sections and less relevant in others. That judgement may also depend on how much information and preparation your department has given you. If you have had plenty, you may just need to practise; if you have had hardly any, or none at all, you should still practise, but seek out more information as a matter of urgency.

The aim of this chapter is to prepare students for talking about the thesis and about the writing process in the viva. An approach to post-viva revisions and corrections is outlined. There is a review of topics covered in the earlier chapters, revisiting points made and language used.

Even after the examination the graduate still has lessons to learn about writing for different audiences and purposes. While the thesis is in many ways a unique form of writing, there are skills learned in the process which are transferable to other writing projects. The viva marks a milestone in the thesis process; but it need not be the end of all writing development. Learning about writing is a lifelong process.

This chapter is not 'all about writing' in the same way that the rest of the book is, but it is about doing justice to your writing in the oral format. For that, you have to translate what you have written in your thesis into oral answers to examiners' questions. In this sense, then, the viva is still very much about your writing. Rather than just hoping to survive the viva, you can prepare to do an excellent – not just adequate – job on the day.

Much of this introduction – perhaps all – could be said to apply to all the chapters of this book. However, the stakes are even higher with the viva. As your writing 'goes public', to the limited extent of your thesis going out to the external examiner, you have to learn the rules of a new game, while still playing the old one well.

More writing?

Oh no. I thought that after the viva I wouldn't have to do any more writing!

This student read the title of this chapter over my shoulder, as I was writing, during a writers' group meeting, and spontaneously expressed horror at the prospect of 'more writing'. Exaggerating more than a little, she explained that she thought she would never have to write again after the viva. She admitted that this was an illusion, but a positive one, in that it kept her writing and progressing towards what she hoped would be 'the end'.

Like this student, you may have been writing for three or more years under the impression that once you got the viva over and done with you would not have to do any more writing. You too may have hung on to this very useful illusion, using it to keep you focused on the submission date. However, clearly, it is not entirely true. It is likely that you will have to do corrections, or revisions, or both. Most people do. This does not constitute a fail; but it does not always feel good, particularly if it comes as a surprise. You may be sick of the sight of your thesis by this stage. You may think that it is now out of date, that it has a glaring weakness and/or naiveté in it. You may be only too aware of the fact that it 'can still be improved'. When the feedback comes, after the viva, the trick is to make sure it is clear about what revisions or corrections are required, and do only those. Then there will be 'more writing' when you try to get your thesis, or part of it, published and that is the subject of the last section of this chapter.

What is a viva?

What the term *viva voce* means is literally 'with the living voice', or in speech, orally. The term 'viva' is used in the UK to refer to the oral examination of a doctoral thesis. In other countries, other terms are used, such as the oral 'defence'. This word is useful in that it reminds us that the primary function of the viva is to give students an opportunity to defend their work.

More developed definitions are provided by different scholars and academics:

On the day a robust performance is required but be careful to avoid dogmatism. Examiners are impressed by thoughtful, reflective candidates who give consideration to constructive criticism and are able to modify their arguments accordingly . . .

Surviving the viva depends fundamentally on preparation and students' ability to demystify the examination procedure.

(Burnham 1994: 33)

What you are expected to do is to be 'robust' in defending your work, but you are not supposed to be dogmatic (even if your examiners are). It is this balance that often strikes students as ambiguous, neither one thing nor the other, strong but not too strong, combining apparent opposites. As for 'constructive criticism', you will have been receiving that for some time, in feedback from your supervisor, but perhaps not orally. Receiving criticism in writing gives you time to prepare – and perhaps disguise your true feelings. In the viva, you will have to respond to feedback and criticism instantly and with people watching you. They may gauge your reaction from your non-verbal behaviours, such as eye contact – or lack of it – facial expressions and hand gestures, as well as your tone of voice and what you actually say. With so many ambiguities and potential unknowns Burnham (1994) is quite right in stating that preparation and demystification are key.

The purpose of the viva is to examine you according to the criteria established for theses at your university or by some other relevant professional group. Criteria were discussed in Chapter 1, and you should know exactly what they are and have discussed them numerous times with different people. Like criteria, however, terms like 'originality' remain open to interpretation: '. . . "an original contribution to knowledge", a nebulous phrase which constitutes a potential ambiguity' (Baldacchino 1995: 72). Yet more ambiguity. However, you have already made your case for the originality of your work – in your thesis – and your task is now to prepare verbally to make that case to the examiners and to defend it against their challenges and probing.

While the focus of the examination is the work you did, as demonstrated in your thesis, you might get – and should be ready for – both product and process questions, i.e. questions about your thesis and questions about your learning and your experiences in conducting your research and writing your thesis.

Purpose of the viva

- Did you do the work yourself?
- Have you done the reading?
- Do you have a good general knowledge of the field?
- Did you write the thesis yourself?
- Can you do research independently?
- Can you communicate your subject to others?
- Can you talk about it professionally?
- Did you receive any training?
- Did you learn anything?
- Have you contributed new knowledge?

Burnham (1994) states that of all the criteria that examiners might – or might not – apply to your thesis, and to yourself as its 'defender', it is possible to narrow it down to three 'most common criteria' (p. 32):

The most common criteria

1 A clear account of the problem addressed in the research
2 Consistent development of this theme in all chapters
3 Clear statement of relevance of conclusion to the discipline

However, while some would argue that there is a 'core' of common elements, there are others who argue that practice is variable. Research has established that, across the university system, there is no single, universal set of definitions of purposes or practices. Perhaps this is one of the causes of the ambiguity associated with the viva.

> There is no consensus regarding the roles of the viva in the PhD examination process. Moreover, our research reveals that there are inconsistencies and contradictions concerning the purposes of the viva, both at the level of policy and practice.
>
> (Jackson and Tinkler 2001: 355)

'No consensus', 'inconsistencies' and 'contradictions' suggest why it is so difficult to get straight answers about the viva. While students are often frustrated that there is no single answer to such a simple question as 'How long will it last?', it should be clear that this is not simply the fault – or guile – of their supervisor. There is no standard practice. This may change, of course, and it may not be true of your institution. You have to find that out.

All of the points covered in this chapter – as in this book – have to be tested in the general context of your institution and the specific context of your supervisor's practice. More importantly, when you do start to research the viva, be ready not for a quick question-and-answer session, but for a more complicated, subtle dialogue.

It cannot be overstated – or repeated too often – how important it is that you should check what happens at your institution. Even if you feel that you really ought to have found out about these matters sooner, do not waste energy being embarrassed. Find out now. Keep asking questions until all your questions are answered.

It may be impossible to start defining the task of the viva if you have not addressed the mystique surrounding it. As far as I can tell, most students approach the viva with mixed emotions and confused expectations. These are not conducive to systematic preparation or excellent performance.

Writing activity

Freewriting: five minutes

- What are your concerns about the viva?
- What do you expect to happen?

The point here is to confront these questions, as part of your preparation. The second question may, in fact, indicate areas where you need more information.

Your supervisors may have told you all they think you need to know about the viva, or all they want to tell you at this time, or they may have simply, and faithfully, answered all your questions. They may think that they are protecting you by not having a full and frank discussion, just as some doctors protect their patients from the knowledge that they have cancer.

If you have not yet had this discussion, it may be that they firmly intended to tell you all this nearer the time – and they may want to stick to that plan – but there is no reason why you should not know more about the thesis examination earlier, right from the start, in fact. It is, after all, generally accepted that assessment influences – some would say 'drives' – learning. At the very least, we have to prepare for the mode of assessment, since it is so very different not only from our mode of working in the research project, but also because it is, for many of us, our first oral examination. For something so important, we want to get it right. We at least want to know what we can expect.

While these are reasonable and sensible expectations, some students find that it is remarkably difficult to get a straight answer to their questions. You may have to be persistent – not easy, when you are feeling vulnerable. Which

is how the viva mystique positions candidates. Note the change of terminology: up to this point you have been a 'student'; from now on you are a
'candidate'.

There are those who argue that the viva should be a much more public affair,
as it is in Sweden, for example. While this might seem, to most students – and
to some viva 'survivors' – as an even more intimidating experience, it would at
least have the effect of opening up an examination process that is often
shrouded in mystery. If the viva were conducted in public, the argument goes,
then everyone would be able to see how examiners – not just candidates –
behave. With this increased visibility, we might even see an end to the 'bad
behaviour' that is part of the mythology of the viva as ordeal. This public
model would have benefits for the candidate:

> The candidate is alerted to any likelihood of failure way before the day and
> a postponement sought . . .
>
> For the candidate, she had had an opportunity publicly to defend and
> display the fruits of her labours before her teachers and those who had
> supported her over five years of study. And for the examiners there was no
> opportunity to intimidate or dismiss the candidate's work behind closed
> doors.
>
> Is a public grilling not a fairer, more accountable way in which to exam-
> ine a PhD student than a private roasting behind closed doors?
>
> (Stephens 2001: 16)

In the context of a system which provides limited guidance and where there
has been almost no research, this proposal – at first sight shocking – has a
certain appeal. It might, in fact, reduce the need for appeals.

That the viva is an examination of your thesis is confirmed by evidence that
the thesis influences the external examiner's judgement well in advance of
your viva:

> Forty per cent of examiners . . . in the non-sciences said that the decision
> about the thesis was made before the viva. In 74% of cases the viva served
> merely to confirm the examiners' opinion of the candidate.
>
> (Jackson and Tinkler 2001: 361)

The argument that your research is up to standard and meets the criteria
should be made in your writing, in your thesis. Once you have found out
about purposes and criteria your thesis becomes the focal point for your
preparation.

Pre-viva

If you have never seen or been to a viva, you can view videos that give an impression of how it works (Green 1998; Murray 1998). Although a video of someone else's viva cannot be guaranteed to provide a programme for yours, it can prompt you to visualize your own viva and to move beyond the 'I don't know what will happen' phase. In some institutions you can sit in on someone else's viva, but you will have to check that and, if necessary, get permission.

While many students have negative feelings prior to their vivas – for many different, understandable reasons – it is not essential to see it in that light. Doing so may prevent you from learning during the viva. It may also make you miss the more positive aspects of the experience. Before the viva, then, try and see your preparation in the same light as preparing for a job interview, rather than a private 'grilling'. For both the job interview and the viva the standard of your work has been judged adequate, though it remains untested.

Find out all you can about the viva at your institution: how it is conducted, what the roles of participants are, what the external examiner does, how you should prepare, other students' experiences. Questions raised again and again by students are gathered together in this section in order to provide an agenda for your further explorations and definitions.

Student questions about the viva

How will it be conducted?

- How long will it last?
- Who will be there?
- What types of question can I expect?
- How do I assess if my answer is correct?
- What if I cannot answer the question?
- Do I have to say how my thesis fits into the broader picture?
- Can I assume by this stage that I have passed?
- How much background knowledge do I need?
- Where do I set the limits?
- Where should I go just before it starts?
- Who's on my side?
- Will my supervisor be there?
- Will anyone help me if I get into difficulties?
- What should I wear?
- If I do badly in the viva, but my thesis is good, will I pass?
- What is the standard I have to achieve?
- Should I admit the weaknesses of the study?

These are all excellent questions. Some simply indicate a lack of information; others reveal a lack of confidence. The power of 'the great unknown' is at its strongest here. For some of these questions, there are specific issues in talking about your study and writing.

'Weaknesses'   You must 'admit the weaknesses' of your study. Is there a study with no weaknesses? Does it exist? If you appear not to see the weaknesses, this may be taken to mean that you do not see that there are weaknesses. It will not look good if you appear not to know the difference between the strong and weak parts of your research or thesis.

'I don't know' Students are often afraid that this will look very bad. They feel it is better to say anything but this. If you do not know the answer, you can say so. The question is how do you say it: 'I'm not sure, but I think it might . . .', so that you give an educated guess, or speculate? Or 'I did not focus on that area in my study, but I wonder if . . .', also illustrating willingness to think. Remember that some examiners see it as their job to probe your knowledge to its limit. That is, for them, one of their roles. Do not panic. Think about the question. Speculate. Make it clear that you are doing so by saying 'If I were to speculate . . .'.

How will supervisors respond to your questions? Will they be willing to help you find answers to these questions? Will they provide contingent answers only, because they feel that even they cannot predict exactly what will happen? Or will they simply remind you that every viva is different?

Many, if not all, of the student questions are worth exploring further. For example, the question of role could be explored for each participant.

Student questions about the viva

- Internal examiner
- External examiner
- Supervisor
- Head of department
- Others?

What are their roles?

The purpose of your exploration of roles is not to prepare the ground for testing them, or critiquing people's performance on the day. The purpose of this role definition is to clarify what you have to do. The core of your work is still to talk about your writing; what is needed is definition of the context in which you will do this. Your starting point is simply to find out who will be there, since this varies from institution to institution.

Defining tasks

The build-up to your viva can also be seen as a process. You can establish your preparation process as a series of tasks.

How you prepare for the viva is an individual thing. For example, some people prefer to spend the ten or fifteen minutes before they are called into the room for their viva in a quiet place, focusing on the task ahead, while others prefer the distractions of the departmental office, to take their minds off what is about to happen.

The final 'countdown' that follows is intended to prompt you to plan ahead. You can use it as a framework to create the steps you need between submission and viva.

Countdown to the thesis examination	
Start of research project	• Find out criteria to be used to evaluate your work.
Three months pre-viva	• Submit thesis. Give final draft of all chapters to supervisor(s). Plan viva practice sessions. Find out about external examiner. Read institution's viva procedures and criteria.
One month pre-viva	• Reread your thesis. Correct typos and other errors. Type list of corrections (to give to examiners). Read recent literature. Write sample questions. Rehearse answers. Have mock viva. Practise what you expect to happen in your viva.
One week before	• Practise 'define–defend' . Practise oral summaries: long and short. Practise oral debate. Decide what to wear. Get it ready. Decide where you will wait just before the viva. Get viva kit: thesis, paper, pens, water, etc. Relax, exercise, eat and sleep well.

One day before	• Eat and sleep well. Spend time with positive, supportive people. Focus on the strengths of your work and writing.
On the day	• Use your best getting up routine. Eat a real breakfast, and/or take food with you.
30 minutes before	• Relax. Drink water. Think positive. Breathe. Focus on the task. Write notes on your strengths. Find somewhere to wait that suits you.
During the viva	• Keep breathing. Slow down. Write down questions. Write notes for answers. Talk about your thesis. Refer to the work you did. Nod. Smile. Look at your notes. Ask for exact definitions of corrections/revisions.
After the viva	• Writing: do corrections/revisions now. Relax. Celebrate. Thank supporters and allies.

However you define the tasks, and that may depend on how your supervisor sees the space between submission and viva, you have to put the tasks in real time. This 'final countdown' should look, in your diary or schedule, much more like a plan of work in itself. As with your plan of work for the research, that you drew up in consultation with your supervisor(s) at the start of your research, so, again, you would be well advised to discuss this plan of work with them. At the very least, you should check that they are available to provide a mock viva well in advance of the real thing.

You may also want to check how your 'case' is progressing through the university administration:

Are the wheels of the system turning?

1 Have my internal and external examiners been approved by the Faculty board, or whatever group has to approve them?
2 Have they been approved by the university Senate, or whatever body approves them in this institution?
3 Has my thesis been sent out to the external?
4 Has the date for my viva been formally approved?

This is not to suggest that you should be suspicious of your supervisor's – or others' – administrative efficiency, but you may learn about how your university works by asking these questions. You could even see this as part of your career development.

Talking about your writing

What's new? This may be your first oral examination, ever. Not only will the examiners ask you questions, they will also ask follow-up questions, to see if you really understand what you've written and what you've said.

But is it completely new? It is a question-and-answer process, as were the many other examinations you sat during your first degree. It is based on the work you have done.

While you have been writing within the scholarly debate for some time, this is when you actually enter the debate. Your thesis enters it before you do, when it goes to the external examiner who reads it – once? twice? – and then brings his or her questions to the oral examination to actually debate them with you. Paradoxically, just as you have achieved maximum closure – though perhaps not certainty – in your writing, it now becomes completely debatable.

You will be examined on the work you have done: the thesis. Your task is to make verbal the written forms, structures and debates in the literature. Your thesis is, therefore, the starting point for the questions of the examiner and for your answers. What you have written is what you will be asked about.

Answering the examiner's questions requires you to cover the same territory as you cover in the thesis. He or she may ask you questions that are beyond the scope of your study, but they will be related to your study in some way and you can take that as your starting point in your answer.

You will by this time know your thesis very well and will be able to talk about it at length. However, this requires an adjustment of style. You cannot simply recite sections of it. You will have to summarize sections, explain decisions and omissions and argue for your conclusions, even though you feel you have already said all there is to say in the thesis. At the end of the day the examiner has to check that you did the work yourself, that you can talk about it competently and professionally and that you are capable of independent research.

Talking tips

1 Use your thesis as your starting point.
2 Connect your answers to specific pages.
3 Decide in advance which pages you want to highlight.
4 Where are the highlights?
5 Make sure you mention these.
6 Choose two or three names (and dates) from the literature.
7 Find a way to link them and your work.

This is what you have been practising all along. In the course of writing, you have become more and more aware of your critical scholarly audience. You have worked hard to structure your writing and have revised it so often that you now know that structure by heart. You have considered the criteria. You have had critical feedback from your supervisor, i.e. detailed, analytical comment and questions. If you have presented at conferences and/or published in journals, you will be well aware of where your work stands, what its strengths and weaknesses are and what professionals and peers are likely to say or ask about it. In other words, everything you have done to produce your thesis, and everything you have read in Chapters 1 to 9, is relevant to your viva.

How you talk about that work may be closer to how you wrote about it; i.e. the viva usually requires formal language, the language of academic debate, much like the language and style you used in writing your thesis.

You may find the viva difficult if you do not have much practice in talking about your work as if you were in a debate, rather than giving a presentation, for example. Find people to practise with who are prepared to interrupt you, to put you under a bit of pressure. Practise dealing with such interruptions politely: 'I'll just finish my answer and then . . .' or perhaps that should be 'May I, very briefly, finish my answer before moving on to that question?' The choice of style is yours, but dealing with contradictory views is not a matter of choice. It will happen.

Finally, there is the difficulty, in talking about your work, that you may feel that it is now old – to you – and likely to be out of date to your examiners. You may even – paradoxically – find that you are a bit 'bored' by your thesis. This may, in fact, be a reaction to the stresses of (1) completing the thesis and (2) the prospect of the examination. Completing your thesis is a great achievement – really – but the 'end' can leave you with a depressing sense of anticlimax, when you were expecting to feel relief.

Talking confidently about your work may be a challenge. You may find that you are uncomfortable using the word 'original' in relation to your research or your thesis, even though you know that this is a key criterion in the examination. You may feel that while you have made a 'contribution', it is not that 'significant'. You may feel that it is certainly a lot more modest an achievement than you set out to realize. To a certain extent, this is par for the course: many new researchers start off with unrealistic research goals. The 'narrowing' (of the topic) process has meant that many good ideas were dropped along the way. It may do you no harm, in your viva, to appear to be quite modest about your work, but you will also have to be clear about where you can see a contribution, however modest. You will have to become comfortable in talking about your work as if it is interesting and important – which it is – and you should take time to practise that quite deliberately. Feedback from peers and supervisors can reassure you that you are striking the right tone. Without that feedback, how can you know? You will only wonder or worry.

You have to find ways of overcoming such barriers in talking about your thesis. You have to find a way to talk confidently – yet not arrogantly – about your research. The process of 'translating' your writing into talking is developed further in this chapter, particularly in the section on anticipating questions. Specific strategies for talking well about your work are covered in the 'During the viva' section of this chapter.

Practice

All of the strategies covered in this chapter for talking about your writing are pretty straightforward. They are fairly uncontentious, though there will be those who disagree. If this disagreement prompts further discussion of the rationale for their views and the specific practices that will result from that rationale – in your viva – then that is no bad thing.

However, while the strategies proposed here are not necessarily intellectually stretching, they do require practice. There is no point in simply understanding a strategy; you really have to put it into practice.

How can you practise for the viva?

1 With friends. With anyone
2 With postgraduates in your area, or any area
3 With a postgraduate who has had a viva
4 With your internal examiner and supervisor(s): 'mock viva'

Working with peers, colleagues or others, prepare a practice session. If you have been a member of a writers' group, they might be willing to help you to practise. You will have to provide material for them to use: general and specific questions, easy and hard questions, follow-up questions. Ask them to interrupt you, to challenge you, to give you lots of non-verbal feedback at some points and none at all at others.

Practice session: one hour

- Aims: discuss what you want to achieve in your practice.
- Which skills do you want to develop or improve?
- Which strategies do you want to practise?
- Prepare questions.
- Run the 'viva' for real, for one hour, without stopping.
- After this, have a full debrief: how did you do?
- How do your colleagues feel you did?
- Where do you need more practice?
- When can you practise this again?

This outline assumes that you have already prepared questions for those friends or colleagues who are acting as your examiners for the purpose of helping you practise. You can – and must – anticipate your examiners' questions. Some are predictable. There will, of course, be different types of question: general and specific. There will be easy questions – to put you at your ease – and hard questions – to probe your understanding of your own work, of the field and of your contribution to it. Any practice session – to be useful – has to include generic and specific questions. You have to practise translating into strong oral statements your answers to questions you may already have answered in your thesis.

If you do not practise, you may get by. You may get lucky. They may ask you questions that you find easy to answer. You may already be quite gifted and/or experienced at talking about your work in a challenging, scholarly forum.

However, if you do practise thoroughly you will give an excellent – not just adequate – performance on the day. You should aim not just to survive the viva, but to give one of your best performances. You will then feel not only relief that it is all over, but satisfaction that you have done yourself justice.

Anticipate the questions

It is not enough simply to recite sections of your thesis. You have to develop convincing answers to the questions asked. You have to answer follow-up questions. You have to answer probing questions that you may have answered more than once in your thesis. You have to rehearse.

General questions

- Would you please summarize your thesis for us?
- Who would you say are the key people in your field?
- Would you say that your thesis has any weaknesses?
- Surely it would have been better to use a different method?
- How do you see research developing in the next five years?

There will also be more detailed questions, possibly working systematically through each chapter. You can anticipate questions about each of your chapters. These may be general or specific, but can be challenging.

Questions the literature review should answer

- Why is this subject important?
- Who else thinks it is important?
- Who has worked on this subject before?
- What had not been done before?
- Who has done something similar to what you did?
- What did you adapt for your study?
- What is your contribution?
- Who will use your material?

These may not be exactly the questions you will be asked in your viva. In fact, they are questions that may be asked of your thesis first and foremost. You may then be asked different versions of these questions. Do not take that as a sign that your original answer – in your thesis – was not adequate or 'wrong'. Do not attempt to second-guess the examiner by trying to work out where he or she sees a flaw in your work. You will be asked about strong sections of your thesis too.

Examiners will almost certainly ask you about the method you chose for addressing your research questions or hypotheses. This part of the discussion should prompt you to restate what you have written in your thesis. Remember that what you have written in your thesis is your starting point in answer to almost all the questions. This means that you should be prepared to talk about anything you have written in any section. You have to show that you fully understand everything you have written. This is particularly true for the methodological dimension of your research and writing, since understanding research methods is so critical for any researcher in any field.

Questions you will be asked may focus on the link between your research questions and your hypothesis. They may ask you to state why you rejected other methods. They may want to test whether you can see the advantages and disadvantages of different methods in different contexts. They may have more probing questions (Partington et al. 1993: 76–7):

Questions about your methodology

- What precautions were taken against likely sources of bias?
- What are the limitations in the design? Is the candidate aware of them?
- Is the methodology for data collection appropriate?
- In the circumstances, has the best design been chosen?
- Has the candidate given an adequate justification for the design used?

If some of the questions do not seem appropriate for your study, adapt them, or invent other probing questions, so that you can practise answering them. Remember that examiners are not looking for you to come up with even stronger reasons for choosing your method, or even stronger procedures for using it; they want to test your understanding of what you have done, what you have written and what you think it all adds up to. They want to know that you know there are limitations – some by design – in your study; they do not want you to cover this up, or explain it away, with excuses and additional defences.

The handbook for external examiners (Partington et al. 1993) – the source of some of the questions listed in this, and other, chapters – includes other questions, on other sections of the thesis. These might help you prepare answers. How they can help is by prompting you to revise and reflect as you translate your writing into talking:

Revision and reflection

- Can you remember all the steps you carried out in your research?
- Can you recall your reasons for choosing your research methods?
- Can you list the five key people in your field?
- Can you explain how they influenced your work?
- Can you think of other questions to help you to revise your research?

Translating your writing into talking

For example, for the question about the steps in your research, take the word 'steps' as your cue:

- Summarize the steps in your research by condensing them into a series of sentences: 'The first step was . . . Then . . . The final step . . .'.
- Use the word 'step' – or some other word – to organize your answer.
- But what if they do not use the word 'steps'?
- This is why it is a good idea to practise more than once, with more than one type of question and more than one way of asking it. Then you can practise more than one way of answering the question.
- All of your answers are based on the work you have written, whatever you have written in your thesis. However, it is easy to be thrown by a question that comes in an unexpected form.
- Do not let that happen to you.
- Write several forms of the same question. Practise answering them all. Orally.

If you prepare for different questions and different versions of the same question you are much more likely to give an excellent performance on the day.

The examiners will also, surely, ask questions that are much more specific to your study. The questions listed here – and in earlier chapters – are all written in general terms. Clearly none of them can refer to your specific study. It is your responsibility to answer the question 'How would the examiner phrase that type of question in relation to my study?' How would you answer?

A study can succeed – or fail – on the strength – or weakness – of its methodology; in many ways it is the most important section of your writing. In this sense, the thesis can be seen as having similar standards to scholarly journals. As in any examination, you should not be distracted by the thought that (1) the examiner has already read your rationale for your method; (2) they know more about it than you do anyway; or (3) it really could have been done better. Instead, remember that, as in other examinations you have taken, your role is to explain what you did and what you know, regardless of what they would have done or what they know. Yes, they will put to you the challenging proposition that – exactly as you expected – you really should have done something different and, they will argue, better, but this is just another prompt for you to define and defend your work.

Specific questions

These are questions that only you can write. They are specific to your study and your writing, using the appropriate terms and points of reference.

- Write questions for every chapter or section of your thesis.
- Do not write vague, general prompts, like 'They will probably ask me about . . .'.
- Write the questions exactly as you think they might ask them.

They may ask you easy questions:

- Please summarize your work for us. Have a two-minute version ready. Prepare a ten-minute version too. Keep talking if they do not appear to want you to stop. Alternatively, you may prefer to give a presentation at the start of the viva.
- How did you develop an interest in this subject? Prepare a narrative of how you developed an interest in your research topic. You could conclude with a statement of where you see yourself going with this subject in future years.
- Tell us what you have learned from conducting your study. Decide in advance what you want to say here.

They will definitely ask you more difficult questions:

- There will be probing questions. These may seem more pointed than the questions you are used to.
- Expect follow-up questions, even when you feel you have given a full answer. Draw on more detail from your thesis.
- They may ask you questions about your whole study experience, writing courses you attended, research training, teaching experience or training.

There may also be a category of questions 'designed to put you at your ease', such as 'Have you enjoyed living in Scotland?' Not every student will appreciate this attempt to calm their nerves:

> The examiners spent far too much time talking about irrelevant matters. They asked me if I found the Scottish people friendly . . . about how I liked the weather. They should have been asking me about my thesis. This wasted time I could have used to talk about it. Why did they do this?

This student was very irate that he had lost time in all that small talk. A positive way of looking at it is that 'the clock was running'. These 'social' questions were using up viva time. In any case, becoming impatient with the questions during the viva is probably not going to endear a candidate to the examiners.

Finally, remember that thesis writers are themselves best placed to anticipate the questions examiners will ask. You know the kinds of things that are questionable in your field – not just in your thesis – and those that are not. Write many types of questions, to give yourself best practice:

1 Write down examples of all of the above types of question.
2 Use words that make them refer specifically to your thesis.
3 Practise answering them with someone else, a fellow student, a friend, anyone.
4 Practise again.
5 Have a debrief: how did you do? What can you improve? What do you need to practise more?

If you do follow these five steps you will be ready to give an excellent – not just adequate – performance on the day. You will then be able to help the next viva candidate with his or her preparation.

Mock viva

The mock viva is when the supervisor, possibly along with the internal examiner, puts you through a simulation of the viva. The word 'mock' does not imply that they do this to make a fool of you, though if you do not prepare well, you may feel foolish and may be made to look foolish. However, that is your responsibility. You can use the questions in the previous section to prepare for the mock viva, as you would with any form of preparation.

The advantage of the mock viva is that it helps you adjust to the more formal verbal style of the oral examination. It helps you develop your skills for more extended focused discussion. Your internal examiner and your supervisor can, since they know the area and/or your thesis, come up with realistic questions. These may be quite similar to or different from the questions you wrote for your practice sessions. You will see how they react when you answer. Because they are there – rather than friends and peers – you will probably find yourself evaluating your answer as you speak. This is not necessarily a good or a bad thing, but it is something that you are likely to do in the real viva and it is therefore important to experience it. In doing so, you will be better prepared to deal with that and will not be thrown by your constant self-evaluation undermining your confidence. You may get some insights into what your viva will really be like on the day.

The disadvantage of the mock viva is that, while it provides realistic practice, it does not guarantee that your external will run things in the same way in your real viva, ask you the same questions or respond to you in the same way. It is still not quite the real thing.

Some students will have a mock viva – and some will have more than one – as part of their ongoing assessment process, but if you have not had this experience, you must set it up now.

Fear

Fear of the real thing, of the elements that cannot be practised and which cannot really be known, makes for a stressful time prior to the viva. We have all heard stories, not many, not necessarily from our departments and possibly not even recent, but they do have an impact on our emotions:

Horror stories

- I didn't get enough feedback on my writing before the viva.
- I didn't know beforehand if I'd done enough work.
- There were too many experts, too many different views about my work.
- I was very nervous, tongue-tied. Had a mental block.
- I had misgivings about my work.
- They asked too many questions about other people's work.
- There were lots of general questions.
- My thesis crosses over two different areas.
- There was rivalry between my examiners and my supervisor.
- I was asked irrelevant questions.

In addition, each of us may have our worst-case scenarios, our nightmare moments, our negative fantasies. We have somehow to turn our thinking around. You can write alternative narratives, picturing a positive version of your viva.

Dealing with pressure is an individual process. Each of us has our own ways of coping. Different people deal with the pressure of the unknown differently:

- The ostrich approach: 'I'd rather not think about it.'
- It's them and us: 'They're out to get me.'
- It is an examination: 'What do I have to do to pass?'
- Discussion: 'I know the kinds of things they'll ask.'
- An ordeal: 'I don't know anything.'
- It's a formality: 'Is that it?'
- It's a test: 'Of what?'

While these reactions raise interesting questions about the viva, they take us further and further away from the writing, which is, after all, the main text to be examined.

Defining the task can help. Knowing our role does help. Talking to others about both our fears and our strategies is sensible, if we can be sure of some reassurance – and not just confirmation of our fears – from them.

High stakes come into play at this point. We have produced an impressive body of work and written an impressive account of it in a thesis, yet the test is still to come.

Ambiguity remains a problem. On the one hand, your thesis has been critiqued, reviewed and revised dozens, perhaps hundreds of times. You have demonstrated your (growing) understanding to your supervisors in hours and hours of discussion. On the other hand, the thesis and you still have to be examined. Even completing the thesis and handing it in felt like an achievement; but that counts for nothing till the examiners decide.

The eternal openness of research is also a factor. It takes time to learn to live with the lack of closure: even once we have created a 'moment' of closure in our writing, we know full well that the debate continues, that we have raised further questions and that we cannot answer our research questions for all times and all places. Some people externalize their feelings of contingency, marking out what they see as the external causes of their insecurities about their work and writing. Sooner rather than later, it would help them – and you – to acknowledge that their contingent feelings about their work – and your contingent feelings about your thesis – are one and the same and are not going to go away. These feelings are embedded in the processes of research and writing. They will not simply disappear once you have passed your viva.

Is fear just a by-product of stress? Any stress management course, book or consultant will teach you the importance of control: those who are most stressed are those who have no control over their circumstances. The trick is to work out what you can control, at this moment in your life, and to plan to do that as well as you can. This may include reminding yourself that the viva is an examination of your thesis.

External examiners are the greatest unknown. For all your defining and practising, they may – assume will – ask something for which you are not prepared. They may not have had any of the conversations that you have had about the viva. Let us assume the worst-case scenario: they have read none of the materials about the viva that you have, even the ones intended to be read by thesis examiners. It can happen. For very good reasons experienced examiners may feel that they know enough about what their role requires. They will certainly feel that they know more about it than you do. How much experience have you had? It would surely be foolish to attempt – in any way – to assess your examiner's competence, although if you are treated unfairly you should appeal.

There are many things that cannot be known about external examiners, but that may be because we cannot know exactly what they will ask, or how they will respond to our answers. This is not to say, however, that the mystique should remain.

The external examiner

Students often ask a string of questions about external examiners. This implies that they have not been given much information about who those people are, how they will be or have been selected and how they will affect the examination. Nor am I the best person to answer these questions; there is no way that I can answer them. I do not have relevant knowledge of every student's context. Each student has, to some extent, to take responsibility for finding out local answers to these – and any other – questions. Therefore, while this section provides some tentative answers, I have avoided being definite about them, in order not to mislead anyone. Even worse, it could leave students thinking that they had enough information just from reading this section, which cannot be true.

The string of questions that students ask me again and again includes:

- Who chooses external examiners?
- How is this done?
- Can I have a say in who it will be?
- When is the best time to start thinking about this?
- How well should I know their work?
- What qualifications/experience/training should they have?
- Will they be experts in my area?
- How final should their copy of the thesis be?
- What are they looking for?
- Should I avoid arguing with them?

You can write sketchy answers to each of these questions, or, if these do not seem to be the right questions, you can write your own.

To what extent can the questions be anticipated, if every thesis is unique? *The Handbook for External Examiners in Higher Education* (Partington et al. 1993) is based on the explicit assumption that while academic staff – including external examiners – see their subjects as unique, 'assessment techniques are to a large extent generalisable' (p. 2). In fact, the authors go as far as to say that 'the issues raised here are those which external examiners could raise as appropriate in any department or course' (p. 2). While this may in principle or in fact be true, is it true in your department? Is it true for the examination of the thesis? A simple test of this assumption would be to ask your supervisor and internal examiner three questions: (1) Have you read this handbook? (2) Do you agree with the statement that thesis 'assessment techniques are to a large extent generalisable'? (3) Are these the types of question I should expect in my viva?

Chapter 4 of the handbook, 'Examining theses in the 1990s', is clearly of most relevance to thesis writers, though, again, your own context may shift the parameters subtly. It is always worth checking your own assumptions and developing understanding with those of your supervisors and their sense of what to expect from your external examiner. Chapter 4 of the handbook lists questions for external examiners to ask about each chapter of the thesis. While these questions are designed to help them form judgements as they read, there is no reason why these – fairly familiar – questions will not be used by examiners in the viva itself. Section 4.6 is, after all, entitled 'Reading and judging a thesis.'

What kinds of answers do they imply? Even if the question seems to invite a categorical answer, you should try to use the language of debate: definition, illustration, occasionally pros and cons, presenting more than one side of the issue, and so on. Be clear, in your answers, about where you can and cannot be definitive and where you should be more propositional in your style. Make this explicit in what you say. Practise talking about your writing in this way. Even parts of your thesis that are pretty definitive may have to be discussed in a more propositional – some hear this as more modest – style than you are used to adopting in discussions with your supervisor, or even at meetings with colleagues and peers.

As always, you should make sure you have a copy of your institution's guidance for thesis examinations. Perhaps you can see the guidelines for external examiners? Then you might have some insight into the viva process. If you cannot find such guidelines, keep asking. Be persistent, as it is likely that there are some, or soon will be: 'Changes in the PhD together with concerns for Quality Assurance are beginning to produce changes in University regulations and notes of guidance for external examiners' (Partington et al. 1993: 71). If that was true in 1993, then it is likely to have become standard practice in many institutions since then. However, Tinkler and Jackson (2000) showed that this might not be true. It is worth checking where your university sits on this evolutionary continuum.

During the viva

Many students believe that, as in previous, undergraduate examinations, they will not be allowed to take anything into the examination with them. This is not true. You can, and should, take your thesis with you, so that you can refer to it and follow the discussion when someone else refers to it. You will also need notepaper and pens, surely for obvious reasons. What might not be so obvious is the practice of writing down the examiners' questions, so that you can be sure to answer them. This means actually writing notes for your answers. You can lay out your notes so that the examiner's question is clearly separate from your notes. In fact, you can use the layout to plan and structure your answer.

Notes layout

Write down the question	Notes for your answer	Specifics
1 Summarize your thesis . . .	Chapter 1 [verb] . . .	Elaborate . . .
	Chapter 2 [verb] . . .	Example . . .
2 Who are the key people in the field?	Name . . .	Date . . .
		Key idea . . .
		Key work . . .
3 . . . weaknesses in your thesis?	Define . . .	Pros . . .
		Cons
		Alternatives

While it may seem pretty basic to be advising postgraduates – experts in their fields – to be 'writing down the question', it is worth emphasizing how useful such a basic activity can be as a coping strategy. The stress of the situation, or, paradoxically, your intense interest in the discussion of the subject you know best, can make you lose track of the question. You can get quite engrossed in the discussion, carried away with the experience of talking to people about your work, people who do not just want a quick answer, but who invite you to develop your points. You can be busily constructing a brilliant argument for something and then suddenly realize that you have lost direction: where was I going with this answer?

There is nothing wrong with being so absorbed in your subject that you forget the question. It is seen by many as a good thing to show enthusiasm for your subject; it might look a bit odd if you showed no such enthusiasm, even if the cause of that were only fatigue. Yet you do have to respond to your audience, in this case the examiner. 'What was your question again?' is a question it would be better not to have to ask too often.

Alternatively, when you write the question down, as it is asked, you give yourself one thing less to hold in your memory as you speak. Moreover, you can then return to the question explicitly as you approach the end of your answer: 'So, to answer your question, the top three people in the field at the moment are . . .'. This is a good time to remind yourself to pause to breathe, to speak clearly, to enunciate your consonants, and so on. Good technique. Much better technique than forgetting the question and having to ask the examiner to repeat it. Even worse if you have to repeat your question, 'What was the question?' Worst of all if you keep having to ask it throughout the viva. It is stressful to be wondering whether, having chosen not to write down the questions, you will be able to remember them as you go along.

The same applies to making notes for your answer, as you write down the question, or as the examiner asks a long question, or as you begin to give your answer: why not sketch out a structure – based on what you have in your thesis, which you know very well – so that your answer is organized? It also helps to have that third column, prompting you to be specific.

If your answers stay at the level of the general, you will appear to have no more than a general knowledge of the field and perhaps of your own work. This will not look good. Be specific. Give examples. Define your terms. Consider more than one side of the issue. Give more than one answer to the question. All of these should, of course, be drawn from your thesis. It has to be said, again, that you should discuss these suggestions with your supervisor(s). They may think it is a good idea to keep your answers short, to the point, general or specific.

In case you felt that all of this might be taken as claiming just a bit too much for your work, remember to speak in the past tense. This means that you are talking – throughout your viva – about work that you have completed, past tense, about how you have interpreted it, past tense, and about what you have argued the importance of that work is, which is still past tense.

The point of this strategy is to make it absolutely clear that you are talking about the work done, the project completed and the finished writing to be found in your thesis. What you avoid by talking about your work in this way is claiming too much for your thesis: if you speak in the present tense, then you immediately take your work out of its context. There is a difference between 'What I took that to mean was . . .' and 'What this means is . . .'. The former locates your point clearly in the past; you can even contrast your thinking then with your thinking now. The latter appears to claim a universal meaning; it is one of those statements that seems timeless in its generality, particularly if it is repeated several times.

Speaking in the past tense: why?

- To give an account of work done
  e.g. 'What I did was. . .'.
- To explain choices and decisions already made
  e.g. 'I did that because. . .'.
- To reveal what you learned
  e.g. 'I thought then that [full explanation]. . . I now think that . . .'.
- To avoid claiming universality
  e.g. 'What this meant was. . .'.

This technique, should you accept it, is yet another verbal strategy for you to practise over and over again, until it becomes automatic, well in advance of your viva.

However, be very, very careful to define your completed work first, before you move beyond it to other possibilities and interpretations. Do not be put off by your own perception that your work is older and more obvious than you are entirely comfortable with.

Of course, you – and your examiners – may change to the future tense in order to discuss what might be the next step in your research, what you will do next, where you see the field as going in the future, and so on.

You will be wondering whether or not you will make as much use of the first person singular – 'I' – as I have used in my examples. There are pros and cons. You might want to discuss this with your supervisor. You might prefer to make some – or exclusive – use of the passive voice: using 'The analyses were conducted' rather than 'I conducted the analyses.' At some stage, however, you have to make absolutely clear that you did the work yourself, and this may require you to be comfortable using 'I', even if it is not your first choice. If you do not use it at all, are you at risk of giving the impression that you did not do it yourself?

Certain strategies that you have used in your writing will be useful in the viva. For example, 'define–defend' is a strategy that helps students answer difficult questions without becoming defensive. Given a difficult, seemingly attacking, question, such as 'Don't you think it would have been better to . . .', the tendency is to start an answer with a defence of what was done.

A stronger strategy – and one that we use in academic writing all the time – is to define what we did first, and why, and then say how it was, if not the best method, then at least an appropriate one for the study. You can then show that you understand both the strengths and the limitations of the approach you chose. You can even go on from this point to consider the pros and cons of the alternative proposed by the questioner. This answering strategy will take more time, but that may be no bad thing, if it helps you to take up more time with a fuller answer. Above all, it saves you from appearing – or actually becoming – defensive. Your role is to defend, not become defensive, when faced with a legitimate set of challenging questions.

Here is one generic example, though you can write some that are specific to your study:

Define–defend

- **Question**
  Why did you not do more detailed analysis of . . . ?
- **Defend answer**
  I did not do that because . . .
- **Define–defend answer**
  What I did was . . . That was because . . . I did not do more detailed analysis because . . .

This strategy has proved popular with students in viva workshops, perhaps because it provides an approach for controlling the flow of your answers, connecting them to the question. Alternatively, its appeal to students may lie in the shift in tone that it engenders, from the students simply reacting to the examiners' provocations to the students managing their answers and their emotions, being more strategic in their contributions. It may be that it makes sense because they recognize that this is a strategy that is well established in scholarly debate; they recognize it from their reading and they have used it in their writing. It may, however, be the first time that the combination of definition and example (as part of a defence) has been explicitly marked as a feature of scholarly style.

At some point, however, you should force – and that may be exactly the right word – the best features of work into the conversation, especially if they have not yet come up in the viva. After all, if the strength of your work does not come up in discussion, it may not be acknowledged, or recognized, as a strength.

Highlight the highlights

- Which parts of your thesis are you proud of?
- Which parts do you want to highlight?
- Practise working them into your answers.

Practise 'expanding as you go': as long as the examiners look as though they want you to continue speaking, do so. Elaborate. Add another example. Link your answer to another section of your thesis, perhaps one of your selected 'highlights'. This may be seen by some as a tactic for 'running down the clock' (and you may see it this way too), but a more positive interpretation is that you are taking control of your speech and not being overly passive. While the balance of power is very much with the examiners, you have developed – in your practice sessions – skills for talking about your work and writing. The examiners are not going to say to you 'Please show us now some of your verbal skills.' You are going to have to find a way to use each question as an opportunity to demonstrate them.

It should be noted that some supervisors and examiners will not approve of this strategy, since it might tempt you to go on at great length and widely off the point. However, if they want you to stop talking and move on to the question, assume that they will ask you to do so. Do not make your answers as short as possible, unless you are explicitly asked to do so. There will, therefore, be an element of 'playing it by ear' – for you – on this point.

As long as you are answering the question, what can be wrong with that? Giving one sentence, or short and to the point answers, will demonstrate admirable conciseness, but will it demonstrate your knowledge? In any case, if the examiners want you to stop talking or to move on to the next question, then they will surely find a way of letting you know that.

Post-viva

Do you know the possible decisions for your viva? Find out what the categories of decision are, from 'pass with no revisions/corrections', to 'pass with minor revisions', to 'pass with major revisions and/or further research', to 'fail/ downgrade to MPhil'. Once you have found out what terms are used in your university, you need to find out exactly what they mean.

The most common result is to have revisions or corrections; this is not a fail. Treat it as a pass. Revisions and corrections are covered later in this chapter.

Endurance

Just when you thought you had written as much as you thought was possible for one person to write in a lifetime, you have *another* '385 yards' to go.

What if the viva has been more than just probing? Whatever your feelings about the viva, if you have been asked to produce corrections and/or revisions, get on with them.

If, however, you feel you were treated unfairly, you have the right to appeal. You should find out the procedures, and above all the grounds, for an appeal in your university. Talk to someone first.

Revisions and corrections

Listen very carefully to what is said at the end of your viva about these. Take notes. Think. Make sure that every revision they are asking for is not already covered in your thesis. You can also question the proposed revisions if you think they are not necessary or useful. You can argue your point: define and defend again. You can state your case for the thesis as it is. After all, you are likely to know it better than anyone else in the room. Negotiate.

When recommendations for revisions have been agreed, make sure you know exactly what you have been asked to change. If they have asked you to 'expand' on a point, does that mean add a sentence or two, or do they want a whole page? It is important to know the scale and scope of the revisions you have to do, not only so that you know what the writing task is before you start, but also so that you provide the type of revision they are looking for. You do not, presumably, want to have to do more revisions after this set.

The external examiner may give you a list of revisions and/or corrections, but you should have your own notes too. Writing them down gives you time to think about your response. Many institutions require that both student and supervisor are given written copies, but you may find it useful to write your own notes as you ask questions for clarification. You may also want to reflect back what they are asking you to do, to check that you have understood.

Even if the required revisions and/or corrections are well defined, it may help you to translate them into writing actions. For example:

- Expand the explanation of step three in the development process (p. 89) becomes
- Add 100 words defining step three to page 89.

The writing task is now clearer. The length has been defined. The purpose has been defined: 'defining' (rather than describing, comparing, analysing, critiquing, etc.). The content is still not defined, however.

Anti-climax

I was examined by two very wise historians who didn't make the nitpicking queries which, while sitting in on vivas, I have heard people raise. It was like coming out of a doctor's surgery after being told that what looked like something nasty on the X-ray was only some coffee spilled on the film.

Sale (2001)

What are the causes of post-viva anti-climax?

1 Having focused your whole life – or much of it – on achieving this one goal, now that you have achieved it there is no focus, for a moment, or a month, or for longer.
2 You have made so many sacrifices – as have your friends, family and loved ones – there is no immediate benefit to you, or to them, as a result of your passing the viva.
3 The viva itself may not have been as challenging as you expected. You may feel that you wasted your time in over-preparing for something that turned out to be a routine discussion among scholars.

Is there life after a thesis?

The PhD process is as much about professional socialisation as it is about producing an original contribution to knowledge.

(Burnham 1994: 33)

Is that what it was? Are we all now socialized into our professions? If only it were so simple.

Was it really worth it?

There may be no tangible reward for completing your thesis. No salary increase. No promotion. No certainty of full-time employment. You will have to invent a sense of achievement to go along with the relief that it is finally over.

Yes, it will all eventually prove to have been worth it. What you learned – about your subject, your academic community and yourself – may only become clear to you over time. You have made contacts that will come in useful over the years. You have developed new skills and have a new qualification.

Recovering

Some students find that they do not want to read – never mind write – anything for a while after the whole process is finally complete. They have been forcing the reading and writing for so long that they have lost the taste for it, they feel. They have lost the motivation for reading once the project is over. This may be partly fatigue and partly the result of achieving a huge goal. It may be that the reading and writing have been so focused that the subject has no appeal. It may be that the subject now seems so old that there seems to be no more to write about it.

However, this is where the conference commitment will prove to have been the smart move. That will keep you involved in scholarly writing and in touch with scholarly readers. If you have planned ahead you will have an abstract submitted and/or a presentation to give a few months after the viva, and the conference paper can be converted into a publication.

Although you are right to take time to recover after your viva, the next section reminds you that you ought to be thinking of publication, though some students will have been published already. Remember also that one of the questions in the viva may be about potential for publication; i.e. examiners want to know, not just whether you have thought about this, but whether you understand publishing in your field well enough to know where and how you are most likely to be published. In some institutions it is seen as the external examiner's responsibility to suggest likely places for publication.

This question is also a further test of how accurately you have been able to assess the strengths and weaknesses of your own work, since you are more likely to publish the most significant features of your thesis. You may, of course, want to publish some of your earlier work that did not make it into your thesis. Or you may have a pilot study that seems readiest for publication.

Whatever the question, and whatever your answer, take time to display your knowledge of publishing in your field. If you have not already visited all the relevant journal websites, if you have not already collected all the instructions for authors, if you have not yet sounded out one or two book publishers and the editors of one or two journals – by email – about possible topics for a book or paper, then you should do so now.

Getting your thesis published

The dissertation system must have laid at its door an enormous squandering of creativity, youth, time, and money each year upon the execution of prose works that do not communicate significantly and are therefore dysfunctional. The publisher, upon whom depends much of the scholar's success, usually refuses even to look at them.

(Harman and Montagnes [1976] 2000: 28)

Exactly how the thesis is 'dysfunctional' is spelled out further: 'amateurism, redundancy, trivialization, specializationalism, reductionism, and arrogance' (Harman and Montagnes 2000: 28).

This section outlines the changes you have to make to your thesis in order to get it published and suggests how you might go about making them.

For future development further learning may be a matter of systematically researching journals and editors in order to develop a personal programme of writing for publication, or developing networks with other researchers in order to share lessons learned about writing and publishing, or it may be a matter of learning further technical skills for academic writing. One of the key skills will be making time for writing, and protecting it, in the workplace, whether that be in a university or in some other environment, and, perhaps equally important, finding others who value writing enough to do so too.

Audience and purpose (again)

As for any piece of writing, your starting point must be defining your audience and purpose. If you are going to translate your thesis into a book, both will change. There is no doubt about that.

A key text here is Harman and Montagnes' *The Thesis and the Book* ([1976] 2000). Though not new, this book has advice that is still useful, as is clear from the number of reprints, up to and including 2000. It is particularly good on the shifts in audience and purpose required to turn your thesis into a book.

Writing activity: 10 minutes' freewriting

- Reflect on what makes for writing problems and blocks at this stage.
- Recontextualize yourself as writer in the research community.
- Convince yourself that you have something to say.
- Why do some people develop the facility for writing for publication?
- Make up topics for a paper/book.

We could study writing habits and concepts: describe them and evaluate them. Take a random sample, across the disciplines, and simply track what they do and what they think about not only their writing process and output but also about themselves as writers.

1 Are there self-concept differences? Is it about confidence and self-esteem?
2 Are there behavioural differences? Do they go about writing, and fitting writing into their lives, in different ways?
3 Is it about differences in peer groups: do productive and/or successful writers have a peer group in place that supports – and rewards? – their writing, while the others do not? Or did that only come once they had a few things in print?
4 Is the difference in how they write? In rhetorical differences? Are the successful writers those who write well? Did they learn how to do this? Did they learn through trial and error?

Finally, is there some interaction of the above factors that is the difference between success and failure in a writer's overall output and self-concept as a writer? Is it true that 'to be an effective and productive writer you need a solid, well-defined sense of yourself' (Hiemstra and Brier 1994: 19)?

Translating the thesis into the book may require the writer to move from being a student, or 'pre-professional', to a professional:

> Tradition has it that rather than being the first act of the scholar, the dissertation is the last act of the student. The dissertation is viewed therefore as the work not of a professional but of a pre-professional. Thus the writer of the dissertation is forced by tradition to resort to the writing of a form that is dysfunctional, because . . . [it] will be read by few and because no publisher will . . . consider publishing it as it stands.
>
> (Armstrong in Harman and Montagnes [1976] 2000: 25)

This may seem overstated, but there is truth in what Armstrong says. However, it may be worth considering whether you need to discard all the lessons you learned about writing in the course of writing a thesis, as is implied here, or whether you can adapt what you have learned. The thesis style may turn out to be appropriate for some journals or publishers. It is likely to be a sensible idea, and a professional strength, to be able to produce more than one style of writing. This brings us back to the position of rhetorical choices, rather than rights and wrongs.

However, moving to writing for publication will require a shift for many thesis writers. Perhaps dissertation/thesis writing is dysfunctional, but no more than any other form of academic writing. Your undergraduate writing was read by even fewer people than your thesis will be and was even less interesting to readers beyond the university. It could be that what is problematic is the mystique surrounding it. There is a similar mystique surrounding writing for publication, unless you have had very good mentoring during your PhD, and very good guidance, once your PhD is completed, on how to translate your work into your first book. The word 'dysfunctional' may be misleading; your writing was subjected to more detailed scrutiny than at any other time, and you may think this scrutiny went too far, yet this process will be repeated every time you submit your writing for peer review. In fact, given the apparent dominance of certain groups, nepotism and various forms of discrimination (documented, in some contexts), the scrutiny is likely to be even harder and, sometimes, unfair.

The question for the new writer is how to join the current community: what are the acceptable ideological forms and discourse practices that dominate in publications in your field today? This is a related question to the ground you covered in your literature review, where you summarized historical and contemporary debates; but it may have a different focus: what are the dominant schools of thought, whether or not you agree with them? How can you join the discussion in which they are participating? It is up to you to develop a professional voice and it may help to analyse how other voices have made themselves heard.

Writing for publication requires a shift in voice from the voice of the thesis. Whole sections may be irrelevant. For example, does the reader need to know – as your supervisor did – the detail of the context for your work or every turn in the argument for your approach?

A shift in style may also be a good idea, in order to move away from the more tentative forms of argument that often feature in a thesis:

> I suspect that the dissertation uses more conditional sentences than does any other prose form in the language. The worst offenders in this respect are the social scientists. In these disciplines the young appear to learn early in their careers an inviolable relationship between truth and tortuous conditionality. Thus: *all things being equal, it would appear to be the case that, under given circumstances, it may not be uncommon for writers of dissertations to execute certain prose styles which those who seem to like their English straight and strong might conceivably call a perversion of the language.*
>
> (Armstrong in Harman and Montagnes [1976] 2000: 29)

Looking for topics

Looking for topics may seem absurd; surely you have more than enough of those? But what is required is a selection that fits the agenda of the publishers or journal editors.

- Convert your conference presentations Use your OHPs or PowerPoint slides as an outline
- Write review papers
- Write about your original research

There is no need to put all your good work into one paper; you can probably carve it up into several papers for different journals. This is how you can become known as an expert in your field: by focusing on one area in your publications.

'Salami slicing' is how some people refer to this, often with the implication that it is in some way cheating. However, it would be foolish – and may not be feasible – to put all of your work in one mammoth paper. Besides, we all know that experts in our field write about related work in their papers.

The ethics of 'recycling' are worth thinking through too: some people will argue that it is unethical to write 'versions' of the same paper for more than one journal. It is true that simply repeating yourself will win you no friends and could have much more serious consequences. However, if you reshape your material as you write about a topic more than once, and if you target the new audience of the next journal, then it is likely that you will develop your thinking about your topic in any case. In other words, writing about your subject more than once can be a way of developing your ideas.

Is one publication in one journal going to bring your work to the attention of all the key people in your field? Probably not. It is important to consider whether you ought to be reaching a wider audience than the readership of one journal. For example, if you have invented a new approach, a new course or a new synthesis, that may be the topic of one paper. It may appear as an appendix in the next paper, or two. In this way, two or three or more sets of readers will see your new invention, even though it has become marginalized in later papers.

The end

Writing a thesis is a massive learning experience for a modest contribution to knowledge. In the beginning, it seemed as though it would be the opposite. We had such grand designs at the start.

But that is part of the learning process too: you now know the limitations of research designs, the constraints of academic writing and the power-plays of academic life. You have learned how to work within these structures.

Paradoxically, in writing a thesis you have learned how to write to the highest standards by writing *well enough*.

Checklist

Before and after the viva

- Find out what your university's code of practice says about the viva. Find out if your department follows the code. Ask your supervisor(s).
- If you don't already know, find out who your examiners are now.
- Find out who will attend your viva. Find out what their roles will be in your viva. Find out who will ask questions and who will not.
- Ask how long it is likely to last.
- Find out what will happen at the end of the viva: will you be told the decision immediately, or not?
- Find out what the categories of decision are. What do they all mean?
- If you would like to give a presentation at the start of your viva, say so. Ask your supervisor(s) if this is OK, how long it can be, etc.
- Ask to see the examiners' report form that will be used in your viva.
- Will the examiner give you a list of corrections/revisions? How and when will you be informed of any further work to be done?
- Set up a mock viva as soon as possible. Practise with friends and peers. Use this practice to 'revise', till you are word perfect on your thesis.

Bibliography

Albert, T. (2000) *Winning the Publications Game: How to Write a Scientific Paper Without Neglecting your Patients*, 2nd edition. Abingdon: Radcliffe.

Anderson, J., Durston, B. and Poole, M. (1970) *Thesis and Assignment Writing*. Brisbane: Wiley.

Baldacchino, G. (1995) Reflections on the status of a doctoral defence, *Journal of Graduate Education*, 1: 71–6.

Ballenger, B. (2004) *The Curious Researcher: A Guide to Writing Research Papers*, 4th edn. New York: Pearson Longman.

Bareham, J., Bourner, T. and Stevens, G.R. (1999) The DBA: What is it for?, British Academy of Management Paper, 75–92.

Becker, H.S. (1986) *Writing for Social Scientists: How to Start and Finish Your Thesis, Book, or Article*. London: University of Chicago.

Becker, H.S. (1998) *Tricks of the Trade: How to Think about Your Research While You're Doing It*. London: University of Chicago.

Bénabou, M. (1996) *Why I Have Not Written Any of My Books*. Lincoln, NE: University of Nebraska.

Black, D., Brown, S., Day, A. and Race, P. (1998) *500 Tips for Getting Published: A Guide for Educators, Researchers and Professionals*. London: Kogan Page.

Blaxter, L., Hughes, C. and Tight, M. (1998) *The Academic Career Handbook*. Buckingham: Open University Press.

Blaxter, L., Hughes, C. and Tight, M. (1998) Writing on academic careers, *Studies in Higher Education*, 23(3): 281–95.

Boice, R. (1987a) A program for facilitating scholarly writing, *Higher Education Research and Development*, 6(1): 9–20.

Boice, R. (1987b) Is released time an effective component of faculty development programs?, *Research in Higher Education*, 26(3): 311–26.

Boice, R. (1990) *Professors as Writers: A Self-Help Guide to Productive Writing*. Stillwater, OK: New Forums.

Boice, R. (1994) *How Writers Journey to Comfort and Fluency: A Psychological Adventure*. London: Praeger.

Bolker, J. (1998) *Writing Your Dissertation in Fifteen Minutes a Day: A Guide to Starting, Revising and Finishing Your Doctoral Thesis*. New York, NY: Henry Holt.

Bolton, G. (2001) *Reflective Practice: Writing and Professional Development*. London: Chapman.

Booth, W., Colomb, G.C. and Williams, J.M. (1995) *The Craft of Research*. London: University of Chicago.

Borg, W.R. and Gall, M.D. (1989) *Educational Research: An Introduction*, 5th edn. New York, NY: Longman.

Boud, D. (1999) Situating development in professional work: using peer learning, *International Journal for Academic Development*, 4(1): 3–10.

Boud, D., Cohen, R. and Sampson, J. (1999) Peer learning and assessment, *Assessment and Evaluation in Higher Education*, 24(4): 413–26.

Bourner, T., Bowden, R. and Laing, S. (1999) Innovation or standardisation in research degree awards, *Higher Education Review*, 31(2): 11–28.

BPS (British Psychological Society) (2000) *Guidelines for Assessment of the PhD in Psychology and Related Disciplines*, revised version. Leicester: British Psychological Society.

Brause, R.S. (2000) *Writing Your Doctoral Dissertation: Invisible Rules for Success*. London: Falmer.

Brent, E.E. (1986) The computer-assisted literature review, *Computers and the Social Sciences*, 2: 137–51.

Brown, G. and Atkins, M. (1988) *Effective Teaching in Higher Education*. London: Routledge.

Brown, R. (1994) The 'big picture' about managing writing, in O. Zuber-Skerritt and Y. Ryan (eds) *Quality in Postgraduate Education*. London: Kogan Page.

Brown, R. (1994/95) Write right first time, *Literati Newsline*, Special Issue, 1–8.

Bruce, C.S. (1994) Research students' early experiences of the dissertation literature review, *Studies in Higher Education*, 19(2): 217–29.

BSI (British Standards Institution) (1990) *Recommendations for the Presentation of Theses*. London: BSI.

Burnham, P. (1994) Surviving the viva: unravelling the mystery of the PhD oral, *Journal of Graduate Education*, 1: 30–4.

Caffarella, R.S. and Barnett, B.G. (2000) Teaching doctoral students to become scholarly writers: the importance of giving and receiving critiques, *Studies in Higher Education*, 25(1): 39–51.

Carlson, R. (1997) *Don't Sweat the Small Stuff . . . and It's All Small Stuff*. London: Hodder and Stoughton.

Collinson, J.A. (1998) Professionally trained researchers? Expectations of competence on social science research training, *Higher Education Review*, 31(1): 59–67.

Committee of Vice-Chancellors and Principals/Committee of Directors of Polytechnics (CVCP/CVP) (1992) *The Management of Higher Degrees Undertaken by Overseas Students*. London: CVCP/CDP.

Cooper, H.M. (1988) The structure of knowledge synthesis, *Knowledge in Society*, 1: 104–26.

Cutts, M. (1995) *The Plain English Guide*. Oxford: Oxford University Press.

Day, A. (1996) *How to Get Research Published in Journals*. Aldershot: Gower.

Delamont, S., Atkinson, P. and Parry, O. (2000) *The Doctoral Experience: Success and Failure in Graduate School*. London: Falmer.

Delamont, S., Atkinson, P. and Parry, O. (2004) *Supervising the Doctorate: A Guide to Success*, 2nd edn. Maidenhead: Open University Press-McGraw-Hill.

Dolence, M.G. and Norris, D.M. (1995) *Transforming Higher Education: A Vision for Learning in the 21st Century*. Ann Arbor, MI: Society for College and University Planning.

Doncaster, K. and Thorne, L. (2000) Reflection and planning: essential elements of professional doctorates, *Reflective Practice*, 1(3): 391–9.

Dreyfus, H.L. (1999) Anonymity versus commitment: the dangers of education on the internet, *Ethics and Information Technology*, 1: 15–21.

Duffy, C.A. (1999) *The World's Wife*. London: Picador.

Elbow, P. (1973) *Writing Without Teachers*. Oxford: Oxford University Press.

Elbow, P. (1981) *Writing with Power: Techniques for Mastering the Writing Process*. Oxford: Oxford University Press.

Elbow, P. (1997) High stakes and low stakes in assigning and responding to writing, in M.D. Sorcinelli and P. Elbow (eds) *Writing to Learn: Strategies for Assigning and Responding to Writing Across the Disciplines*. San Fancisco, CA: Jossey-Bass.

Elbow, P. (1998) http://www.tc.cc.va.us/writcent/handouts/writing/pelbow.htm

Elliott, G. (1999) *Lifelong Learning: The Politics of the New Learning Environment*. London: Jessica Kingsley.

Ely, M., Vinz, R., Downing, M. and Anzul, M. (1997) *On Writing Qualitative Research: Living by Words*. London: Falmer.

Emerson, C. (1996) *The 30-Minute Writer*. Cincinnati, OH: Writers' Digest.

Emerson, R.M., Fretz, R.I. and Shaw, L.L. (1995) *Writing Ethnographic Fieldnotes*. London: University of Chicago.

Emig, J. (1977) Writing as a mode of learning, *College Composition and Communication*, 28: 122–8.

Fahnestock, J. and Secor, M. (1990) *A Rhetoric of Argument*, 2nd edn. New York, NY: McGraw-Hill.

Fitzpatrick, J., Secrist, J. and Wright, D.J. (1998) *Secrets for a Successful Dissertation*. London: Sage.

Flower, L. (1989) *Problem-Solving Strategies for Writing*. London: Harcourt Brace Jovanovich.

Flower, L. and Hayes, J.R. (1981) A cognitive process theory of writing, *College Composition and Communication*, 32: 365–87.

Fowler, H.W. ([1965] 1984) *Fowler's Modern English Usage*. Oxford: Oxford University Press.

Flynn, E. (1986) Composing responses to literary texts, in A. Young and T. Fulwiler (eds) *Writing Across the Disciplines*. Upper Montclair, NJ: Boynton/Cook.

Friedman, A. (2001) *Writing for Visual Media*. Oxford: Focal Press.

Gere, A.R. (1987) *Writing Groups: History, Theory, and Implications*. Carbondale, IL: Southern Illinois University Press.

Gillon, E. (1998) We demand too much from the traditional PhD, *Research Fortnight*, 8 April: 13.

Gillon, E. and Hoad, J. (2000) *What Questions Should I Ask? Some Guidance for the Prospective Postgraduate Student*. http://www.npc.org.uk/page/1003798926: National Postgraduate Committee.

Glatthorn, A.A. (1998) *Writing the Winning Dissertation: A Step-by-Step Guide*. Thousand Oaks, CA: Corwin.

Grant, B. and Knowles, S. (2000) Flights of imagination: academic writers be(com)ing writers, *International Journal for Academic Development*, 5(1): 6–19.

Graves, N. and Varma, V. (eds) (1997) *Working for a Doctorate: A Guide for the Humanities and Social Sciences*. London: Routledge.

Green, D.H. (1998) *The Postgraduate Viva: A Closer Look* [video]. Leeds: Leeds Metropolitan University.

Greenfield, N. (ed.) (2000) *How I Got My Postgraduate Degree Part Time*. Lancaster: School of Independent Studies, University of Lancaster.

Griffiths, M. (1993) Productive writing, *The New Academic*, Autumn, 29–30.

Haines, D.D., Newcomer, S. and Raphael, J. (1997) *Writing Together: How to Transform Your Writing in a Writing Group*. New York, NY: Perigree.

Hall, G.M. (ed.) (1998) *How to Write a Paper*, 2nd edn. London: BMJ.

Hampson, L. (1994) *How's Your Dissertation Going? Students Share the Rough Reality of Dissertation and Project Work*. Lancaster: Unit for Innovation in Higher Education.

Harman, E. and Montagnes, I. ([1976] 2000) *The Thesis and the Book*. Toronto: University of Toronto Press.

Hart, C. (1998) *Doing a Literature Review: Releasing the Social Science Imagination*. London: Sage.

Harwood, W.S. (1996) The one-minute paper: a communication tool for large lecture classes, *Journal of Chemical Education*, 73(3): 229–30.

Herrington, A.J. (1981) Writing to learn: writing across the disciplines, *College English*, 43(4): 379–87.

Herrington, A.J. (1985) Writing in academic settings: a study of the contexts for writing in two college chemical engineering courses, *Research in the Teaching of English*, 19(4): 331–61.

Herrington, A.J. (1988) Teaching, writing and learning: a naturalistic study of writing in an undergraduate literature course, in D.A. Jolliffe (ed.) *Advances in Writing Research, Vol. 2: Writing in Academic Disciplines*. Norwood, NJ: Ablex.

Herrington, A.J. (1992) Composing one's self in a discipline: students' and teachers' negotiations, in M. Secor and D. Charney (eds) *Constructing Rhetorical Education*, Carbondale, IL: Southern Illinois University Press.

Hicks, W. (1999) *Writing for Journalists*. London: Routledge.

Hiemstra, R. and Brier, E.M. (1994) *Professional Writing: Processes, Strategies, and Tips for Publishing in Educational Journals*. Malabar, FL: Krieger.

Hiney, T. and MacShane, F. (2000) *The Raymond Chandler Papers: Selected Letters and Non-fiction, 1909–1959*. London: Hamish Hamilton.

Hockey, J. (1994) New territory: problems of adjusting to the first year of a social science PhD, *Studies in Higher Education*, 19(2): 177–90.

Hockey, J. (1995) *Strategies and Tactics in the Supervision of Research Students* [video]. Cheltenham: Cheltenham and Gloucester College of Education.

hooks, b. (1999) *remembered rapture: the writer at work*. New York, NY: Henry Holt.

Hounsell, D. and Murray, R. (1992) *Essay Writing for Active Learning*. Sheffield: CVCP Universities' Staff Development and Training Unit.

Huff, A.S. (1999) *Writing for Scholarly Publication*. London: Sage.

Jackson, M.W. (1991) Writing as learning: reflections on developing students' writing strategies, *Higher Education Research and Development*, 10(1): 41–52.

Jackson, C. and Tinkler, P. (2000) The PhD examination: an exercise in community-building and gatekeeping?, in Ian McNay (ed.) *Higher Education and its Communities*. Buckingham: Society for Research into Higher Education and Open University Press.

Jackson, C., and Tinkler, P. (2001) Back to basics: a consideration of the purposes of the PhD viva, *Studies in Higher Education*, 26(4): 354–66.

James, T. and Woodsmall, W. (1988) *Time Line Therapy and the Basis of Personality*. Capitola, CA: Meta Publications.

Johnston, B. and Murray, R. (2004) New routes to the PhD: cause for concern?, *Higher Education Quarterly*, 58(1): 31–42.

Johnston, S. (1997) Examining the examiners: an analysis of examiners' reports on doctoral theses, *Studies in Higher Education*, 22(3): 333–47.

Kaye, S. (1989) *Writing Under Pressure: The Quick Writing Process*. Oxford: Oxford University Press.

Ketefian, S. and McKenna, H.P. (2005) *Doctoral Education in Nursing: International Perspectives*. London: Routledge.

King, S. (2000) *On Writing, a Memoir of the Craft*. London: Hodder and Stoughton.

Lee, A. (1998) Doctoral research as writing, in Joy Higgs (ed.) *Writing Qualitative Research*. Sydney: Hampden.

Lee, M. and Street, B. (1998) Student writing in higher education: an academic literacies approach, *Studies in Higher Education*, 23(2): 157–72.

Leedy, P. (1989) *Practical Research: Planning and Design*, 4th edn. New York, NY: Macmillan.

Leonard, D. (2001) *A Woman's Guide to Doctoral Studies*. Buckingham: Open University Press.

Lowe, A. and Murray, R. (1995) Reflexivity in postgraduate research training: the Strathclyde Business Faculty experience, *Journal of Graduate Education*, 1: 77–84.

McNeill, D. (1998) Writing the new Barcelona, in T. Hall and P. Hubbard (eds) *The Entrepreneurial City: Geographies of Politics, Regime and Representation*. Chichester: John Wiley.

Marshall, S. (2001) Reference management software: it's your choice, *Technical Computing*, 22 (Summer): 16.

Merriam, S.B. (1988) *Case Study Research in Education: A Qualitative Approach*. San Francisco, CA: Jossey-Bass.

Moon, J. (1999) *Learning Journals: A Handbook for Academics, Students and Professional Development*. London: Kogan Page.

Morss, K. and Murray, R. (2001) Researching academic writing within a structured programme: insights and outcomes, *Studies in Higher Education*, 26(1): 35–52.

Moxley, J.M. and Taylor, T. (1997) *Writing and Publishing for Academic Authors*, 2nd edn. London: Rowman and Littlefield.

Mullen, C.A. (2000) Linking research and teaching: a study of graduate student engagement, *Teaching in Higher Education*, 5(1): 5–21.

Murray, R. (1992) *An Introduction to Writing Skills*. Glasgow: Department of Adult and Continuing Education, University of Glasgow.

Murray, R. (1995) *Thesis Writing* (video and notes). Glasgow: University of Strathclyde.

Murray, R. (1998) *The Viva* (video and notes). Glasgow: University of Strathclyde.

Murray, R. (2000) *Writing for Publication* (video and notes). Glasgow: University of Strathclyde.

Murray, R. (2001) Integrating teaching and research through writing development for students and staff, *Active Learning*, 2(1): 31–45.

Murray, R. (2003) *How to Survive your Viva*. Maidenhead: Open University Press-McGraw-Hill.

Murray, R. (2005) *Writing for Academic Journals*. Maidenhead: Open University Press-McGraw-Hill.

Murray, R. and Lowe, A. (1995) Writing and dialogue for the PhD, *Journal of Graduate Education*, 1(4): 103–9.

Murray, R. and MacKay, G. (1998a) Supporting academic development in public output: reflections and propositions, *International Journal for Academic Development*, 3(1): 54–63.

Murray, R. and MacKay, G. (1998b) *Writers' Groups for Researchers and How to Run Them*, Universities' and Colleges' Staff Development Agency [now Higher Education Staff Development Agency] Briefing Paper 60. Sheffield: UCOSDA.

Navarra, T. (1998) *Toward Painless Writing: A Guide for Health Professionals*. Thorofare, NJ: SLACK.

Neuman, R. (2005) Doctoral differences: professional doctorates and PhDs compared, *Journal of Higher Education Policy and Management*, 27(2): 173–88.

Nightingale, P. (1988) Understanding processes and problems in student writing, *Studies in Higher Education*, 13(3): 263–83.

NPC (National Postgraduate Committee) (1992) *Guidelines on Codes of Practice for Post-graduate Research*. Nottingham: NPC.

NPC (National Postgraduate Committee) (1995) *Guidelines for the Conduct of Research Degree Appeals*. Nottingham: NPC.

Nystrand, M. (1982) *What Writers Know: The Language, Process, and Structure of Written Discourse*. London: Harcourt Brace Jovanovich.

Orna, E. and Stevens, G. (1995) *Managing Information for Research*. Buckingham: Open University Press.

Palumbo, D. (2000) *Writing from the Inside Out: Transforming Your Psychological Blocks to Release the Writer Within*. Chichester: John Wiley.

Park, C. (2005) New variant PhD: the changing nature of the doctorate in the UK, *Journal of Higher Education Policy and Management*, 27(2): 189–207.

Partington, J., Brown, G. and Gordon, G. (1993) *Handbook for External Examiners in Higher Education*. Sheffield: UK Universities' Staff Development Unit and the Universities of Kent and Leeds.

Pearce, L. (2005) *How to Examine a Thesis*. Maidenhead: Open University Press-McGraw-Hill.

Phillips, E.M. and Pugh, D.S. (2000) *How to Get a PhD: A Handbook for Students and their Supervisors*, 3rd edn. Buckingham: Open University Press.

Plomin, J. (2001) Way ahead clear? *The Guardian*, 13 March: 1.

Powell, W.W. (1985) *Getting Into Print: The Decision Making Process in Scholarly Publishing*. London: University of Chicago.

Quality Assurance Agency (1999) *Code of Practice for the Assurance of Academic Quality and Standards in Higher Education: Postgraduate Research Programmes*. Gloucester: Quality Assurance Agency for Higher Education.

Reif-Lehrer, L. (2000) *The Beauty of Outlines*. http://nextwave-uk.sciencemag.org/cgi/content/full/2000/06/07/2.

Rekulak, J. (2001) *The Writer's Block: 786 Ideas to Jump-Start your Imagination*. London: Running Press.

Rodrigues, D. (1997) *The Research Paper and the World Wide Web*. Upper Saddle River, NJ: Prentice-Hall.

Rozakis, L. (1999) *Writing Great Research Papers*. London: McGraw-Hill.

Rudd, E. (1985) *A New Look at Postgraduate Failure*. Guildford: Society for Research in Higher Education, NFER/Nelson.

Ruggeri-Stevens, G., Bareham, J. and Bourner, T. (2001) The DBA in British universities: assessment and standards, *Quality Assurance in Education*, 9(2): 61–71.

Sadler, D.R. (1990) *Up the Publication Road: A Guide to Publishing in Scholarly Journals for Academics, Researchers and Graduate Students*, 2nd edn., Green Guide No. 2. Campbelltown, NSW: Higher Education Research and Development Society of Australasia.

Sale, J. (2001) The PhD gave me cunning, Education Supplement, *The Independent*, 27 September: 9.

Sarros, J.C., Willis, R.J., Fisher, R. and Storen, A. (2005) DBA examination procedures and protocols, *Journal of Higher Education Policy and Management*, 27(2): 151–72.

Seijts, G., Taylor, L. and Latham, G. (1998) Enhancing teaching performance through goal setting, implementation and seeking feedback, *International Journal for Academic Development*, 3(2): 156–68.

Selzer, J. (1981) Merit and degree in Webster's *The Duchess of Malfi, English Literary Renaissance*, 11(1): 70–80.

Shakespeare, W. ([1607] 1974) *The Riverside Shakespeare*. Boston: Houghton Mifflin.

Sorcinelli, M.D. and Elbow, P. (1997) *Writing to Learn: Strategies for Assigning and Responding to Writing Across the Disciplines*. San Francisco, CA: Jossey-Bass.

Spark, M. (2001) Monday Review, *The Independent*, 17 September: 7.

Steinbeck, J. (1962) *Travels with Charley, In Search of America*. London: Pan.

Stephens, D. (2001) Why I . . . believe all PhD students should be grilled in public, *Times Higher Education Supplement*, 20 April: 16.

Strunk, W. and White, E.B. ([1959] 1979) *The Elements of Style*. London: Collier Macmillan (http://www.diku.dk/students/myth/EOS).

Sullivan, G. (2005) *Art Practice as Research: Inquiry in the Visual Arts*. London: Sage.

Swales, J.M. (1990) *Genre Analysis: English in Academic and Research Settings*. Cambridge: Cambridge University Press.

Swales, J.M. and Feak, C.B. (1994) *Academic Writing for Graduate Students: Essential Tasks and Skills*. Ann Arbor, MI: University of Michigan.

Thyer, B.A. (1994) *Successful Publishing in Scholarly Journals*. London: Sage.

Tiberio, M. (2000) The value of self-acquaintance, *Personal Journaling*, December, 42–7.

Tight, M. (1999) Writing in British higher education journals 1993–98: concerns and omissions, *Higher Education Review*, 31(3): 27–44.

Tinkler, P. and Jackson, C. (2000) Examining the doctorate: institutional policy and the PhD examination process in Britain, *Studies in Higher Education*, 25(2): 167–80.

Torrance, M., Thomas, G.V. and Robinson, E.J. (1992) The writing experiences of social science research students, *Studies in Higher Education*, 17(2): 155–67.

Torrance, M., Thomas, M. and Robinson, E.J. (1993) Training in thesis writing: an evaluation of three conceptual orientations, *British Journal of Educational Psychology*, 63: 170–84.

UKCGE (UK Council for Graduate Education) (1995) *Graduate Schools*. Warwick: UKCGE.

UKCGE (UK Council for Graduate Education) (1996) *The Award of the Degree of PhD on the Basis of Published Work*. Warwick: UKCGE.

Wakeford, J. (2001) Nowhere to turn, *Guardian Education*, 25 September: 2–3

Williams, J. (1996) Writing in concert, in H.A. Veeser (ed.) *Confessions of the Critics*. London: Routledge.

Williams, J. and Coldron, J. (eds) (1996) *Writing for Publication: An Introductory Guide for People Working in Education*. Sheffield: PAVIC.

Wilson, W.L. (1999a) *Gathering and Evaluating Information from Secondary Sources*. Glasgow: Universities of Edinburgh, Glasgow and Strathclyde.

Wilson, W.L. (1999b) *Interpreting and Documenting Research and Findings*. Glasgow: Universities of Edinburgh, Glasgow and Strathclyde.

Winter, R., Buck, A. and Sobiechowska, P. (1999) *Professional Experience and the Investigative Imagination: The Art of Reflective Writing*. London: Routledge.

Winter, R., Griffiths, M. and Green, K. (2000) The 'academic' qualities of practice: what are the criteria for a practice-based PhD?, *Studies in Higher Education*, 25(1): 26–37.

Woolf. V. ([1928] 1993) *Orlando*. Harmondsworth: Penguin.

Zuber-Skerrit, O. and Ryan, Y. (eds) (1994) *Quality in Postgraduate Education*. London: Kogan Page.

Index